Critical Essays on
Saul Bellow

Critical Essays on Saul Bellow

Stanley Trachtenberg

G. K. Hall & Co. ● Boston, Massachusetts

Copyright © 1979 by Stanley Trachtenberg

Library of Congress Cataloging in Publication Data
Main entry under title:

Critical essays on Saul Bellow.

(Critical essays on American literature)
Includes bibliographical references and index.
1. Bellow, Saul—Criticism and
interpretation—Addresses, essays, lectures.
I. Trachtenberg, Stanley. II. Series.
PS3503.E4488Z615   813'.5'2   79-2556
ISBN 0-8161-8281-7

This publication is printed on permanent/durable acid-free paper
MANUFACTURED IN THE UNITED STATES OF AMERICA

For
Israel and Bessie Trachtenberg
and
Robby and Dina Eisenberg

CRITICAL ESSAYS ON AMERICAN LITERATURE

This series seeks to publish the most important reprinted criticism on writers and topics in American Literature along with, in various volumes, original essays, interviews, bibliographies, letters, manuscript sections, and other materials brought to public attention for the first time. Stanley Trachtenberg's volume on Saul Bellow is not only the most substantial collection of criticism yet assembled on this Nobel Prize winning author, but offers several new essays as well. In addition to Professor Trachtenberg's important introduction, there is a revised review by Irvin Stock and original criticism by Philip Stevick, Eusebio Rodrigues, and Daniel Fuchs, whose analysis rests on hitherto unknown Bellow manuscripts. We are confident that this collection will make a permanent and significant contribution to American literary scholarship.

James Nagel, GENERAL EDITOR

Northeastern University

CONTENTS

INTRODUCTION

From its appearance in the mid forties, critics have found in Saul Bellow's fiction a quality of intelligence that gave imaginative form to the central concerns of a literary generation. Commenting on his "intellectual animation," for example, Elizabeth Hardwick looked to Bellow to become the "redeeming novelist of his period," while for Norman Podhoretz, "the self esteem of his generation seemed to depend on whether Bellow would succeed as a novelist."[1] What could be seen in this almost messianic critical reception was a reaction to the then dominant esthetic formalism of I. A. Richards and the new critics for whom poetry had to be dissociated from belief, the work imaginatively invented rather than imaginatively perceived. Stephen Spender has noted that the modernist sensibility, responsive to a past as yet uncorrupted by commerce, hoped to realize its art forms through a combination of unconscious processes and the exercise of critical consciousness.[2] Rational processes of arriving at meaning were abandoned for intuitive ones or epiphanies. The resulting insights remained elusive despite an exhaustive concentration on the subjective processes from which they emerged. Bellow has attributed the literary response of the period to the heritage of an ascetic tradition he described as

> dominated by a tone of elegy from the twenties to the fifties the atmosphere of Eliot in "The Waste Land" and that of Joyce in the *Portrait of the Artist as a Young Man*. Sensibility absorbed this sadness, this view of the artist as the only contemporary link with an age of gold, forced to watch the sewage flowing in the Thames, every aspect of modern civilization doing violence to this (artist-patrician) feeling.[3]

In contrast to this claustrophobic climate, Bellow has been concerned with "the connection between the understanding and the imagination and the future place of intelligence in imaginative literature."[4] As part of that subject, however, he has seen the need to incorporate the social reality he quotes the Spanish-born filmmaker Luis Buñuel as wishing to deal with in his own work: "the fundamental problems of today's man, taken not as a particular case, but in relation to other men."[5] In balancing the particular case against the collective reality, Bellow reflected the interests of a new generation, a generation, as his friend Delmore Schwartz put it, which came to maturity "during the depression, the sanguine period of the New Deal, the days of the Popular Front and the days of Munich and the slow, loud ticking imminence of a new war." To evoke the American experience, an experience he described as "that murky, burdensome, chaotic thing," Bellow abandoned the ironic mode of alienation adopted by the modernists in favor of a moral judgment that emerged from the attempt to allow ideas a dramatic expression. Characteristically, that expression has required a specific social environment, usually urban—Chicago or New York—people who belong to identifiable social levels, who have jobs in which we can recognize both levels of intelligence and economic condition—who dress, own things, travel in a certain style, all of which tells us about them. Who, above all, address themselves to the difficulties of thinking and feeling in the framework of circumstances outside their own consciousnesses. In this examination of the look and feel of things, Bellow attempts to establish the importance of action, to see who is hurt, who benefited, who has acted with innocent motive, who with calculation.

Bellow has been responsive to a naturalistic sense of social conditions, often commenting on the constricting pressures of public life. Writing in the early fifties, he found the writer particularly vulnerable to these pressures and to the social institutions which "by their size and force too thoroughly determine." Barring such rare literary exceptions as Ralph Ellison's *Invisible Man*, the reader could expect to find that

> family and class, university, fashion, the giants of publicity and manufacture, have had a larger share in the creation of someone called a writer than truth or imagination—that Bendix and Studebaker and the nylon division of DuPont, and the University of Chicago, or Columbia or Harvard or Kenyon College, have once more proved mightier than the single soul of an individual: to find that one more lightly manned position has been taken.[6]

The military metaphor more than anything else reinforces Bellow's sense of the adversary relation of the writer and society. It is a relation, however, which echoes as well the pressures exerted within the successful structure. "There are so many of us," Bellow has acknowledged with only partial irony, "such a multitude, that it is difficult if not impossible to give each man his full measure of attention."[7] This theme echoes throughout his fiction. In *The Victim*, Kirby Allbee talks of the crowded cemeteries, Basteshaw, the mad ship's carpenter in *Augie March* of crowded swimming pools; Herzog is made aware of the press of humanity through subway turnstiles, Sammler reminded of the anonymity of extinction of those forced by the Nazis to dig their own graves. Often this oppressive quality of death is identified in the image of the modern city, which equally is associated with the protagonist who attempts to resist it. "I'm an American, Chicago born," Augie March begins and in *Humboldt's Gift*, Charlie Citrine ends his adventures with the wry acknowledgement that his familiarity with life's mysteries—death prominent among them—must be understood in terms of his urban background.[8] Bellow himself has acknowledged the influence of the city on his fiction. "I don't know," he has claimed, "how I could possibly separate my knowledge of life such as it is, from the city. I could no more tell you how deeply it's gotten into my bones than the lady who paints radium dials in the clock factory can tell you."[9] Despite this ominous image, however, Bellow has not found in such urban knowledge solely the victimizing force of naturalistic determinism. Though he has identified its pressures, he has equally seen in the streets, the people, the restaurants, the stores, the nostalgic echo of family connections it supports, a reassuring familiarity sometimes illusory, just as often real, that sustains its residents. The city in Bellow's fiction is often vital, vigorous, enterprising; the towns (he writes of them during a journey through the midwest during which he looked for evidence of cultural development), in Illinois at least, are places of failure and decay, inhabited by those too old or apathetic to escape.[10]

The contrasting attitudes toward the city are paralleled by oppositions in both style and theme that appear throughout Bellow's fiction, among them the desire for an extended life in contrast to the willingness to accept the limits the world imposes on the self; the concern for a rational view of experience in contrast to the potential isolation such a view enforces and a corresponding recognition of the need to record the particularity of commonplace events and to range beyond the limits of fact to imaginative justification of them. At the same time as Bellow has maintained the human obligation to accommodate rather than avoid the prospect of death, he has been reluctant to identify a common bond of humanity on the basis of its shared sense of helplessness, a feeling he has scornfully referred to as potato love. Instead, he has continued to insist on a separate destiny as an element of dignity, a destiny realized through the deceptions of a nonetheless vital earthly power. "Human greatness," he has remarked, "can still be seen by us. And it is not a question of the gnat who sees the elephant. We are not members of a different species."[11] Even the notion of greatness, however, becomes qualified by Bellow's sense of the pressures of public life which, he has claimed, in the form of "vivid and formless turbulence, news, slogans mysterious crises, and unreal configurations dissolves coherence in all but the most resistant of minds."[12] The formlessness and mystery, the incoherence that Bellow finds characteristic of these pressures suggests that, for the most part, they have not been the economic or even social ones described in the proletarian fiction of the thirties. Rather they are the result of more abstract, cultural conditions which Bellow has seen grow increasingly more insistent, noisier he has called them, since the First World War. Recently he has found this noise of public life has reached a crescendo in the "unreal issues, ideologies, rationalizations, errors, delusions, nonsituations that look real, nonquestions demanding consideration, opinions, analyses in the press, on the air, expertise, inside dope, factional disagreement, official rhetoric, information,"[13] characteristics of a sophisticated rather than philistine society. By the late fifties, they had led Bellow's critical emphasis to shift to a concern for narrative development from the scientific or social questions he accuses intellectuals of substituting for a "serious consideration of literature." The character of the public, he felt, had changed, become more intellectual. "Writers themselves have more intellectual interests . . . they have become as concerned to analyze, to investigate problems or to consider ideological questions as to tell stories."[14]

The thematic consequences of this perception emerge in Bellow's recognition that the consummation of the heart's ultimate need can be found only in letting go. He has attempted in his fiction to reach beyond the world of appearances to the psychic unity that links men to one another. In an address delivered in 1975 at The Institute of Verdi Studies, Bellow emphasized that the visionary if disciplined intention of art must be to resist the obsessive materialism of our time by taking us into "transcendental static states, states of unity."[15]

Yet throughout his career, Bellow has also been responsive to the urging of the spirit for what he has called a fate good enough, which is to say one which distinguishes the individual from all others and so makes his life necessary, above all, a fate which is self determined.

Structurally, the longing for unified states of feeling has led Bellow to the conviction that the artist must rely on his imagination to lead him to his story, must arrive at what things are real by means of "enduring intuitions."[16] The artist, in fact, resists the pragmatic interest in technology by inhabiting what Bellow terms a "dream sphere."[17] Alternatively, Bellow has argued that art must in Irving Kristol's words "question or affirm the legitimacy of society's basic institutions . . . criticize or amend the original assumptions on which political life proceeds."[18] The resulting complex, even contradictory notions of reality in Bellow's fiction and the notions of the approach the writer must adopt to it—the insistence at times on a rational, a factual authority, at other times on one projected by a single consciousness—these have been the focus of the central critical issues raised in connection with Bellow's work.

Bellow himself has characteristically been uncomfortable with such criticism, more, he has indicated, because it complicates rather than clarifies his own imaginative approach to his material than because of any quarrel he has with the critics.[19] Nonetheless he has shown a strongly partisan attitude toward the way he feels literature should be both written and read. Bellow has noted with regret the fading of the nineteenth and early twentieth century view of the novelist as public spokesman in the manner of Tolstoy, Victor Hugo, or, the last of the tradition, of Bernard Shaw or H. G. Wells, whose work addressed itself to public issues and to the social conditions from which they emerged. The modernists who succeeded them—Eliot, Lawrence, Valery among them—were inclined to view literature either as a form of a compensatory estheticism, as did Flaubert, or, like Proust or Joyce, in terms of encyclopedic fidelity to the receptive consciousness, a consciousness described only by random activity and so, far removed from the actuality of life.[20] The attempt to comprehend all experience in this way, for Bellow, leads to an unacceptable surrender of moral judgment; but though it is to the consequent lack of clarity in the author's intention that he objects in *Ulysses*,[21] Bellow has adopted a similar strategy throughout much of his fiction, so that it is often difficult to determine who or what is the object of its laughter and where responsibility lies for the comic vulnerability it exposes.
major figure Herzog has been likened.

As the American culture became less confident than Marcus Klein described it in one of the influential early essays on Bellow's fiction, the mood of hopeful accommodation to the social equilibrium of the late 1940s and early 1950s became for many critics increasingly parochial, even pessimistic.[22] What Bellow objects to, at least as much as the slippery nature of the characteristic irony of modernism, is the consequent exaggeration it has received at the hands of critics who have translated its major works into less accessible forms of discourse and whose intention is "to redescribe everything downward, blackening the present age and denying creative scope to their contemporaries."[23]

Bellow's resistance to alienation has for the most part taken the form of an individual's struggle to define those qualities which identify him as human, qualities which, for Bellow, emerge sometimes in opposition to, sometimes as a function of, the belief that goodness can be achieved only in the company of other men. In exploring these alternatives, Bellow has demonstrated an overriding concern for the ordinary circumstances of daily reality. "While our need for meanings is certainly great," he has written, "our need for concreteness, for particulars, is even greater."[24] In approaching the reality of individuals who actually live and actually die, however, Bellow has evidenced a good deal of anxiety about a facticity that smothers the imagination. "The facts begin to crowd me," Henderson complains, "and soon I get a pressure in the chest." Bellow has responded to the same pressure. American fiction, he complained not long after the publication of *Henderson*, had become characterized by a concern for documentation animated neither by the theoretical structure that informed Zola's naturalism nor the feeling or the view of fate that described Dreiser's social novels.[25] More recently, he has objected to the accountability to fact which the society holds the demands of the artist no less than of the scientist or the technical expert in any field. Writing of the difficulty of the artist in a modern, technological society, Bellow has remarked that "the artist has less power to resist the facts than other men. He is obliged to note the particulars. One may even say that he is condemned to see them."[26] In this shift from the artist's need to the social demand for fact as a compelling principle of composition, Bellow anticipated a tendency which, as Pearl K. Bell has recently noted,[27] has come to extend even to the popular novel—Bell cites as representative examples Arthur Hailey's *Wheels*, James Michener's *Centennial*, James Clavell's *Shogun*, and prominently, Herman Wouk's *War and Remembrance*—which formerly defined itself by a concern for narrative movement. Though Bellow continues to insist on the importance of giving weight to the particular, such weight, he argues, need not be in quantifiable terms any more than art should fulfill a compensatory function in restoring the alienated modern individual to psychic health. Rather, factual authority proceeds from an imaginative faculty that, with Henry James, Bellow insists must maintain its regard for the story as story and must express man's "intuition that his own existence is peculiarly significant."[28] In his Nobel lecture, Bellow quotes with approval Joseph Conrad's belief that the artist must descend within himself to invent the visible universe and starting out in Chicago, where he wrote sitting at a bridge table facing the back of his mother-in-law's home. Bellow struggled with the necessity of remaining independent of the cultural noise that threatened the writer on all sides with the material values it pressed him to adopt.[29]

Accordingly, despite his concern for social conditions, Bellow has shown little interest in specific social movements or political issues. Environment has functioned less as an influence on events and characters than as a projection of their inner conflict, a symbol as well as an agent of inhuman darkness. Bellow's protagonists are thus placed in a social environment but oppressed by personal and natural forces that obscure the resulting tensions by developing them in oblique relation to their framing situations. Allbee, the protagonist's alter ego in

The Victim, to take one example, does not confront Leventhal with social realities but with an inverted view of the personal truths whose existence Leventhal has not entirely been successful in repressing. The ruin of Herzog's country estate both contributes to and reflects the personal breakdown he experiences. There is, then, in Bellow's fiction a fundamental division between a moral concern for the way things look and feel and an insistence on a more meaningful ideality, antecedent to such everyday striving and projected by characters indistinguishable from the authorial voice, whose narrow consciousness of a world displaces its portrayal through an independent perspective.[30]

In developing his fiction independently of the social realism of the thirties and equally of the modernist alienation that immediately preceded it, Bellow, as M. A. Klug argues, has remained in the American tradition by balancing a naturalistic pessimism with an equally American romantic quest for self-perfection. Objectifying as well as internalizing the conflicts which the naturalists assigned to separate characters, Bellow, Klug continues, allows his heroes to contain both the heroic and ordinary self. It is as an expression of the debate between these selves that the real conflict of Bellow's novels emerges. That is to say that not only do Bellow's protagonists struggle with life; they struggle, most of all, to make sense of it as well, struggle with the difficulty of articulating that struggle. Bellow's characters do not merely attempt to get something done; they attempt to make something clear—clear, above all, to themselves. Like Joseph in *Dangling Man,* they seem drawn "to know what we are and what we are for, to know our purpose, to seek grace." Often the search for all this knowledge has not yielded a belief in the evolution of a character as a product of his developing experience but as an expression of a mystical stillness that exists at its axial center. In looking to this mysterious center as an alternative to man's frantic striving and to the disguises he often adopts to conceal it from himself no less than from others, Bellow, particularly since the fifties seemed responsive, if at times playfully so, to metaphysical more than social explanations of human behavior.

Such philosophical concerns in Bellow's fiction have clustered chiefly around the fictional interest in Rudolf Steiner or Wilhelm Reich, to whose ideas Bellow was reputedly introduced by his friend the late Isaac Rosenfeld. Bellow has played down the importance of his own commitment to this as well as other literary influences on his fiction. Of Rosenfeld he has explained that "In some of his strange beliefs I often followed him because I loved him and did not want to lose my connection with him."[31] Pointing to a later version of the essay in which these remarks were made, Eusebio Rodrigues shows that Reichianism was an important if not always successfully handled element in his fiction. In fact, the furious struggle for self realization that describes the central action of much of Bellow's fiction is marked by a decided ambivalence toward what constitutes a human response and consequently toward where to locate the nobility Bellow attempts to invest in his protagonists. He has invested such nobility in the conviction Augie March is led to by observing his brother Simon and fellow machiavellians that "one is only ostensibly born to remain within limits," and in the parallel desire of Eugene Henderson for Grun tu Molani—the notion that man wants to live. Alternatively it emerges with Wilky, with Herzog, Artur Sammler, with Charlie Citrine, in acknowledging the contract man signs with life—with God—as a condition of his existence. It is this later conviction that has seemed to dominate Bellow's more recent fiction, where, for the most part, the striving for a separate destiny changes direction, if it does not stop altogether, and becomes the hope for a semi-mystical transformation, an "inspired condition."

In tracing the composition of *Herzog*, Daniel Fuchs sees a progression from realism to lyricism in which the protagonist is able to approach such a state. Examining both verbal changes as well as larger, structural revisions, Fuchs demonstrates Herzog's conversion from madness to sanity by declaring his allegiance to a "moral authority greater than that of the individual ego." Unlike Tommy Wilhelm, who similarly comes to a recognition of the transcendent unity of being, Herzog is aware of the comic aspects of his predicament. As Bellow continues to address it, however, there has developed an increasing distance between the affirmation of human possibility he has stubbornly attempted to maintain and the successful dramatization of such an affirmation in the face of life's desperate conditions. Noting that Bellow has not brought his fiction within a single dramatic focus, John Aldridge identifies in it two concurrent statements: one of a speculative nature which expresses Bellow's faith in a cosmic place for man; the other a more earthly statement in which "success is measured by the standards of the con game." For Aldridge, Bellow's success in objectifying in *Humboldt's Gift* the condition of wishfulness if not the basis for hope is a function of his recognition that such reconciliation of the opposing strands of optimism and perception result from the acknowledgement that it is a gift and not an earned change proceeding from the character's experience.

This transcendent impulse as a moral yardstick for human behavior, however, at times leads Bellow to something like the alienation he has seen in the modernist reaction to middle-class values and which, he has maintained, resulted in a fragmented view of the self and a complementary weakening of the narrative principle, a concern for what happens next. Bellow has complained of the consequent passivity in the fiction of Lawrence, Joyce, or Proust, but though in contrast to what he describes as their didactic view of experience he argues for the expression of ideas most opposite to those of the author and for the dynamic ranging of these ideas against each other, he envisions the creative act through which these ideas are arrived at as itself fundamentally passive. Fictional ideas, he insists, must be discovered not invented.[32] In contrast to Philip Roth's sense that writers were unable to find sustaining social values and became preoccupied with examinations of the private life as a fictional subject, Bellow, surveying the fiction of the early sixties, objects that such examinations have yielded a contempt for the possibilities of the self, particularly as it is seen to represent conventional, humanistic values. In novelists such as Roth, J. F. Powers, James Jones, John Updike, J. P. Donleavy, and William Burroughs among others, he finds a submissiveness similar to Ernest Hemingway's eager acceptance of the restrictions imposed more by his image of man—terse and elliptical—than by the demonstrated impact of feelings and emotions.[33] Bellow's objection to the inability of these writers to arrive at a rational affirmation of contemporary life is, however, complemented by his sense that since "almost nothing of a spiritual ennobling character is brought into the internal life of a modern American by his social institutions. He must discover it in his own experience, by his own luck as an explorer, or not at all."[34] Yet he has also maintained that it is just such exaggerated notions of the self that result in the distortions of life's true meaning. As early as *Dangling Man*, he has identified our preoccupation with the insubstantial, with distortions of reality on a heritage of Romanticism which leads us to compare unfavorably our present situation with the models of greatness history offers. "It is because we have been taught there is no limit to what a man can be," the narrator explains. Accordingly Herzog, like Tommy Wilhelm before him and Artur Sammler and Charlie Citrine after, is content to end his furious struggle for self realization content merely to accept things as willed. Earthly power no longer steals but resides chiefly in women and in the judiciary. Even the phallic majesty which Bellow invests in a black pickpocket who ironically carries an echo of D. H. Lawrence's notion of blood consciousness, even such primitive power is overcome by the singleminded and brutal efficiency of commercial purpose.

Jeffrey Meyers indicates an iconographic focus for this pessimism in Bellow's use of Breughel's painting "The Misanthrope," while Philip Stevick shows how in Bellow's short fiction the voices—its true subject—are limited in their attempt to get beyond the confusion of society and nature. For Stevick, such confusion is concentrated in the variety of rhetorical devices that Bellow employs, few if any of which permit the exchange of definitive understanding. Stevick thus makes a radical departure from the more traditional view of Bellow's style which has regarded it as a liberating element in his fiction, particularly as it reflects Bellow's immersion in a Jewish literary and cultural tradition.[35] Though, as Frank Kermode indicates, Bellow's themes establish the representative dilemma of the urban Jew, the bouncy texture of his prose with its scrambling of formal and colloquial diction and forcing of conventional syntax and its underlying ironic intonation yield an energy that calls attention to the quality of life rather than to its limits. Irving Howe compares the style to action painting and Bellow himself in a well-known review of Sholom Aleichem's *Mottel the Cantor's Son* has claimed for Yiddish the ability to reconcile greatness of thought with poverty of condition and so enable ghetto minorities to maintain their connection with the world and to overcome its penalties.[36] Yet the rush and flow of his language lends itself more to an impressionistic feeling, as Howe points out, to the sense of the felt moment than to what happens next or to the fully developed drama of ideas.[37]

Speaking of his play, *The Last Analysis*, Bellow has remarked that "its real subject is the mind's comic struggle for survival in an environment of ideas," and it is with the rational engagement of moral issues that Bellow's fiction is most intimately identified.[38] "Unless we think," Bellow insisted in accepting the

National Book Award for *Herzog,* "unless we make a clearer estimate of our condition, we will continue to write kid stuff, to fail in our function; we will lack serious interests and become truly irrelevant."[39] This is the fate, he comes close to saying, that threatens such writers as Ernest Hemingway, who, Bellow notes ironically, "was not satisfied with arriving at a satisfactory idea of his existence" and correspondingly, along with his heroes, resisted "the passivity and impotence that result from the prevalence of thought."[40] Yet Bellow has refused to identify himself as an intellectual, repeatedly challenging what he has taken to be the estrangement of the intellectual tradition from the common world of feeling. The writer must not allow himself to become distracted from what, quoting Melville, Bellow describes as "the low enjoying power." What made this resistance to distraction particularly difficult for Bellow was the indifference with which he found society regarded true art[41] and the complementary impotence of the writer in affecting public policy, a decline in importance he saw from the literary position closer to the center of things in the eighteenth and even the nineteenth centuries.[42] A decade after the now famous symposium conducted by the *Partisan Review* revealed a widespread belief that the writer could no longer discover his values in opposition to society, Bellow saw the influence of the intellectual limited to providing government with a symbolic legitimacy.[43] Even at that the now vastly more numerous intellectuals were concentrated in the university—Bellow described it as a hospital of literature—which was preoccupied with translating literature into alternate and less accessible forms of discourse. Yet if art has been assimilated by a technological society, Bellow recognized that it was nonetheless unintelligible to it. In the sixties, he noted with concern that the modern writer has lost his interest in narrative and substituted for it a vision of experience for which the dominant metaphor became the principle of entropy taken from modern physics.[44] Bellow attributes this tendency to the modernist reaction to an oppressive middle class and to the complementary desire it fostered in the public to be marvelous. On the one hand, he sees the result of this to be "a dark literature, a literature of victimization, of old people sitting in ash cans waiting for the breath of life to depart." On the other, it results in a loss of the exemplary figure of action.[45] Bellow is thus led both to reject the influence of modernism and to bemoan the isolation of the contemporary writer from the great modernist figures, to complain at the same time of the desire for a unique fate and of the inability to realize that desire.

One striking manifestation, for Bellow, of the eagerness with which culture assimilated the appearance of thought was the adoption of a popularized Freudianism as a staple of Hollywood psychology. Bellow saw in the formulaic application of psychological insights that characterized American movies a dehumanization in which motive came to dominate not only the characters portrayed, but even the actors themselves. Having lost all human qualities, they served, like models, "merely [to] wear merchandise." Particularly troubling to Bellow was the idea that the unrestricted expression of sexual feeling was a requisite of healthy human development, a belief he saw as an extention of a philosophy formerly limited to radical artists and thinkers, so that, ironically, he is led to acknowledge the superiority of movies which celebrated action for its own sake to those freighted with intellectual significance.[46] On a broader scale, he was moved to observe derisively that "art in the twentieth century is more greatly appreciated if it is directly translatable into intellectual interests, if it stimulates ideas, if it lends itself to discourse. Because intellectuals do not like to suspend themselves in works of the imagination."[47] The opposition to the imagination of intellect no less than of fact emerges in Bellow's fiction not only in the struggle of ideas with each other but in the struggle of the fiction against the notion of approaching reality through them at all.[48]

Emphasizing the principle of self-transcendence particularly as it emerges in the Hasidic strain of Jewish spirituality in the later novels in contrast to the concern for social circumstances that often had been seen as a definitive element of the earlier ones, Nathan Scott, Jr. has noted Bellow's "penchant for viewing with alarm the brutalizing power of the intellect and the desiccating effects of modern rationalism."[49] Bellow has spoken of the didactic purpose as a function of the "calculating principle in modern life," and has seen the literary breakdown of character, action, and language as an aspect of the cultural tendency toward abstraction. "Not only books, paintings, and musical compositions, but love affairs, marriages, and even religious convictions often originate in an idea," he has pointed out, "so that the *idea* of love is more common than love, and the *idea* of belief is more often met with than faith."[50] Bellow has seen such ideation as an individuating principle, obscuring the true understanding of an axial connection which unifies all humanity. Tommy Wilhelm, for example, describes the consequences of the private language each man's ideas allow him to speak:

> If you wanted to talk about a glass of water, you had to start back with God creating the heavens and earth; the apple; Abraham; Moses and Jesus; Rome; the Middle Ages; gunpowder; the Revolution; back to Newton; up to Einstein; then war and Lenin and Hitler. After reviewing this and getting it all straight again you could proceed to talk about a glass of water. "I'm fainting, please get me a little water."[51]

Expanded into a cultural style, the effect is a rise in consciousness which paradoxically serves only to further isolate the artist from the community:

> We are not sold real apples or real ice cream (Bellow observes) we are sold the idea of an apple, the memory of ice cream. Most people, for their fifteen cents, buy the idea of a newspaper. On other levels, still, they hear the idea of music in elevators. They are presented with the idea of honor, patriotism, and sincerity in politics, or, in law, the shadows of justice. The media offer flimsy ideas of human attachment, the films produce the spooks of passion and of love. Then there are impresarios, performers, painters and writers who offer in various packages the thinnest recollection, the phantom of art.[52]

The conflict between a regard for ideas, particularly in a social context of religion, science, philosophy, and politics, and a suspicion both of the society in which those ideas are given shape and of the intellectual tendency to submerge reality in the act of the mind has often emerged in Bellow's concern for the

writer and for the nature and condition of his art. Bellow's realistic tight struc-
tured novels had begun with the sense of the individual as a victim of social
conditions he could nonetheless not afford to alienate himself from. By the
beginning of the seventies, culture itself had become the victim of an intellectual orthodoxy and influenced by European theories of phenomenology and
structuralism suffered from a "corruption of consciousness," which Bellow saw
as "the worst disease of the mind." "Modern writers sin," Bellow claimed,
"where they suppose they know as they conceive that physics knows or that
history knows."[53] Such supposed knowledge results, for Bellow, in an idea
of literature whose view of reality accommodates only a desperate striving
for individual distinctions or in the conviction of hopelessness against
which such striving appears to struggle. Bellow's objection to this literature
of ideas, then, is not that it allows for exaggerated notions of individual
possibility but that it fulfills its own gloomy prophecies by ignoring the
uncertainty with which life confounds our scepticism about these same
possibilities. When modern writers "knock at the door of mystery with the
knuckles of cognition," Bellow has remarked, "it is quite right that the door
should open and some mysterious power should squirt them in the eye."[54]
attempts to translate his ideas about it into parity with such mysterious power
becomes incorporated as a central thematic element of the narrative. Ben Siegel
points out that in Charlie Citrine's attempt to get beyond the formulaic categories of knowledge that determine the cultural notions of success, he comes to
realize that the ideas with which both he and his mentor, Humboldt, started out
are themselves the means by which man victimizes himself. Only in parodic
form as they address what Siegel sees as Citrine's withdrawal from his immediate environment no less than from history to the safety of ideas can these ideas
become nourishing once again.

Citrine is thus not an artist who must sacrifice his unorthodox views to
obtain the tolerance or even the rewards society has to offer. It is rather
unorthodoxy that accounts for his success. Even his exclusionary concern for
that success, his intention to examine social ailments, the boredom it generates
contributes to his value to society. Citrine's interest in anthroposophy and his
parallel vulnerability to small time, even comic gangsterism, here humorously
associated with academic ambition, becomes the focus of this intellectuality
and as it affects his life and his art becomes as well the subject of Bellow's satire.

The comic tone in Bellow's treatment of Citrine's troubled consciousness,
like that in *Herzog*, emerges as the defining element of Bellow's fiction. It
informs to some degree his concern for social realism as well as the more lyrical
evocations of consciousness which Robert Alter has seen supplying the conventionally objective realism of the present with the richness of the personal past
and thereby constituting one of the continuing notions of value Bellow expresses.[55] Along with the discovery of a comic subject in the limits of art as well
as those of men, Bellow has animated his comedy with romantic figures who are
not held to one social class or level of society and who do not allow themselves to
be defined by such affiliation. He has himself written ironically of the tendency

in modern American comic fiction to parody the romantic conception of the self. The roots of this tendency he has identified in the modernist repudiation of the middle class, extending from Dostoevski to Chaplin and including James Joyce. *Ulysses*, to whose protagonist Herzog has oftentimes been compared and which has been cited as the source of his name, Bellow disparagingly termed a "comedy of information," held together by slurs (in the musical sense) of ambiguous laughter."[56] In the novels of Nabokov, Donleavy, and Bruce J. Friedman among more recent novelists, Bellow has similarly objected to the reduction of private life to an interchangeable and equally inessential series of observations, a subject of comic acceptance rather than of comic protest. In finding his comic subject in the limits of art as well as in those of men, Bellow extends the scope of his comic imagination, beyond that of the solvent Delmore Schwartz has seen in it for both unqualified affirmation and satirical rejection. Lionel Trilling sees in Bellow a conscious commitment to the comic tradition which excludes the exaggerated capacity and expectations of the heroic personality. Writing of the idiosyncratic figure in William Morris's romance, who expresses some dissatisfactions with utopian conditions, Trilling notes that "although [Morris] sees to it that this subversive person is refused and gently mocked, [he] pays through him his own tribute to the comic and expresses his momentary uneasy sense that the impulse to an organized human perfection might mean a dimunition of human reality and interest.[57] Trilling's sense of comedy thus involves an acceptance as well as a recognition of the limited conditions that circumscribe what we ordinarily think of as reality, that is the ability to find some redeeming aspect of those limitations and so, in some sense, overcome them. But for Bellow the comic sensibility, even in its ironic mode, is more complex and serves as well in a liberating function, even as Augie's refusal to be bound by any of the official roles with which society hopes to structure his experience makes him a comic prototype for all those heroes who hope to rise beyond the restrictive circumstances of their birth—metaphysical no less than social or economic. "If you *think*," Einhorn advises Augie, "the least of the consolation prizes is the world," and even wise old Marcus Schlossberg, who sees as schizophrenic the attempt to deny death, recognizes the unlimited power of thought. This comic motion which takes as its thrust a belief in realized opportunities is, however, counterpointed by a sense that the ambition which informs them is only a boast, fostered by a false perception of what we can get away with. It is this perception that is filtered through our dealings with society and comes to us sometimes in the form of sugars, other times in blows. Bellow tells Jo Brans that though Herzog has come to a point of rest, he will have to deal with people again and so once more assume roles himself. Bellow does not resolve the contradiction between the belief in the attempt to realize a separate and unique destiny and the corresponding search for such a destiny in both resistance to and acceptance of the conditions of being. Like Leopold Bloom, who, he observed, seeks relief from the undifferentiated ocean of fact in "digression, in evasion, and in wit,"[58] Bellow's comedy is evasive, turning finally to parody its inclusive tendency. With it least partial approval, Bellow has quoted Harold Rosenberg's belief that "the artist is the only figure in this society who is able not to be alienated, because he works directly with the materials of his own experience and transforms them."[59] Transforms them into what, Rosenberg does not say. Neither does Bellow. It is unlikely that either one meant transforms them into someone else's experience, though the point of Rosenberg's remarks is to protest the separation of the intellectual from the way the rest of society thinks and feels. Bellow does, it is true, not always seem sure this would be such a bad idea, especially when the social experience is dominated by an admiration for technology that imposes itself even on the aims of literary representation. In opposition to the democratic principle, he quotes Goethe's view of the writer's responsibility. "I have never bothered to ask in what way I was useful in society as a whole," Goethe remarked, "I contented myself with what I recognized as good or true." The transformation Bellow had in mind, then, must not have been of experience at all, but of the material which, through art, becomes no longer inert but vital. It is a comic transformation that leads Bellow from his pursuit of what he thinks of as an awareness of what all men have in common— our true condition—back to the world. For this is what comedy always does. The brilliant African chief in *Henderson*, like so many similar brilliant figures of Bellow's fiction, insists on the need for striving by which he can convert the ideal to actual. And such effort becomes translated even into the texture of Bellow's prose and in the narrative technique, which, like Melville's, is speculative, dissolving the world of particularly in antecedent meanings. Bellow's comedy does not let the world and its noise blot out the individual truth. For this, too, is what comedy always does. And in this way, both in the world and outside of it, Bellow's comedy reaches beyond the threatening appearances— the personal and social crises of our time—to that state where all striving stops, but in which man can not be still, and touches in the verdict of his art the living human principle that continues to engage us all.

Notes

1. Elizabeth Hardwick, "Fiction Chronicle," *Partisan Review*, 15 (1948), 114. Norman Podhoretz, *Making It*.

2. Stephen Spender, *The Struggle of the Modern*, (London: Hamish Hamilton, 1963), p. 48.

3. Gordon Lloyd Harper, "The Art of Fiction XXXVII: An Interview with Saul Bellow," *The Paris Review*, 36 (1966), 62–63.

4. Saul Bellow "Where Do We Go From Here: The Future of Fiction," *Michigan Quarterly*, 1 (1962), 27–33; repr. *Saul Bellow and the Critics*, ed. Irving Malin (New York: New York Univ. Press, 1967), pp. 211–20.

5. Saul Bellow, "Buñuel's Unsparing Vision," *Horizon*, 5 (Nov. 1962), 110–12.

6. Saul Bellow, "Man Underground," *Commentary*, 13 (1952), 608.

7. Saul Bellow, "The Writer and the Audience," *Perspectives USA*, 9 (1954), 100–01.

8. Drawing on Ralph Freedman's ground-breaking recognition of environment as both influence on as well as index to the hero's consciousness ("Saul Bellow: The Illusion of Environment," *Wisconsin Studies in Contemporary Literature*, 1 [1960], 50–65.), Mark Christhilf advances an argument for the city in Bellow's fiction as both an image of oppressive social conditions and as a projection or mirror of man's destructive instincts. The city, Christhilf concludes, serves as a symbol

of the inhuman force, "a terrorfilled underworld which constantly offers up some encounter with death" ("Death and Deliverance in Saul Bellow's Symbolic City," *Ball State University Forum*, 18 [1977], 9–23). Throughout his fiction, Bellow has, however, resisted the view of the individual as dominated or even shaped by an environment for which he is nonetheless in part responsible. Wandering around Chicago, Joseph in *Dangling Man* anticipates the striving for a good opinion of human prospects that culminates in *Herzog*. "There could be no doubt," Joseph thinks, "that these billboards, streets, tracks, houses, ugly and blind were related to interior life. And yet, I told myself, there had to be a doubt. There were human lives organized around these ways and houses, and that they, the houses, say, were the analogue, that what men created they also were, through some transcendent means, I could not bring myself to concede. There must be a difference, a quality that eluded me, somehow, a difference between things and persons and even between acts and persons. Otherwise the people who lived here were actually a reflection of the things they lived among. I had always striven to avoid blaming them. Was that not in effect behind my daily reading of the paper? In their business and politics, their taverns, movies, assaults, divorces, murders, I tried continually to find clear signs of their common humanity" (Saul Bellow, *Dangling Man* [New York: Meridian Books, 1960], pp. 24–25).

9. Harper, p. 65.

10. Saul Bellow, "Illinois Journey," *Holiday*, 22 (Sept. 1959), 62, 102–07. Along with Bellow's estrangement from the city, Sarah Cohen ("Saul Bellow's Chicago," *Modern Fiction Studies*, 24 [1974], 139–46) notes that its menace, in Chicago at least, is leavened with a vitality that compels Bellow's imagination into a luminous evocation of place. Sanford Pinsker, similarly, notes the sustaining aspect of urban environment along with its complexity. Writing of Bellow's most recent fiction, Pinsker sees that complexity as a stage the hero must pass through on his way to a more transcendent simplicity. ("Sustaining Community of 'Reality Instructor': The City in Saul Bellow's Later Fiction," *Studies in American Jewish Literature*, 3 [1977], 25–30). Bellow summed up his own view of Chicago in recalling that right from the start it gave him "a sense of painful emptiness and discontinuity," but adding immediately that "its great energy uncomfortably demanded participation" ("A Writer and His City," *National Observer*, Nov. 11, 1972).

11. Saul Bellow, "The Sealed Treasure," *Times Literary Supplement*, July 1, 1960, p. 414.

12. Saul Bellow, "Recent American Fiction," *Gertrude Clarke Whittall Lecture* (The Library of Congress: Washington. D.C., 1963), 2.

13. Saul Bellow, "Starting Out in the Thirties," p. 77.

14. Saul Bellow, "A World Too Much With Us," *Critical Inquiry*, 2 (1975), 9.

15. Saul Bellow, "A Matter of the Soul," *Opera News*, 11 (1975), 28.

16. Saul Bellow, "The Writer and the Audience," p. 102.

17. Saul Bellow, "Machines and Storybooks," *Harper's*, Aug. 1974, p. 50.

18. "Cloister Culture," in "An Interview with Myself," *New Review*, 18 (1975), 44–45.

19. Letter from Saul Bellow to Stanley Trachtenberg, Jan. 15, 1979.

20. Bellow, "Machines and Storybooks," pp. 48–59.

21. Bellow, "Machines and Storybooks," p. 53.

22. Marcus Klein, "A Discipline of Nobility: Saul Bellow's Fiction," *Kenyon Review*, 24 (1967), 203–26.

23. Bellow, "Cloister Culture," p. 2.

24. Saul Bellow, "Deep Readers of the World, Beware," *New York Times Book Review*, 15 Feb. 1959, p. 1.

25. Saul Bellow, "Facts That Put Fancy to Flight," *New York Times Book Review*, 11 Feb. 1962, pp. 1, 28.

26. Bellow, "Machines and Storybooks," p. 53.

27. Pearl K. Bell, "Good-Bad and Bad-Bad," *Commentary*, 66 (1978), 70–73.

28. Bellow, "Machines and Storybooks," p. 54.

29. Saul Bellow, "Starting Out in Chicago," *American Scholar*, 44 (1974/5), 71–77.

30. Although Bellow is generally acknowledged to have found his authentic voice with *The Adventures of Augie March*, it is with the publication of this novel that significant criticism of his structural unity and conception of character begins. Mark Schorer, for example, notes that Augie's commitment is mainly to self-discovery despite the seemingly picaresque quality of his adventures and the densely social texture of the novel and concludes that Augie's character does not develop but only "becomes more articulately aware of what he already is" ("A Book of Yes and No," *Hudson Review*, 7 [1954], 136–41). Richard Chase similarly sees a weakness in the novel's structural unity as a result of Bellow's failure to subordinate the circumstances to a controlling vision ("The Adventures of Saul Bellow: Progress of a Novelist," *Commentary*, 27 [1959], 326–7, 330). More recently Robert Boyers accuses Bellow of making irrelevant to the conclusion of *Mr. Sammler's Planet* the central issues earlier raised by the novel. Boyers sees these as the relation between natural unity and social diversity and the attempt of the critical intellect to resolve the split. "In the view to which Mr. Sammler subscribes," Boyers remarks, "we come to know what is necessary through an operation of the mind which is not exercised by specific phenomena, the accumulation and consideration of sensible experience." He concludes that "Mr. Sammler disappoints us in his continuing incapacity to get beyond the realm of sentimental affirmation to a more accurate apprehension of social reality" ("Nature and Social Reality in Bellow's *Sammler*," *Critical Quarterly*, 15 [1973], 260, 270). Theodore Solotaroff has seen a parallel evasion of and insulation from the social issues raised in *Herzog* by means of the protagonist's feeling ("Napoleon St. and After," *Commentary*, 38 [1964], 63–66.) while Roger Shattuck has maintained that Bellow by means of spoof evades these larger questions raised in *Humboldt's Gift* ("A Higher Selfishness?" *The New York Review of Books*, 22 [Sept. 18, 1975], 21–25). Much of the recent criticism of Bellow's fiction has been directed at what has been perceived to be the author's growing conservatism. Among the more extreme of these judgments are those of Richard Poirier, "Bellows to Herzog," *Partisan Review*, 32 (1965), 264–71; David Gallaway, "*Mr. Sammler's Planet*: Bellow's Failure of Nerve," *Modern Fiction Studies*, 19 (1973), 17–28; and Jack Richardson, "A Burnt-out Case," *Commentary*, 60 (1975), 74–78. Attributing much of this criticism to the partisan view of the "New Left," Allan Guttmann takes a more positive view of Bellow's achievement, arguing in *Mr. Sammler*, at least, that Bellow has separated his views from those of his protagonist.

31. Saul Bellow, "Isaac Rosenfeld," *Partisan Review*, 23 (1956), 565–67. Critics have seen in Bellow's fiction the influence of Dostoevsky, Camus, and Sartre, whose philosophy Bellow has felt, so overwhelmed the dramatic element in the work that "not even his stubbornest admirers can read his novels." See Saul Bellow "Theatre Chronicle," *Partisan Review*, 21 (1954), 315. Bellow has acknowledged an admiration for Edgar Lee Masters, Sherwood Anderson, and Vachel Lindsay, writers who "resisted the material weight of American society" ("Starting Out in Chicago," *American Scholar*, 44 [1974/5], 73). And for Theodore Dreiser, whose "great lifting power," of feeling and concern for man's struggle to admit an *amor fati*, Bellow regarded as the source of his power (Saul Bellow, "Dreiser and the Triumph of Art," *Commentary*, 11 [1951], 502–03).

32. Bellow, "Where Do We Go From Here," p. 210.

33. Bellow, "Recent American Fiction," pp. 1–12. See also Saul Bellow, "Hemingway and the Image of Man," *Partisan Review*, 20 (1953), 338–42. For Bellow's sense that Hemingway "wants to be praised for offenses that he does not commit," see Bellow, "Dreiser and the Triumph of Art," p. 503.

34. Bellow, "Where Do We Go From Here," p. 215.

35. Among the many observations on the Jewish background in Bellow's fiction are Sarah Blacher Cohen, *Saul Bellow's Enigmatic Laughter* (Urbana: Univ. of Illinois Press, 1974), pp. 18–21, 66–67, 199; Allan Guttmann, "Mr. Bellow's America," *The Jewish Writer in America* (New York: Oxford Univ. Press, 1971), pp. 243–61; Irving Malin, *Jews and Americans* (Carbondale, Southern Illinois Univ. Press, 1965), pp. 73–75, 97–98; and Keith Opdahl, *The Novels of Saul Bellow* (University Park: The Pennsylvania State Univ. Press, 1967), pp. 25–26. Stephen Axelrod's note "The Jewishness of Bellow's *Henderson*," *American Literature*, 47 (1975), 439–43, provides an interesting reading of the one Bellow protagonist clearly not intended to be Jewish. Bellow has

responded cautiously to attempts to deal with his fiction reductively as determined by its Jewish quality and has ironically referred to himself along with Malamud and Roth as "the Hart, Shaffner and Marx of our trade" (Bellow, "Starting Out in the Thirties," p. 72).

36. Saul Bellow, "Laughter in the Ghetto," *Saturday Review of Literature*, 30 May 1953, p. 15.

37. In "The Stature of Saul Bellow," *Midstream*, 10 (1964), 3–15, Robert Alter makes an important distinction between the necessity of living with suffering that characterizes much of the Jewish diaspora and the modern view of the Jew as an archetype of alienation which implies fulfillment through such suffering. Writing of the fragmentation of style in *Herzog*, however, Alter points out that "the reader's traditional question about what happens next is replaced by our curiosity about what piece of Moses Herzog we will get next."

38. Alan Guttmann makes this point in "Saul Bellow's Humane Comedy," *Comic Relief Humor in Contemporary American Fiction* (Urbana: Univ. of Illinois Press, 1978), pp. 127–51.

39. Saul Bellow, "Thinking Man's Wasteland," *Saturday Review*, 3 April, 1965, p. 20.

40. Bellow, "Hemingway and the Image of Man," p. 339.

41. Saul Bellow, "Pleasures and Pains of Playgoing," *Partisan Review*, p. 317.

42. Bellow, "A World Too Much With Us," p. 5.

43. Bellow, "Cloister Culture," in "An Interview with Myself," *New Review*, 18 (1975), 53–56, Bellow comments on the difficulty experienced by writers who, ornamental in the world of influence and power and isolated from the world of literary culture in which the novel's "ideas, its symbolic structure, its position in the history of Romanticism or Realism or Modernism, its higher relevance require devout study," is nonetheless "no more an Ivory Tower than Time magazine."

44. Bellow, "Where do We Go From Here," p. 213. See also Bellow, "Recent American Fiction," p. 2. For Bellow's concern about the effects of the concept of entropy on the romantic idea of the Self see Bellow, "Recent American Fiction," p. 2. The effects of the university and of fashionable intellectuality on both the writer and the culture can be seen prominently in Saul Bellow, "The University as Villain," *The Nation*, 185 (1957), 361–63, and in Saul Bellow, "Culture Now: Some Animadversions, Some Laughs, *Modern Occasions*, 1 (1971), 162–71.

45. Bellow, "Where Do We Go From Here," p. 219; Bellow, "Culture Now," pp. 177–78.

46. Saul Bellow, "The Mass-produced Insight," *Horizon*, 5 (1963), 111–13.

47. Bellow, "Machines and Storybooks," p. 54.

48. In a particularly incisive treatment of the ambivalent treatment of thought in Bellow's fiction, Ronald Weber has pointed out that Bellow's hero must "pass beyond mental explanation altogether and renew his grasp on ordinary human reality" (Ronald Weber, "Bellow's Thinkers," *Western Humanities Review*, 22 [1968], 305–13). Shaun O'Connell also writes of the limits of thought, particularly self reflection and of the unlikelihood of controlling experience by ideas. O'Connell, however, does not so much question the intrinsic value of intellect in Bellow's fiction as he does point to the author's scepticism about whether ideas can make anything happen. (Shaun O'Connell, "Bellow: Logic's Limits," *Massachusetts Review*, 10 [1969], 182–87). See also Tony Tanner, "Saul Bellow: The Flight from Monologue," *Encounter*, February 1965, pp. 58–70.

49. Nathan Scott, Jr., "Sola Gratia: The Principle of Bellow's Fiction," in *Craters of the Spirit* (Washington, D.C.: M. Corpus Publications, 1968), pp. 233–65.

50. Bellow, "Where Do We Go From Here," pp. 217–18.

51. Saul Bellow, *Seize the Day* (Fawcett: Greenwich, Conn., 1956), p. 91.

52. Bellow, "A Matter of the Soul," p. 29.

53. Bellow, "Recent American Fiction," p. 12. See also "Culture Now: Some Animadversions, Some Laughs," pp. 162–71, for Bellow's view of the literary decadence spawned by "an amusement society."

54. Saul Bellow, Harper, "The Art of Fiction," 67.

55. Robert Alter, "Stature of Saul Bellow," pp. 5–7. Alter sees the innovative use of flashback in

Bellow's narrative method as dramatic enactment rather than, as in, say, Proust, an adventitious discovery.

56. Bellow, "Machines and Storybooks," pp. 52–53.

57. Lionel Trilling, Introduction to *The Adventures of Augie March* (New York: Modern Library, 1965), pp. vii–xiii.

58. Bellow, "Machines and Storybooks," p. 53.

59. Saul Bellow, "A World Too Much With Us," *Critical Inquiry*, 2 (1975), 1.

REVIEWS

REVIEWS

A Man in His Time

Delmore Schwartz[*]

Here, for the first time I think, the experience of a new generation has been seized and recorded. It is one thing simply to have lost one's faith; it is quite another to begin with the sober and necessary lack of illusion afforded by Marxism, and then to land in what seems to be utter disillusion, only to be forced, stage by stage, to even greater depths of disillusion. This is the experience of the generation that has come to maturity during the depression, the sanguine period of the New Deal, the days of the Popular Front and the days of Munich, and the slow, loud, ticking imminence of a new war. With the advent of war, every conceivable temptation not to be honest, not to look directly at experience, not to remember the essential vows of allegiance to the intelligence and to human possibility and dignity—every conceivable temptation and every plea of convenience, safety and casuistry has presented itself.

Joseph, the hero of *Dangling Man*, is remarkable because he has the strength (and it is his only strength) to keep his eyes open and his mind awake to the quality of his experience. He has been for a time a member of the Communist Party and he has been offered a business career by a successful older brother. He has rejected both. With the coming of the war, he undergoes the slow strangulation of being drafted but not inducted into the army because of various bureaucratic formalities. During this period in the inter-regnum between civilian and army life, he is gradually stripped of the few pretenses and protections left to him. A Communist refuses to speak to him; his brother attempts to lend him money; his niece taunts him as a beggar; his friends who have made their "meek adjustments" are repelled by his unwillingness to accept things as they are; he quarrels with his friends, his relatives, his wife who is supporting him and the people who live in the rooming house in which he spends his idle days. And finally, unable to endure the continuous emptiness and humiliation of his life, he sees to it that he is immediately taken into the army.

Is it necessary to emphasize the extent to which this experience is characteristic? Here are the typical objects of a generation's sensibility: the phonograph records, the studio couch, the reproductions of Van Gogh, the cafeteria; and the typical relationships: the small intellectual circle which gradually

[*]Reprinted from *Partisan Review*, 11 (1944), 348–50.

breaks up, the easy and meaningless love affair, the marriage which is neither important nor necessary, the party which ends in hysterical outbreaks or sickness of heart, the gulf separating this generation from the previous one and the family life from which it came.

What is not typical is Joseph's stubborn confrontation and evaluation of the character of his life. He insists on making explicit his dependency on his wife. He tells himself again and again that his days are wasted. He seizes the Communist party-member who tries to snub him, and insists that as a human being he has a right to be greeted. He tells himself and anyone who will listen that he does not like the kind of life his society has made possible. And he refuses to yield to the philistinism and the organized lack of imagination that consoles itself by saying: "It might be worse," "It is worse elsewhere," "It cannot be other than it is," "This is the lesser evil, hence it is good."

As a novel, the faults of *Dangling Man* come mainly from the fact that it is somewhat too linear in its movement and contained within too small an orbit. Thus, in seeking to keep Joseph's frame of mind constantly in the foreground, Bellow brushes over a number of dramatic possibilities, particularly those inherent in Joseph's marriage relation and his rejection of financial success. The narrative is perhaps too spare in its use of detail and background. And the use of the journal as a form blocks off the interesting shift of perspective that could be gained by presenting Joseph through the eyes of some person of the preceding generation. But, given Bellow's choice of a diary for conveying a larger social pattern, these limitations were perhaps, hardly to be avoided, and this small book is an important effort to describe the situation of the younger generation.

Fiction in Review

Diana Trilling*

It is a special pleasure for a reviewer who did not admire Saul Bellow's first novel, "Dangling Man," to report of his second, "The Victim" (Vanguard, $2.75), that it is not only in every way a striking advance over its predecessor but also hard to match, in recent fiction, for brilliance, skill, and originality. There are of course certain clear connections between the two performances: Mr. Bellow still writes of a world where the sunlight penetrates only with difficulty and of people whose nerves are rubbed almost raw. But however cheerless the universe of "The Victim," the new novel is not open to the charge, as the earlier volume was, of reducing the world to the mean stature of some of its least expansive inhabitants or of neglecting to suggest the reprieve from misery which is always the promise of art. Mr. Bellow has remarkably transcended, in his second book, the self-pitying literalness which robbed his first of scale. He is still puritanically fearful of charming us, but he is at least willing to excite our emotional participation.

So much of the virtue of "The Victim" lies in its wonderful physical evocations—the domestic detail, for example, of its hero's existence: the dreadful decency of his apartment, the ghastliness of his quick, solitary meals, the suffocating routine of his habits of personal cleanliness—that not to linger over them is to do Mr. Bellow's sheer novelistic talent a grave injustice. But it is also impossible to deal adequately with the philosophical content of Mr. Bellow's book in a short review: like all good novels, it can be read on so many levels of meaning that to stay with only one or two of them is to put false boundaries on a very large experience.

Mr. Bellow tells the story of a young man; a Jew named Asa Leventhal, who is suddenly accused of having ruined another man's life in revenge for some anti-Semitic remarks. Several years before, when Leventhal had been out of a job, a Gentile acquaintance, Kirby Allbee, had given him an introduction to his employer, the editor of a chain of publications. The editor had received Leventhal so coldly that Leventhal had turned the interview into a violent quarrel. Now Allbee reappears in Leventhal's life and announces that the reason Leventhal had attacked his boss was that Allbee had once spoken offensively about Jews; he insists that as a consequence of Leventhal's misconduct he, who

*Reprinted from *Nation*, Jan. 3, 1948, pp. 24–25.

had introduced Leventhal to the editor, had himself been fired; out of work, he had taken to drinking heavily, lost his wife, and become a complete down-and-outer. He places the responsibility for this débâcle squarely upon Leventhal, attaches himself to him, and demands that his persecutor make restitution for the ruin he has caused.

The dramatic problem of Mr. Bellow's novel is to figure out who, in this complex of circumstances, is the "victim" of the book's title. There is certainly no doubt that Leventhal is being madly persecuted by Allbee, who has suddenly appeared out of nowhere to drop the full burden of his disintegrated life upon the other man. Leventhal remembers all the incidents of his former association with Allbee; but there is no reason for him to feel that when he lost his temper with Allbee's boss he was acting to affect the fate of a third person. And even supposing that Allbee had been fired as a result of Leventhal's behavior, is it Leventhal's responsibility that Allbee then went to pieces? On the other hand, not only is Allbee himself convinced that *he* was victimized by Leventhal; there are mutual friends, whom Leventhal respects, who—it turns out—agree that he had an important share in precipitating Allbee's downfall. The accusations and defenses move back and forth between the two men: each is forced farther and farther into examination of his motives both conscious and unconscious, while Mr. Bellow brilliantly explores the whole problem of guilt. What emerges from the investigation is a beautiful balance of forces: no man is without responsibility for his neighbor, but neither is any man really responsible for his neighbor or free of responsibility for himself. In addition, there is accident or, if you will, the biological determination which it would be hopeless to suppose one can entirely master, for oneself or anyone else.

Obviously not the least impressive aspect of Mr. Bellow's novel is that he dares to place this study of the difficult problem of responsibility in that most difficult of spheres, the sphere of interracial relationships. More and more these days, under the guise of increasing our "realism" about minority situations, progressive thought has actually been lending itself to myth-making. Teaching us to defend the rights of minorities, it also teaches us that members of minorities are not adult human beings like other citizens, with as much responsibility for their own destinies, but born victims—the innocent sufferers of the will of the dominant groups. Probably there is no less fashionable idea in current liberalism than that Jews exist in reciprocal relationship with Gentiles or Negroes with white people. But Mr. Bellow cuts across this pleasant fantasy to confront us with the disturbing idea that the social "victim" may himself assist in the creation of his unhappy condition. It would be a mistake to read "The Victim" as only a novel about anti-Semitism: its implications are much wider, and its insights are as relevant to members of majority groups—that is, to any human being—as to members of oppressed minorities. But even apart from these wider references, and read solely as a novel about the Jewish situation, it is morally one of the farthest-reaching books our contemporary culture has produced.

A good deal of nonsense is written by the book reviewers about the novel of ideas. Our professional readers like to assume that there is an unbridgeable separation between the novel of thought and the novel of feeling, that a book must be one or the other. But the simple truth is of course that not only do ideas necessarily adhere in emotions and emotions in ideas, but also that there is no such thing as a novel *without* ideas: a good novel has good ideas, a bad novel has bad ideas. And actually what the reviewers are protesting against when they protest against the novel of thought, is the confrontation with new, serious, or provocative thinking; we see that a book has only to be sufficiently soft or shoddy in its thinking—as, say, in the case of an "A Bell for Adano" or an "Arch of Triumph"—for the reviewer to acknowledge himself deeply stirred by its message. "The Victim" is solidly built of fine, important ideas; it also generates fine and important, if uncomfortable, emotions. Indeed, one has only to compare it to Mr. Bellow's earlier "Dangling Man" to have a striking lesson in the way in which intellect has the power to alter the quality of a novelist's feeling and even enhance his art.

Adventure in America

Delmore Schwartz[*]

Saul Bellow's new novel is a new kind of book. The only other American novels to which it can be compared with any profit are *Huckleberry Finn* and *U.S.A.*, and it is superior to the first by virtue of the complexity of its subject matter and to the second by virtue of a realized unity of composition. In all three books, the real theme is America, a fact which is not as clear in this new work as it is in its predecessors, perhaps because of its very newness. The sheer bigness of America as a theme and as a country has always made the novelist's task difficult, which may be the reason that Thomas Wolfe was so excited by trains, just as it certainly has something to do with the fact that *U.S.A.* does not possess complete narrative unity.

In other American novels of the same seriousness and ambition, the theme of America and of being an American is narrowed to a region—Hawthorne is writing about New England, Faulkner is writing about the South—or the novels are about Americans in Europe, which is almost as true of Hemingway as it is of James; or there is, in any case, a concentration upon a particular American *milieu.* Moreover, the classic choice of the American writer has been either uncritical affirmation on the one hand, or on the other hand some form of rejection, the rejection of satire in Lewis, the rejection of social protest in Dos Passos, or the rejection of tragedy in Dreiser and Fitzgerald. The point can hardly be overemphasized: Huck Finn is in flight from civilization; Milly Theale is swindled of, above all, her desire to live; Lambert Strether (or William Dean Howells) discovers in middle age that he has not really lived at all; Lily Bart commits suicide; Richard Cory blows out his brains; J. Alfred Prufrock feels that he "should have been a pair of ragged claws"; Frederic Henry makes "a separate peace"; Quentin Compson has to say four times that he does not hate the South; Clyde Griffiths is electrocuted; Jay Gatsby is murdered. There are many other instances of the same kind, almost none of which can be considered purely as tragedy, but more precisely as catastrophe: Clyde Griffiths and Jay Gatsby perish because they are Americans, Agamemnon and Macbeth because they are human beings.

The Adventures of Augie March is a new kind of book first of all because Augie March possesses a new attitude toward experience in America: instead of the blindness of affirmation and the poverty of rejection, Augie March rises

[*]Reprinted from *Partisan Review*, 21 (1954), 112–15.

from the streets of the modern city to encounter the reality of experience with an attitude of satirical acceptance, ironic affirmation, the comic transcendence of affirmation and rejection. As he says at the very start: "I am an American, Chicago-born—Chicago, that somber city—" (the adjective should make it clear that to be an American is far from the same thing as being a 100 percent American) "and go at things as I have taught myself, free style, and will make the record in my own way: first to knock, first admitted; sometimes an innocent knock, sometimes a not so innocent . . .," and it is soon clear that Augie has identified America and adventure, an identification which functions as both method and insight. Augie's style of speech is the kind of speech necessary for going everywhere and talking to all kinds of Americans: he is a highbrow of sorts, but he does not talk like one, knowing that if he did, there would be the wrong kind of distance between himself and most other human beings. Being a pure product of the big city, he talks like a wise guy and he is a wise guy, like the other guys on the block; but he does not entirely like being a wise guy, and he is one not for the sake of any sense of self it gives him, but because it is a way of staying alive if you live in twentieth-century America, staying alive and getting around. Augie is an adventurer in every sense of the word, including the not so innocent sense, because adventure is the only way to the reality of experience in America. This essential fact about Augie has been the cause of misgivings in several critics who have otherwise expressed much admiration for the book, and who feel that there is something wrong about Augie's resistance to commitments, or what Augie himself calls being recruited. Augie does not want to be recruited or committed to the commitments which others have decided are desirable for him, one of which is a wealthy marriage. To be committed is to be pinned down and cut off from the adventure of reality and of America, to be cut off from hope and from freedom and from the freedom to move on to new hopes when some hopes collapse. Once you are committed, the frontier is gone. This may not be the most desirable moral attitude, but it certainly gives Augie a degree of awareness which none of the other characters possess. The critics who felt misgivings about Augie's being uncommitted recognized the overwhelming reality of a dozen other characters. But since their reality is given solely through Augie's mind, there must be a necessary connection between Augie's uncommitted or free mind and his perception of their reality. Moreover, as Augie himself might say, you have got to be sure that you are not committing yourself to what that guy Erich Fromm calls "escape from freedom." To which it must be added that Kierkegaard, in pointing the necessity of choice and commitment, attacked the very commitments which Augie resists, the conformist, conventional, and official roles which are characteristic forms of inauthenticity, a term which anticipates the stuffed shirt.

And the connection between Augie's chief attitude and his grasp of experience comes to a climax in the wonderful episode of the eagle who, like Augie, refuses in his own way to be committed. Any paraphrase of the episode would violate its narrative tact and subtlety, but the main thing about the eagle is his refusal to be dominated beyond a certain point by another being: which seems quite sensible to Augie and outrageous cowardice to the girl who is training him and who is also trying to impose another kind of domination upon Augie. Augie does not want to be dominated and he does not want to dominate anyone else: this is a free country, and to dominate or to be dominated is to be cut off from the reality of experience and of human beings in America, however else it may be in a hierarchical society. Augie is precisely like the veterans of the last war who once the war was over wanted to get out of the army because no matter how high your rank, there was always someone else to boss you around: freedom is existence, as America is adventure. Since America began as an adventure, Augie is right to conclude as he does:

> Why, I am a sort of Columbus of those near-at-hand and believe you can come to them in this immediate *terra incognita* that spreads out in every gaze. I may well be a flop at this line of endeavor. Columbus, too, thought he was a flop, probably, when they sent him back in chains. Which didn't prove there was no America.

Thus, by hoping for the best and being prepared for the worst, Augie proves that there is an America, a country in which anything might happen, wonderful or awful, but a guy has a fighting chance to be himself, find out things for himself, and find out what's what. For the first time in fiction America's social mobility has been transformed into a spiritual energy which is not doomed to flight, renunciation, exile, denunciation, the agonized hyper-intelligence of Henry James, or the hysterical cheering of Walter Whitman.

The Man With
No Commitments

Robert Penn Warren[*]

The Adventures of Augie March is the third of Saul Bellow's novels, and by far the best one. It is, in my opinion a rich, various, fascinating, and important book, and from now on any discussion of fiction in America in our time will have to take account of it. To praise this novel should not, however, be to speak in derogation of the two earlier ones, *The Dangling Man* and *The Victim*. Both of these novels clearly indicated Saul Bellow's talent, his sense of character, structure, and style. Though *The Dangling Man* did lack narrative drive, it was constantly interesting in other departments, in flashes of characterization, in social and psychological comment. In *The Victim*, however, Bellow developed a high degree of narrative power and suspense in dealing with materials that in less skillful hands would have invited an analytic and static treatment. These were not merely books of promise. They represented—especially *The Victim*—a solid achievement, a truly distinguished achievement, and should have been enough to win the author a public far larger than became his. They did win the attention of critics and of a hard core of discriminating readers, but they were not popular.

The Dangling Man and *The Victim* were finely wrought novels of what we may, for lack of a more accurate term, call the Flaubert-James tradition. Especially *The Victim* depended much on intensification of effect by tightness of structure, by limitations on time, by rigid economy in structure of scene, by placement and juxtaposition of scenes, by the unsaid and withheld, by a muting of action, by a scrupulous reserved style. The novel proved that the author had a masterful control of the method, not merely fictional good manners, the meticulous good breeding which we ordinarily damn by the praise "intelligent."

It would be interesting to know what led Saul Bellow to turn suddenly from a method in which he was expert and in which, certainly, he would have scored triumphs. It would be easy to say that it had been from the beginning a mistake for him to cultivate this method, to say that he was a victim of the critical self-consciousness of the novel in our time, to say that in his youthful innocence he had fallen among the thieves of promise, the theorizers. Or it would be easy to say that the method of the earlier books did not accommodate

[*]Reprinted from *New Republic*, Nov. 2, 1953, pp. 22–23.

11

his real self, his deepest inspiration and that as soon as he liberated himself from the restriction of the method he discovered his own best talent.

These things would be easy to say but hard to prove. It would be equally easy to say that the long self-discipline in the more obviously rigorous method had made it possible for Bellow now to score a triumph in the apparent formlessness of the autobiographical-picaresque novel, and to remember, as a parallel, that almost all the really good writers of free verse had cultivated an ear by practice in formal metrics. I should, as a matter of fact, be inclined to say that *The Adventures of Augie March* may be the profit on the investment of *The Dangling Man* and *The Victim*, and to add that in a novel of the present type we can't live merely in the hand-to-mouth way of incidental interests in scene and character, that if such a novel is to be fully effective the sense of improvisation must be a dramatic illusion, the last sophistication of the writer, and that the improvisation is really a pseudo-improvisation, and that the random scene or casual character that imitates the accidental quality of life must really have a relevance, and that the discovery, usually belated, of this relevance is the characteristic excitement of the genre. That is, in this genre the relevance is deeper and more obscure, and there is, in the finest examples of the genre, a greater tension between the random life force of the materials and the shaping intuition of the writer.

It is the final distinction, I think, of *The Adventures of Augie March* that we do feel this tension, and that it is a meaningful fact. It is meaningful because it dramatizes the very central notion of the novel. The hero Augie March is a very special kind of adventurer, a kind of latter-day example of the Emersonian ideal Yankee who could do a little of this and a little of that, a Chicago pragmatist happily experimenting in all departments of life, work, pleasure, thought, a hero who is the very antithesis of one of the most famous heroes of our time, the Hemingway hero, in that his only code is codelessness and his relish for experience is instinctive and not programmatic. This character is, of course, the character made for the random shocks and aimless corners of experience, but he is not merely irresponsible. If he wants freedom from commitment, he also wants wisdom, and in the end utters a philosophy, the philosophy embodied by the French serving maid Jacqueline, big-legged and red-nosed and ugly, standing in a snowy field in Normandy, hugging still her irrepressibly romantic dream of going to Mexico.

But is this comic and heroic philosophy quite enough, even for Augie? Augie himself, I hazard, scarcely thinks so. He is still a seeker, a hoper, but a seeker and hoper aware of the comedy of seeking and hoping. He is, in fact, a comic inversion of the modern stoic, and the comedy lies in the tautology of his wisdom—our best hope is hope. For there is a deep and undercutting irony in the wisdom and hope, and a sadness even in Augie's high-heartedness, as we leave him standing with Jacqueline in the winter field on the road toward Dunkerque and Ostend. But to return to the proposition with which this discussion opened: if Augie plunges into the aimless ruck of experience, in the end we see that Saul Bellow has led him through experience toward philosophy. That is, the aimless ruck had a shape, after all, and the shape is not that of Augie's life but of Saul Bellow's mind. Without that shape, and the shaping mind, we would have only the limited interest in the random incidents.

The interest in the individual incidents is, however, great. In *The Victim* the interest in any one episode was primarily an interest in the over-all pattern, but here most incidents, and incidental characters, appeal first because of their intrinsic qualities, and, as we have said, our awareness of their place in the over-all pattern dawns late on us. In incident after incident, there is brilliant narrative pacing, expert atmospheric effect, a fine sense of structure of the individual scene. In other words, the lessons learned in writing the earlier books are here applied in another context.

As for characterization, we find the same local fascination. The mother, the grandmother, the feeble-minded brother, the brother drunk on success, the whole Einhorn family, Thea, the Greek girl—they are fully realized, they compel our faithful attention and, in the end, our sympathy. As a creator of character, Saul Bellow is in the great tradition of the English and American novel, he has the fine old relish of character for character's sake, and the sort of tolerance which Santayana commented on in Dickens by saying that it was the naturalistic understanding that is the nearest thing to Christian charity.

It is, in a way, a tribute, though a back-handed one, to point out the faults of Saul Bellow's novel, for the faults merely make the virtues more impressive. The novel is uneven. Toward the last third the inspiration seems to flag now and then. Several episodes are not carried off with the characteristic elan, and do not, for me at least, take their place in the thematic pattern. For instance, the Trotsky episode or the whole Stella affair, especially in the earlier stages. And a few of the characters are stereotypes, for example, Stella again. In fact, it is hard to see how she got into the book at all except by auctorial fiat, and I am completely baffled to know what the author thought he was doing with her, a sort of vagrant from some literary province lying north- northeast of the *Cosmopolitan Magazine*. Furthermore, several critics have already said that the character of Augie himself is somewhat shadowy. This, I think, is true, and I think I know the reason: it is hard to give substance to a character who has no commitments, and by definition Augie is the man with no commitments. This fact is a consequence of Bellow's basic conception, but wouldn't the very conception have been stronger if Augie had been given the capacity for deeper commitments, for more joy and sorrow? He might, at least, have tried the adventurer's experiment in those things? That is, the character tends now to be static, and the lesson that Augie has learned in the end is not much different from the intuition with which he started out. He has merely learned to phrase it. There is one important reservation which, however, I should make in my criticism of Augie. His very style is a powerful device of characterization. It does give us a temper, a texture of mind, a perspective of feeling, and it is, by and large, carried off with a grand air. Which leads me to the last observation that the chief release Saul Bellow has found in this book may be the release of a style, for he has found, when he is at his best, humor and eloquence to add to his former virtues.

The Language of Life

Norman Podhoretz°

At first sight, *The Adventures of Augie March* is very different from *Dangling Man* and *The Victim*, Saul's Bellow's first two novels. They were disciplined, abstract, subjective, and somber. But Mr. Bellow lets the reins go in this one. *Dangling Man* hardly ventured beyond the consciousness of its narrator; *Augie March* covers continents and the whole range of American society. *The Victim* restricted itself to the evocation of a nerve-pulling anxiety never adequately defined; *Augie March* is all variety, hopping from farce to melodrama, from abstract speculation to the most minute descriptions of faces, figures, and things. Its atmosphere, if not genial, is expansive, charged, effervescent. One senses the joy with which Mr. Bellow breathes the freer air; he writes like a man set loose from prison. Every page in his earlier books had a look of nervousness, as if expecting to be challenged to justify its presence in the total conception. In *Augie March*, every word exhales a devil-may-care, reckless confidence coming from the discovery of its right to exist solely for the sake of its own immediate impact. Mr. Bellow can't spurt out the images fast enough; the book is almost bursting at the seams in an effort to be exuberant:

"The rest of us had to go to the dispensary—which was like the dream of a multitude of dentists' chairs, hundreds of them in a space as enormous as an armory, and green bowls with designs of glass grapes, drills lifted zigzag as insects' legs, and gas flames on the porcelain swivel trays—a thundery gloom in Harrison Street of limestone county buildings and cumbersome red streetcars with metal grillwork on their windows and monarchical iron whiskers of cowcatchers front and rear. They lumbered and clanged, and their brake tanks panted in the slushy brown of a winter afternoon or the bare stone brown of a summer's, salted with ash, smoke, and prairie dust, with long stops at the clinics to let off clumpers, cripples, hunchbacks, brace-legs, crutch-wielders, tooth and eye sufferers, and all the rest."

Thomas Urquart (17th-century translator of Rabelais) and Smollett and Dickens are behind the raciness, pace, and thickness of that prose, not Flaubert or James or Forster—and that in itself indicates pretty well what Mr. Bellow is up to. He is trying to put blood into contemporary fiction and break through the hidebound conventions of the well-made novel. This is a herculean job that will have to be done if we are to have a living literature at all. But our sympathy

°Reprinted from *Commentary*, 16 (1953), 378–80.

with Mr. Bellow's ambition and our admiration for his pioneering spirit should not lead us to confuse the high intention with the realization.

The strain is apparent not only in many lapses, where Mr. Bellow tugs at syntax frantically, as if squeezing and twisting the language were enough to get all the juices out of it, but even in a passage as good as the one quoted. In a comparable paragraph of Urquart or Smollett, we get the sense of an endlessly flowing fountain; the stuff comes quickly and easily, with an effect rather like a Brueghel painting. But the feeling conveyed by Mr. Bellow's exuberance is an overwhelming impulse to get in as many adjectives and details as possible, regardless of considerations of rhythm, modulation, or, for that matter, meaning. Like Milton in *Paradise Lost*, who was trying to do the near impossible too, Mr. Bellow seems frightened of letting up; a moment's relaxation might give the game away. The result is that we are far more aware of the words than the objects, of Mr. Bellow than of the world—which is the reverse of how he would like us to respond. His language lacks the suction to draw us into its stream.

Exuberance isn't the only quality he strains for; he wants detachment and impersonality too. Mr. Bellow apparently knows that *Dangling Man* was ruined by its non-dramatic subjectivity, and *The Victim* marred by its failure to relate Leventhal's anxiety to the world outside. This time every precaution, we feel, has been taken to insure that *Augie March* shall be rich with life and mature in viewpoint. It proliferates in people, and Mr. Bellow also uses a narrator quite unlike himself in order to increase the distance between him and his material. I find it extremely difficult, however, to determine how often and how much he takes Augie at face value, and I think Mr. Bellow himself would be hard pressed to answer the question. It isn't that Augie lacks a personality of his own. Actually, considering how inherently incredible a character he is— tough as nails and sensitive as a poet, a handsome sex-hero and a profound moralist, a bum and a sophisticated man-about-town—he comes off very well on the realistic level. But he doesn't represent a point of view independent of Mr. Bellow's.

The jargon Augie speaks—it's the language of the autodidact—is a device that permits Mr. Bellow to get away with his uncertainty: "I am an American, Chicago born—Chicago, that somber city—and go at things as I have taught myself, free-style, and will make the record in my own way: first to knock, first admitted; sometimes an innocent knock, sometimes a not so innocent. But a man's character is his fate, says Heraclitus, and in the end there isn't any way to disguise the nature of the knocks by acoustical work on the door or gloving the knuckles."

Mr. Bellow is no doubt poking fun at his narrator here through mimicry, but we are supposed to be taking what Augie says very seriously: it's the theme of the novel, after all. The main effect of the mimicry is to give Mr. Bellow an out (he *knows* what sort of character his narrator is), not to qualify our response to Augie in any significant way. This kind of trick we are familiar with from Auden's early poetry, in which self-mockery becomes an excuse for the self-indulgent refusal to make up his mind.

Consequently, two things are always going on in *Augie March*. We are actually permitted to see the world only from Augie's perspective—and it is a very limited one—while being aware that Mr. Bellow shifts constantly in his attitude toward Augie, sometimes identifying with him completely, sometimes standing off with an equivocal neutrality very far from the detachment he's after.

Consider, for example, the love affairs in the book. They are obviously drawn not from life but from day-dream. It's impossible to believe that Mr. Bellow is unaware of this: from internal evidence we know that he is a first-hand authority on street-corner legend and pool-room mythology. But he gives us in Lucy Magnus the tired old image of the calculating, frigid rich girl who has always served as the scapegoat for her class in the bull sessions of the pool-room. And there is Mimi, the waitress who can be "one of the boys" (Augie of course doesn't sleep with her—another proof that Mr. Bellow knows the conventions of the pool-room). Thea is the most blatant example. Unbelievably beautiful, she runs after Augie (even coming to his room while he's in bed with a working girl), loves him madly, supports him in wealth and style in exotic Mexico, gives him a chance to show his stuff as a he-man trainer of eagles, and then clears out leaving him with the luxury of a broken heart and a gorgeous movie star to sleep with.

Is Mr. Bellow offering us some sort of comment on the fantasies of Americans? If so, what is it? Is Augie's jargon intended as the barometer to register the author's changes in attitude? If so, there must be more than mere mimicry in the standoffish passages to overpower or at least balance the pull of the action. The suspicion forces itself upon one that Mr. Bellow is resorting to a convenient trick only to sneak in a titillating appeal to our self-dramatizing day-dreams and his own.

The detachment Mr. Bellow is most often capable of is that of the caricaturist: "As she had great size and terrific energy of constitution she produced all kinds of excesses. Even physical ones: moles, blebs, hairs, bumps in her forehead, huge concentration in her neck; she had spiraling reddish hair springing with no negligible beauty and definiteness from her scalp, tangling as it widened up and out, cut duck-tail fashion in the back and scrawled out high above her ears."

Obviously, there is a great sensitivity here to the way things look and feel. The same energetic eye is very good at capturing mannerisms and tricks of speech too. But Mr. Bellow's relish in his own performance and his fascination with externals combine somehow to prevent reverberations below the surface from forcing their way through—as they do force their way through in Dickens' Mr. Podsnap, for instance, or George Eliot's Mrs. Glegg. As a result, most of Mr. Bellow's characters are one-dimensional: they exhibit not individuality but peculiarity. This simplicity of characterization is of course reinforced by the fact that Augie's point of view is not used to brighten the light thrown on the characters but to dim it to a flicker.

The portrayal of the cynical old Russian Jewish matriarch who raises Augie and tries to teach him how to become a gentleman is a case in point. We know in great detail what she looks like, how she speaks, what her notions about life are. But we get no sense of her as a complex, contradictory, rounded human being. Mr. Bellow never asks himself the question: What would it be like to be Grandma Lausch? He doesn't care, contenting himself merely with a vivid sketch of an eccentric old woman, to whom he asks us to respond not as we might to a real Grandma Lausch, but only to one figure who exists in the imagination of Augie March. And Augie, of course, is taken in by her. The awe of the child clings to his descriptions of her, and its impact is far more powerful than his assurances that he really understands her now.

The point to be drawn from all this is that Mr. Bellow hasn't yet worked his way out of the non-dramatic solipsism of his earlier books: the most successfully drawn character in *Augie March* is not a human being but an ego. Yet Mr. Bellow has made some real strides forward. I know of no modern novel which speaks up more wonderfully for the necessity of love and charity than *Augie March*. The way that compassion wins out over envy in the portrayal of Augie's brother Simon is a triumph of the moral will: "He was ashamed, stony with shame. His secrets were being told. His secrets! What did they amount to? You'd think they were as towering as the Himalayas. But all they were about was his mismanaged effort to live. To live and not die. And this was what he had to be ashamed of." There is hope that this note will grow into the kind of compassion that makes a great novelist. The novelist begins with pity—in which his own emotions are more important than the object which has called them forth—but he moves on to sympathy, in which detachment has been achieved without a diminution of feeling. It is the most difficult of all attitudes to reach; that is why we have so few genuine novelists. So far Mr. Bellow is closer to pity than to sympathy.

It would be misleading to suggest that Mr. Bellow is another Smollett. *Augie March* makes a bid for a greater style of picaresque than Smollett's, for it is also a novel of ideas. The book is about America, or, more specifically, the problem of the individual in a conformist society.

Augie March stands for the American dream of the inviolable individual who has the courage to resist his culture—that figure whom Tocqueville doubted could survive the realities of American life and whom David Riesman has lately tried to reinstate as an ideal. His quest is for happiness through self-realization. The power to find oneself and then to submit to what one *is*—that is the superior fate Augie believes he can achieve. He rejects an enormous range of flattering temptations—power, wealth, devotion to cause—because his will to oppose is stronger than his will to be a recruit and conform.

But Augie is a representative American in other ways too, the image of modern man living in a hopelessly fluid society, forced to choose an identity because he has inherited none. Augie is fatherless, Jewish, and penniless. He starts with nothing and is eventually propelled into everything, but he won't stay put and he won't admit defeat: "I may well be a flop at this line of endeavor. Columbus too thought he was a flop, probably, when they sent him back in chains, which didn't prove there was no America."

Mr. Bellow probably intended this book as a parable of American optimism. He is saying, and rightly, that the American dream is a faith which, like any other, can only be maintained stubbornly in spite of the evidence. Augie's optimism is not blind. You cannot argue with his belief in the American abstractions by telling him how completely at odds they are with nature, human, social, and physical. He knows all your arguments and uses them against himself. What's more, he has been through hell and back, he has touched bottom, he has seen cruelty and rottenness and degradation. He is a first-hand authority on evil. Or would be, if he were human. But he remains a mere device, not a test case at all. Augie reminds us of those animals in the cartoons who get burned to cinders, flattened out like pancakes, exploded, and generally made a mess of, yet who turn up intact after every catastrophe, as if nothing had happened. Though he goes through everything, he undergoes nothing. He doesn't change in the course of the novel; he doesn't even learn, for all his great show of having learned. He merely resists the apparent lessons of his experience. So that Mr. Bellow's failure to explore concretely the impact of experience on faith makes that faith—with which, incidentally, I am very much in sympathy—seem merely willful. He has written a deeper parable than he may have intended, and Tocqueville, alas, still hasn't been proved wrong.

Augie March is an impressive *tour de force*, impressive enough to earn the right to be criticized as a criticism of life. Mr. Bellow deserves our admiration and gratitude for showing us the direction serious fiction must take if it is to come alive: it will have to get in touch with day-to-day concerns, it will have to set itself rigorous standards of detachment and complexity that do not result in a shrivelled and straitjacketed transcription of petty worries, and it will have to open up the sources of vitality in American life.

Mr. Bellow has the very genuine distinction of giving us a sense of what a real American idiom might look like. It is no disgrace to have failed in a pioneer attempt.

Henderson's Bellow

Richard G. Stern[*]

The first forty pages of *Henderson the Rain King*, are packed with enough material for two or three novels, odd, intricate relationships between husbands and wives, fathers and children, landlords and tenants, all suspenseful, and all disposed of with a quick easy brilliance that is the first of this book's surprises. The next three hundred pages leap from this material into territory few novelists in the world are brave or energetic enough to enter. Or rather, to construct; for here lies the bravery: scanting a gift of which he has more than any writer alive, the gift of soaking in and then returning with shine the detail of the world, Bellow propels his book into the jungles of possibility to hack out a country that will both stage his hero's quest and partially slake his appetite, a country constructed for discovery.

> The way grew more and more stony and this made me suspicious. If we were approaching a town we ought by now to have found a path. Instead there were these jumbled white stones that looked as if they has been combed out by an ignorant hand from the elements that make least sense. There must be stupid portions of heaven, too, and these had rolled straight down from it. I am no geologist but the word calcareous seemed to fit them. They were composed of lime and my guess was that they must have originated in a body of water. Now they were ultra-dry but filled with little caves from which cooler air was exhaled—ideal places for a siesta in the heat of noon, provided no snakes came. But the sun was in decline, trumpeting downward. The cave mouths were open and there was this coarse and clumsy gnarled white stone.

This country is neither conscientiously symbolic nor artificial; seen through the eyes of the regal, knowledgeable, keening slob who narrates the book, its topography has personality, one which seems to both objectify and nourish the novel's bizarre notions.

Are there precedents for this sort of construction? In a way, there aren't. Utopians, satirists, dream visionaries have been contriving countries for millenia, but, to greater or lesser degree, their contrivances are unlikely. Either the landscape is unearthly and the brute creation articulate, or the hero arrives by time machine or dream. In Bellow's Africa, custom and belief are strange, but all—including a semi-domesticated lion—it seems, is real. The fantasy is kept in

[*]Reprinted from *Kenyon Review*, 21 (1959) 655–61 by permission of Wallace & Sheil Agency, Inc. Copyright 1959 by Richard G. Stern.

the realm of ideas where it can be legitimately accommodated as an early stage of knowledge.

There is a much more important difference in *Henderson*, and that is its hero. The Gullivers, Candides, and Connecticut Yankees may be scalpels, sensitometers, blank slates, mechanical pens, victims, physicians, P.A. systems, or even types, eccentric and amusing, but they are never characters whose fates mean more than their discoveries and situations. Eugene Henderson outlasts both what he learns and what happens to him, and constantly he pulls the book out of the perilous abstract. His American memories corkscrew through the African present tense with a backtracking ease which makes Ford and Conrad look elephantine; his grabbag miseries and splendors—battered hulk, largesse, sweet ambitions, ever-aching conscience—weight the unfamiliar with familiar presence, and the book stays grounded in the real. *Henderson* is composed out of the expression of the narrator's want, its complicated genesis—he's had the world and found it wanting—and its satisfaction. It is partly the nature of the want and of the food which the novelist who instilled the want is obligated to supply for it that makes *Henderson* a different sort of reading experience for faithful Bellovians.

An account of the difference might begin with a paragraph from *Augie March*:

> In his office Simon wore his hat like a Member of Parliament, and while he phoned his alligator-skin shoes knocked things off the desk. He was in on a deal to buy some macaroni in Brazil and sell it in Helsinki. Then he was interested in some mining machinery from Sudbury, Ontario, that was wanted by an Indo-Chinese company. The nephew of a cabinet minister came in with a proposition about waterproof material. And after him some sharp character interested Simon in distressed yard-goods from Muncie, Indiana. He bought it. Then he sold it as lining to a manufacturer of leather jackets. All this while he carried on over the phone and cursed and bullied, but that was just style, not anger, for he laughed often.

There in a single paragraph out of Augie's thousand or so, the great know-how is at work, the skipping facts, the bunched variety more lively than life ever is, four or five different sorts of sentence, all held in and charged with Augie's tone. Places, things, people, pointed description, key movements—the alligator-skin shoes knocking things off the desk—and the characterizing summary, this is the way the novel goes, more brilliantly packed with the commodity and stuff of the world than anything in American literature. "It was like giving birth to Gargantua," Bellow said of it, and that comparison may indicate the reason it stopped, for, to the reader, it looks as if it might go on as long as the world supplied Augie with objects to handle and people to watch.

Henderson starts where Augie leaves off; where Augie was a knocker at doors, a Columbus of the "near-at-hand," Henderson is a Columbus of the absolute, fifty-five, not twenty, a man for whom doors have opened and whom the rooms have not satisfied. The problem for the writer here is that the absolute is barely furnished, and what furniture it has consists of those Biedermeier hulks of fiction, ideas.

When realist writers write novels in which ideas play important roles, the procedure is usually a form of concealment: the action is tied-into the idea either as illustration or contradiction of it. The big, organizing idea of a novel close to *Henderson*, Mann's *Felix Krull*, is something like the reality of fakery, and the book is cluttered with such detail as glorious-looking champagne bottles containing miserable champagne, actors seen first under the lights and then backstage, crooks, magicians, illusionists of all sorts, a whole Mann spectrum drawn from department stores to interstellar space. The picaresque adventures are sunk into this detail which is assembled to illustrate, or rather, to compose the themes. On the other hand, in such a book as *The Magic Mountain*, the characters in action contradict the notions they expound and for which they sometimes seem to stand. (A humanitarian pacifist challenges a Jesuit convert to a duel, and the latter kills himself.) *Henderson* takes neither one of these classic routes; its actions are discrete from the notions which make up no small part of the book, those of Henderson himself, or of the two beautiful obesities, the women of Bittahness, or of the almost-MD, William James-reading totem king, Dahfu. The notions of *Henderson* glow like actions and the actions like ideas. This needs illustration.

Towards the end of the novel, King Dahfu is in the midst of a kind of Reichian analysis of Henderson's posture:

> . . . You appear cast in one piece. The midriff dominates. Can you move the different portions? Minus yourself of some of your heavy reluctance of attitude. Why so sad and so earthen? Now you are a lion. Mentally, conceive of the environment. The sky, the sun, and creatures of the bush. You are related to all. The very gnats are your cousins. The sky is your thoughts. The leaves are your insurance, and you need no other. There is no interruption all night to the speech of the stars. Are you with me? I say, Mr. Henderson, have you consumed much amounts of alcohol in your life? The face suggests you have, the nose especially. It is nothing personal. Much can be changed. By no means all, but very much. You can have a new poise. It will resemble the voice of Caruso, which I have heard on records, never tired because the function is as natural as to the birds.

Then Dahfu tells him to get down on his hands and knees and bellow. "Be the beast!"

> And so I was the beast. I gave myself to it, and all my sorrow came out in the roaring. My lungs supplied the air but the note came from my soul. The roaring scalded my throat and hurt the corners of my mouth and presently I filled the den like a base organ pipe. This is where my heart had sent me, with its clamor. Oh, Nebuchadnezzar! How well I understood that prophecy of Daniel. For I had claws, and hair, and some teeth, and I was bursting with hot noise . . . .

Dahfu's speech is so wily a mixture of the lyric and admonitory, the descriptive and conceptual, that even if it were not couched in gorgeous Bellafrikanisch, it would seem to further the book's progress as more obviously dramatic action would. Indeed, as it is idea moving toward action, so the roaring of Henderson moves toward idea. "I was the beast . . . . [I roared] . . . . the note came from my soul . . . . This is where my heart had sent me . . . ." The scenic extravagance, a large man on hands and knees bellowing like a maniac, is implanted in an idea-context which not only makes it right but moving. Behind the action is the sort of momentum Swift supplied for the scene in which Gulliver kisses his Master's hoof, perhaps the most touching in 18th Century fiction.

As for the ideas themselves, they exist in terms of Henderson's need, and have as much relation to belief as Bellow's Africa to Tom Mboyo's. The major one—a version of the notion that we are in no small part the product of the images we absorb—can be found in such different places as the beginning of Plutarch's life of Timoleon, *Felix Krull*, and the somatic psychology of Wilhelm Reich. What counts in the novel is that Henderson's reaction to them is part of the revelation of his personality, and for Bellow, as for Malamud and some of the other fine novelists of the time, personality is back in the middle of the novel, not where their great predecessors—Proust, Joyce, and to somewhat lesser extent, Mann—put it, as part of a thematic scheme which apportions the size and intensity of every element. *Henderson* is a kind of bridge between *Augie*, *Seize the Day*, and these thematic novels; the difficulty is that the bridge must bear the weight of constant invention, invention which can draw hardly at all on the home detail in which the other novels luxuriate. An original like Bellow can't lean on the second-hand views of travellers and movies, and must be on the qui vive for the cliches which always threaten writing about the exotic. Consequently, much of Henderson's detail is landscape, physiognomy and a few clothing props, and the investment there is great. Bellow readers, used to commodity markets, Mexican resorts, Evanston haberdasheries, and the Machiavellians and con-men who in vintage Bellow load the pages, must go into another gear. They will be helped by the fact that *Henderson* is a stylistic masterpiece.

The Henderson prose had a kind of trial—and somewhat barren—run in a long story, "Leaving the Yellow House," which appeared a year or so ago in *Esquire*. The story's about a sort of female Henderson—but on her last legs—who drips out like hourglass sand in the Utah desert. The clean sentences of that story are now somehow galvanized by the popping energy of *Augie*, and the result is such paragraphs as this:

> Itelo protruded his lips to show that I was expected to kiss her on the belly. To dry my mouth first, I swallowed. The fall I had taken while wrestling had split my underlip. Then I kissed, giving a shiver at the heat I encountered. The knot of the lion's skin was pushed aside by my face, which sank inward. I was aware of the old lady's navel and her internal organs as they made sounds of submergence. I felt as though I were riding in a balloon above the Spice Islands, soaring in hot clouds while exotic odors rose from below. My own whiskers pierced me inward, in the lip. When I drew back from this significant experience (having made contact with a certain power—unmistakeable!—which emanated from the woman's middle), Mtalba also reached for my head, wishing to do the same, as indicated by her gentle gestures, but I pretended I didn't understand and said to Itelo, "How come when everybody else is in mourning, your aunts are both so gay?"

There are, in my view, three very different sorts of literary experience, the writer's, the reader's, and the critic's, the last two being as distinct as the first from them. If we analogize the writer to an assassin, the reader may be thought of as the corpse, and the critic as the coroner-detective. The feelings of the assassin and his victim are notably different, but, at least for our purposes, they may be said to be powerful ones, and in the former's case organized by a sense of purpose as in the latter's by force—(scarcely conceived and rapidly terminated). The coroner-critic is the rationalist, the reconstructionist, and although he cannot alter the responses of the reader-victim, he can, in a sense, alter those of future readers in such fashion that their reactions will be shaped in part by his notions. An early Monet critic could instruct viewers to stand back from the canvasses. (Indeed, the feelings of someone who knows he has been murdered—knows, because "murder" is defined—are most likely different from the feelings he would have if he thought he were dying a natural death.) I bring this up because my reactions first as reader, and then as critic of *Henderson*, are distinct.[1] As reader, I respond more easily to the Bellow I am used to, the parts of *Henderson* which deal with that hero's American experience—his pig farm, bad teeth, Sevçik violin exercizes, his fights on Highway Seven, his high rides with the bear Smolak, his wives and children. As critic, however, that part of me which reading has not yet slain, I admire immensely the boldness and brilliance of the whole, admire the "originality" and the style and the other tributaries of great narrative, and I am hopeful that my feelings will in future readings catch up with my admiration. This is the least credit one can extend to greatness.

Notes

1. As a matter of fact, I feel in small part with the assassin, perhaps as accessory after the fact. I know Bellow, and have talked with him about this novel among other things. Indeed, I read an earlier version, and some of my initial reactions to it turned out to be similar to Bellow's as he went over the book, so that changes were made which make me feel—for no good reason—implicated. The point here is that I feel I know what effects were wanted at certain moments; I also feel "in" on such genetic factors as Bellow's interest in Reich. Such knowledge alters, and alters seriously, my responsiveness to the "magic" of the book and might well be taken into account by readers of the review.

The Search for Freedom and Salvation

Melvin Maddocks°

Saul Bellow's new novel describes a visit to a bizarre wilderness by an odd holy man in search of salvation. Eugene Henderson is an intensely self-concerned Connecticut millionaire of 55, whose violent efforts to "burst the spirit's sleep" drive him to the remotest parts of Africa.

His is hardly a contemplative withdrawal. A big, profane, rearing bull of a man nagged by an inner voice that cries "I want, I want, I want." he marches to his retreat with the irresistible energy of an American go-getter who has never understood where he was going or what he hoped to get. Before he is through, he has blown up a tribal village's reservoir, befriended a lion, and lifted a mammoth wooden goddess, thereby becoming rain king of the Wariri.

Described in the style Mr. Bellow established in "The Adventures of Augie March," these events supply the picaresque narrative to drape over what is essentially a spiritual exploration. For in his headlong wanderings, Henderson seeks nothing less than a second birth. . . .

His American and European past, about which he reminisces constantly and compulsively in the midst of his African present, is a blotted page with great blanks on it. The rejected son of a millionaire, he has married twice—once under explicitly sordid circumstances—and distinguished himself only by eccentric stunts like drunkenly shooting bottles at a swank beach resort and raising pigs on his gentleman's estate.

But underneath, a more significant rebellion has been fomenting sporadically, involving the struggles and frustrations of a worthier Henderson, who has taken violin lessons, wept in French cathedrals, and dreamed of modeling himself after Sir Wilfred Grenfell.

In his wild African odyssey, Henderson yields himself to chaos in the hope of finding order, in a universal as well as a private sense. As he lugs about a broken dental bridge, one deaf ear, and a leg and a stomach scarred by World War II, he trumpets his own personal response to the problem of evil: "I really do not wish to live by any law of decay.". . .

Chief among the influences Henderson encounters is Dahfu, king of the

---

Wariri, to whom Henderson, as rain king, becomes second in command. "Disease," the king, a former medical student, tells him, "is a speech of the psyche." Dahfu even goes so far as to speculate: "Nature might be a mentality."

Henderson is not totally convinced. But he is sufficiently encouraged to believe that ideas of goodness, firmly understood, can be projected into experience. In short, he has discovered faith in a law of regeneration to replace his law of decay—even if he has not discovered the law itself.

As a novelist, Mr. Bellow moves in lunges and plunges, a bit like his hero. He sputters out action in a breezy slang that often seems forced and awkward. As a philosopher, he tends to maintain the same butch-haircut pose and prose. At worst, he can sound like Daddy Warbucks trying to explain Spinoza. He is self-conscious in a way that a great picaresque natural like Celine is not, whose stories never seem an illustration of his ideas but the very stuff from which ideas spring.

But this is still an exceptional novel. There is an energy and earnestness to Mr. Bellow's writing that can make a reader as grateful for what he has intended as for what he sometimes achieves.

Bellow Comes of Age

Robert Baker°

It is a peculiarity of our age that the more significant statements about man are being made by people who speak in terms of the uptake of strontium-90 in human bone, or the release rate of serotonin in the brain. The throne once occupied by literature has seemingly been usurped (or abdicated—as you will) and so it is with some relief that we greet a new work by a novelist capable of saying something meaningful about life. With the novella from which this collection takes its title Saul Bellow demonstrates his attainment of full artistic maturity.

Briefly, "Seize the Day" depicts one crucial day in the life of a middle-aged New Yorker, Tommy Wilhelm (né Adler), whose own impulsiveness has brought him to the end of the trail, shorn of the conventional badges of identity. Jobless, separated from his wife, unable to marry his mistress, in conflict with his aged, successful father, Tommy is about to founder in the heavy seas of his financial and emotional obligations. The day in question is spent in frantic efforts to recoup his monetary losses by gambling his last seven hundred dollars in the commodities market under the guidance of a fascinating charlatan, Dr. Tamkin, with whom he has become embroiled. Interspersed with all this are Wilhelm's equally desperate attempts to review his past and discover some faint glimmer of meaning. Finally, at the funeral of a stranger he achieves a purgation, a sense of the value of merely being alive. But the action of "Seize the Day," so badly stated, conveys nothing of the work's concentrated power; it is all in the telling. Bellow has at last gained control of his never-questioned force: in earlier work he seemed unable to resist the temptation to digress, but here Bellow has piled scene upon scene, image upon image, building a marvelous focused crescendo that leaves the reader nearly as shattered as Wilhelm.

The three short stories and the one-act play that pad out the collection have all—like the title-piece—been previously published in periodicals. The principle (if such there be) behind their selection remains obscure, unless it is their common concern with the oppressive burden of the material world as symbolized by money: "Money surrounds you in life as the earth does in death," muses the protagonist of "A Father-to-Be." Undoubtedly competent, these stories do not match the brilliance of "Seize the Day," and so the less said about them the better.

°Reprinted from *Chicago Review*, 11 (1957), 107–10.

"Seize the Day" logically culminates a line of development begun with *Dangling Man* (1944), and continued through *The Victim* (1947), and *The Adventures of Augie March,* Bellow's *Bildungsroman* that won the 1954 National Book Award. Horace's *Carpe diem* furnishes the title for "Seize the Day"; for his work as a whole, Bellow could well adopt another Latin tag, the one found on the coins of his adopted country—*E pluribus unum.* For Bellow has tried to lasso the universe, to explore the splendid, profligate diversity of human experience, and to seek the ties that bind. His all-inclusiveness forces him to skip about from one level to another; the swift leaps from the sublime to the ridiculous and back have the flavor of the best Jewish humor—and are equally productive of brilliant insights into the human condition. Romantic at root, this impulse to embrace the world leads to, in his own phrase, "a mysterious adoration of what occurs." As Joseph says in *Dangling Man,* "In a sense everything is good because it exists. Or, good or not good, it exists, it is ineffable and, for that reason, marvelous." Bellow, recipient of a Guggenheim award, knockabout intellectual, and an intimate of the greatest living con man, Yellow Kid Weil, sees his role, as does Augie March, as that of "a Columbus of those near-at-hand." Since "judgment is second to wonder," in his work celebration of life takes precedence over criticism. (In "Day," all the major characters are partially right, partially justified. Bellow's compassion is the greater for being non-selective.) But what distinguishes this author from other "acceptors" is that with him acceptance is an outgrowth of full knowledge, not a substitute for it.

So much for *pluribus.* It is the vast tract Bellow must traverse in his search for the *unum.* Each man *is* an island, entire unto himself, and it is no good pretending otherwise. Bellow has few peers in delineating the particularity, the uniqueness of the topography of a single individual. But he also insists that individuals form archipelagos, and far beneath the surface all are rooted to the same ocean floor. Out of this awareness he draws two themes that pervade his work—the horrible price of insularity (far from rare in modern fiction) and, transcending this, the common humanity shared by all.

In his drive to illumine this latter motif Bellow has passed through four phases. Since each is organically related to the one preceding, they are not *that* sharply divided; they are, however, apparent enough to warrant noting. In *Dangling Man* the emphasis is ideational; what we get is mostly Joseph's thought and some of his speech. In *The Victim* ideas and action revolving around the theme of the difficulty of being human are neatly correlated, almost in a one to one ratio. In the sprawling *Augie* Bellow seems more confident of his abilities to convey attitudes through action rather than discourse, so that thought becomes the pungent seasoning and not the whole stew. Finally, in "Day" he descends deeply to a primal level of atmosphere and feeling that communicates in a way that defies analysis but that carries the moist, hot sting of truth.

The growth and ripening of Bellow's attitudes have been paralleled by the perfecting of his medium of expression. He has fused the varied and often conflicting elements of American English into a natural whole that is ours and yet remains peculiarly his own. Almost alone among today's writers he can select words and phrases, here from the gutter, there from the ivory tower, without the slightest hint of embarassment or awkwardness.

For all his virtues (and they are considerable), Bellow is by no means flawless. If writing were dancing, the symbol of much postwar American fiction would be Fred Astaire: urbane, a bit wistful, it camouflages its lack of committment behind a dazzling command of techniques. Bellow, on the other hand, is a Nijinsky, but one who takes an occasional pratfall. If at times he falls heavily, it is because he leaps higher, dares more, than those who are content to stay within the confines of competence.

The most apparent of Bellow's faults is his incapacity to deal convincingly with women. The female figures in his novels repeatedly fall into one of two categories; they are either nags or nymphomaniacs, and the Bellow hero is too often a passive figure, condemned to suffer verbal abuse on the one hand or a physical embarassment of riches on the other. No Bellow novel has a heroine and in none of them does the protagonist's fate directly hinge upon his relationship with a woman. Joseph's wife Iva "has a way about her that discourages talk," and is alternately colorless and irritating. Joseph also has a mistress, Kitty, but it is noteworthy that she seduces him. The central action of *Victim* could not have occurred at all without the absence of Mary, wife of the protagonist, Asa Leventhal; and the little that we know about her relates almost entirely to the weird, abortive period of their engagement. In *Augie* many of the episodes that in other novels would be called "love scenes" are little more than rape fantasies with Augie as the assaulted. In the final chapters Augie is married to Stella, but matrimony seems to have transformed her from nympho to nag: "She sits and listens . . . and refuses me—for the time being, anyway—the most important things I ask of her." If and when Augie lights out for the territory, Stella will probably be left behind. In "Day," Tommy's wife Margaret, from whom he is separated, never gets closer than letters and telephone calls to refuse him a divorce and badger him for money. Nor is Tommy's mistress, Olive, ever clearly visualized.

The argument could be advanced that all this is intended, that Bellow uses these women as an analogue of the animal, natural side of life. Thus the abortive heterosexual relationships symbolize the twentieth-century American's failure to cope effectively with Nature. But if this be true, need it happen in all four of Bellow's novels? Surely, with the slow erasure of the distinction between the sexes that has been occurring in the past half-century, women are not incomprehensible and one could serve as *the*, or at least *a*, central figure in a Bellow novel.

Bellow's second failure—that his books don't end, they just stop—is perhaps more easily explained. With his avowal that "character is fate," sheer plot, the arrangement of events, has a diminished importance. Since life won't fit the neat forms of art, Bellow's flaw probably stems from his greater devotion to the former than the latter. It remains to be seen whether these faults can be transcended or whether they are logically outgrowths of the author's deepest beliefs. One rather suspects that his perceptions of women will remain the same, while predicting better resolutions for his future books. Bellow is certainly not insensitive to aesthetic issues, and the ending of "Seize the Day" is several cuts above those of the other three novels.

These strictures aside, it must be said that Saul Bellow is perhaps the major talent of the past decade. He has displayed magnificent fulfilment of his early promise and is now at an age—chronological and artistic—to produce his best work. Publication of his two works-in-progress will be awaited with uncommon eagerness, for he may very well be the fair-haired boy, *El Bello*, of current American letters.

Odysseus, Flat on His Back

Irving Howe°

Where shall a contemporary novel begin? Perhaps unavoidably: with the busted hero reeling from a messy divorce and moaning in a malodorous furnished room; picking at his psyche's wounds like a boy at knee scabs; rehearsing the mighty shambles of ambition ("how I rose from humble origins to complete disaster"); cursing the heart-and-ball breakers, both wives and volunteers, who have, he claims, laid him low; snarling contempt at his own self-pity with a Johnsonian epigram, "Grief, Sir, is a species of idleness"; and yet, amidst all this woe, bubbling with intellectual hope, as also with intellectual gas, and consoling himself with the truth that indeed "there were worse cripples around."

This is Moses Herzog, hero-patsy of Saul Bellow's extremely, if also unevenly; brilliant new novel. Herzog is a representative man of the sixties, eaten away by those "personal relations" which form the glory and the foolishness of a post-political intelligentsia. He is a good scholar, but cannot complete his books. He rips off imaginary letters to great men, finessing their wisdom and patronizing their mistakes. He is a lady-killer, "aging" at 47 and worried about his potency. He is a loving father twice-divorced, who each time has left behind him a child as token of good will. He is a true-blue Jewish groaner, and perversely, groans against fashionable despair. Inside or outside our skins, we all know Herzog: *Hypocrite lecteur—mon semblable—mein schlemiehl.* Hungering for a life of large significance, eager for "a politics in the Aristotelian sense," he nevertheless keeps melting into the mercies of women, each of whom, in sequence, really understands him.

Herzog is Bellow's sixth novel and in many ways the most remarkable. All of his books—whether melancholy realism, moral fable or picaresque fantasia—represent for him a new departure, a chosen risk in form and perception. Bellow has the most powerful mind among contemporary American novelists, or at least, he is the American novelist who best assimilates his intelligence to creative purpose. This might have been foreseen at the beginning of his career, for he has always been able to turn out a first-rate piece of discursive prose; what could not have been foreseen was that he would also become a virtuoso of fictional technique and language.

Behind Bellow's writing there is always a serious intention, but as he grows

°Reprinted from *New Republic*, Sept. 19, 1964, pp. 21–26.

older he becomes increasingly devoted to the idea of the novel as sheer spectacle. His last few books comprise a hectic and at times ghastly bazaar of contemporary experience; they ring with the noise of struggle; characters dash in and out, glistening with bravura; adventures pile up merrily, as if the decline of the West had not been definitely proclaimed; the male characters plunge and rise, mad for transcendence; the women (a little tiresomely) are all very beautiful and mostly very damaging. And the language spins.

Before and, I hope, after everything else has been said, *Herzog* should be praised as a marvellously animated performance. It is a book that makes one greedy for the next page, the next character. Racing ahead like a sped-up movie, the action covers a brief time in the life of Herzog and nimbly reaches back and forth to segments of his immigrant childhood in Montreal, his failed marriages, his intellectual spirallings, and his recent lady-hopping. The minor figures are drawn as sharp caricature, without the distraction of psychological probe or nuance, and sometimes, when Bellow's zest becomes compulsive, a little over-focused. There are foul-mouth lawyers, boiling with drug-store wisdom, professional chicanery and "potato love"; a couple of tough-spirited aunts; a sadly ineffectual father fumbling at bootleggery; a professor who loves, solely but purely, his monkey. There are Herzog's ladies of the season: Sono, a Japanese doll who soothes the spirit and, Oriental-style, washes the back of Master Moses in an Upper West Side bathtub while cooing at him in baby French, "mon professeur d'amour," and Ramona, bravely marching into middle age with an overload of "understanding" and graduate credentials in sex, who "entered a room provocatively . . . one hand touching her thigh, as though she carried a knife in her garter belt."

And then the demons, the evil spirits: Madeleine, the wife who betrays; Valentine Gersbach, the best friend with whom she does it.

A talentless buffoon-double of the talented hero, Valentine Gersbach (what a name!) booms out the latest highbrow cant in his great bearish voice and ends by lecturing to Hadassah clubs on Martin Buber. Toward, Valentine, Bellow is merciless, yet one is seldom troubled by this open display of aggression; for there is no pretense in this novel that we are being shown a world which exists, self-sufficient, apart from the neurotic inflammations of the central figure, Gersbach is a clown, a windbag, a traitor, the kind of man who makes intellectuals wish they were dead when they hear him parroting their words; yet he is utterly alive, one waits for him to reappear on the page, and finally even he wins a moment of humane redemption: secretly, angrily Herzog watches Gersbach bathing his (Herzog's) little girl and must admit to himself that the act, though done by a betrayer, is yet done with tenderness.

Madeleine is drawn with pure venom, a sentiment capable of generating in writers, as in other men, great quantities of energy. She is, naturally, a beauty; she fiddles in Russian intellectual history and Catholic conversion; she outmaneuvers the slumping Herzog not merely at sexual games (where she has, after all, the advantage of youth) but also in intellectual competition. When Herzog complains about her extravagance, her arrogance, her paranoia, she replies with the great modern rationale: "Anyway, it'll never be boring." A moony schoolgirl meets Madeleine, and describes her in a phrase embodying the great modern cant: "She gives a sense of significant encounter." With her postures of depth, screeches of enthusiasm, learned references and distinguished airs, Madeleine is the female pseudo-intellectual done, and done in, once and for all. The portrait is unjust, an utter libel, but a classic of male retaliation.

Herzog himself is not, in the traditional sense, a novelistic character at all. He is observed neither from a cool distance nor through intimate psychological penetration. We experience him intensely, entering his very bones; yet, trapped as we are in his inner turmoil, we cannot be certain that finally we know him. For Bellow has not provided a critical check: there is no way of learning what any of the other characters, by way of Jamesian correction, might think or feel about Herzog. Bellow offers not a full-scale characterization but a full-length exposure of a state of being. We do not see Herzog acting in the world, we are made captive in the world of Herzog. The final picture is that of Herzog in cross-section, bleeding from the cut.

In one sense, then, there is a complete identification between Bellow and Herzog: the consciousness of the character forms the enclosing medium of the novel. But in a more important respect Bellow manages skillfully to avoid the kind of identification which might lead one to conclude that he "favors" his central character or fails to see through his weaknesses and falsities—a fault that could radically distort the line of vision by which everything is to be considered. That Herzog cannot accurately perceive the other figures in the novel and that we are closely confined to his sense of them, is true and in ways I shall later suggest, a limitation. But not a crippling limitation. For it soon becomes clear that, while totally committed to Herzog's experience, Bellow is not nearly so committed to his estimate of that experience.

Things, to be sure, do not always work out neatly. There are sections in which the malice toward Madeleine gets out of hand, so much so that one suspects Bellow of settling private scores. And while the device of having Herzog compose imaginary letters is often amusing—

> "Dear Doktor Professor Heidegger, I should like to know what you mean by the expression 'the fall into the quotidian.' When did this fall occur? Where were we standing when it happened?"

—one becomes somewhat irked at being unable, at times, to grasp which of the letters are serious, that is, Bellow's opinions, and which are not, that is, Herzog's conniptions. Ambiguity? No doubt. We all know about this prime blessing of modern literature; but there are occasions when the uses of ambiguity can themselves be ambiguous, shading off into confusion or evasiveness.

For the most part, however, *Herzog* marks a notable advance in technique over Bellow's previous books. He has become a master of something that is rarely discussed in criticism because it is hard to do more than point toward it: the art of timing, which concerns the massing, centering and disposition of the characters and creates a sense of delight in the sheer motion of the narrative.

Bellow has also found a good solution to a technical problem which keeps arising in the contemporary novel. Most readers, I imagine, groan a little when they see a novelist wheeling into position one of those lengthy and leaden flashbacks in which, we know in advance, the trauma will be unveiled that is to explain the troubles of time-present. These flashbacks, by now one of the dreariest conventions of the novel, result in a lumpiness of narrative surface and blockage of narrative flow. But Bellow has managed to work out a form in which the illusion of simultaneity of time—a blend of past with the present-moving-into-future—is nicely maintained. Instead of the full-scale flashback, which often rests on the mistaken premise that a novelist needs to provide a psychiatric or sociological casebook on his characters, Bellow allows the consciousness of his narrator to flit about in time, restlessly, nervously, thereby capturing essential fragments of the past as they break into the awareness of the present. Through these interlockings of time—brief, dramatic and made to appear simultaneous—he creates the impression of a sustained rush of experience.

Bellow began his career as a novelist of somber intellectuality: his impressive early book *The Victim* asks almost to be read as a fable concerning the difficulties of attempting a secure moral judgment in our day. With *Augie March* he made a sharp turn, casting aside the urban contemplativeness and melancholy of his previous work, and deciding to regard American life as wonderfully "open," a great big shapeless orange bursting with the juices of vitality. Though in some ways his most virtuoso performance, *Augie March* suffers from a programatic exuberance: it is fun to watch the turns and tricks the suddenly acrobatic Bellow can execute, yet hard to suppress a touch of anxiety concerning his heart-beat.

With *Augie March* Bellow also began to work out a new fictional style, for which there may be some predecessors—just possibly Daniel Fuchs and Nathanael West—but which in the main is an original achievement. By now it has come to be imitated by many American Jewish novelists as well as by a few gentiles trying wistfully to pass, but none of these manages it nearly so well as Bellow himself.

What Bellow did was to leave behind him the bleak neutrality of naturalistic prose and the quavering sensibility of the Jamesian novel: the first, he seemed to feel, was too lifeless and the second insufficiently masculine. Beginning with *Augie March*—but none of this applies to his masterful novella, *Seize the Day*—Bellow's prose becomes strongly anti-literary, a roughing up of diction and breaking down of syntax in order to avoid familiar patterns and expectations. The prose now consists of a rich, thick impasto of verbal color in which a splatter of sidewalk eloquence is mixed with erudite by-play. Together with this planned coarsening of texture, there is a great emphasis on speed, a violent wrenching and even forcing of images, all the consequence of his wish to break away from the stateliness of the literary sentence. Analytic refinement is sacrificed to sensuous vigor, careful psychological notation to the brawling of energy, syntactical qualification to kinesthetic thrust. (One is reminded a bit of action painting.) Psychology is out, absolutely out: for to psychologize means to reflect, to hesitate, to qualify, to modulate, to analyze. By contrast, the aim of Bellow's neo-baroque style is to communicate sensations of immediacy and intensity, even when dealing with abstract intellectual topics—to communicate, above all, the sense that men are still alive. Toward this end he is prepared to yield niceties of phrasing, surface finish, sometimes even coherence of structure.

It is a style admirably suited to the flaming set-piece, the rapid vignette, the picaresque excursion. But it is not so well suited to a sustained and complex action, or a lengthy flow of experience, or a tragic plot, or what George Moore, in discussing the nature of fiction, called the "rhythmic sequence of events." In *Augie March* there is a run of action but hardly a plot; in *Herzog* a superbly-realized situation but hardly a developing action; and in both of these novels, as well as in *Henderson*, not much of a "rhythmic sequence of events." That is why, I think, none of them has a fully satisfying denouement, an organic fulfillment of the action. In principle these books could continue forever, and that is one reason Bellow finds it hard to end them. He simply stops, much against one's will.

Finally, Bellow's style draws heavily from the Yiddish, not so much in borrowed diction as in underlying intonation and rhythm. Bellow's relation to Yiddish is much more easy and authoritative than that of most other American Jewish writers. The jabbing interplay of ironies, the intimate vulgarities, the strange blend of sentimental and sardonic which characterizes Yiddish speech are lassoed into Bellow's English: so that what we get is not a sick exploitation of folk memory but a vibrant linguistic and cultural transmutation. (Precisely at the moment when Yiddish is dying off as an independent language, it has experienced an astonishing, and not always happy, migration into American culture. In two or three decades students of American literature may have to study Yiddish for reasons no worse than those for which students of English literature study Anglo-Saxon.)

One of the most pleasing aspects of *Herzog* is that Bellow has brought together his two earlier manners: the melancholy and the bouncy, the "Russian" and the "American," *Seize the Day* and *Augie March*. *Herzog* is almost free of the gratuitous verbalism which marred *Augie March*, yet retains its vividness and richness of texture. The writing is now purer, chastened and a great deal more disciplined.

There is a similar marshalling of Bellow's earlier themes. For some years now he has been obsessed with that fatigue of spirit which hangs so dismally over contemporary life. *Seize the Day* shows a man utterly exhausted, unable so much as to feel his despair until the wrenching final page. *Augie March* shows a man composing a self out of a belief in life's possibilities. Of the two books *Seize the Day* seems to me the more convincing and authentic, perhaps because despair is easier to portray than joy, perhaps because the experience of our time, as well as its literature, predisposes us to associate truth with gloom. In any case, what seems notable about *Herzog* is that nothing is here blinked or evaded, rhetoric does not black out reality (Herzog declares himself "aging, vain, terribly narcissistic, suffering without proper dignity"); yet the will to struggle, the insistence upon human possibility, is maintained, and not as a mere flourish but as the award of agony. Herzog learns that

> ". . . To look for fulfillment in another . . . was a feminine game. And the man who shops from woman to woman, though his heart aches with idealism, with the desire for pure love, has entered the female realm."

Not, perhaps, a very remarkable lesson, but worth learning when the cost comes high. More importantly, Herzog says about himself, wryly but truthfully, that he is a man who "thought and cared about belief." To think and care about belief: that is the first step toward salvation.

For all its vividness as performance, *Herzog* is a novel driven by an idea. It is a serious idea, though, in my judgment, neither worked out with sufficient care nor worked into the grain of the book with sufficient depth. Herzog, he tells us, means to write something that will deal "with a new angle on the modern condition, showing how life could be lived by renewing universal connections, overturning the last of the Romantic errors about the uniqueness of the Self, revising the old Western, Faustian ideology. . . ." This time clearly speaking for Bellow, Herzog declares himself opposed to

> "The canned sauerkraut of Spengler's 'Prussian Socialism,' the commonplaces of the Wasteland outlook, the cheap mental stimulants of Alienation, the cant and rant of pipsqueaks about Inauthenticity and Forlornness. I can't accept this foolish dreariness. We are talking about the whole life of mankind. The subject is too great, too deep for such weakness, cowardice. . . ."

And in the magazine *Location* Bellow has recently written an attack on "the 'doom of the West' [which] is the Established Church in modern literature." It is a Church, he says, which asserts the individual to be helpless among the impersonal mechanisms and sterilities of modern life; it cultivates self-pity and surrender; and it is wrong.

Bellow has touched on something real. Talk about "the decline of the West" can be elitist rubbish. The posture of alienation, like any other, can collapse into social accommodation. Cries of despair can become mere notes of fashion. Where the motif of alienation in the literature of modernism during the late 19th and early 20th Centuries signified an act of truth, courage and sometimes rebellion too, now it can easily become the occasion for a mixture of private snobbism and public passivity. Yet may not all ideas suffer this sort of outcome in a culture which seems endlessly capable of assimilating and devitalizing everything? Suppose Bellow's assault upon alienation becomes fashionable (it is not hard to imagine the positive thinkers who will hasten to applaud): will it not then suffer a public fate similar to that of the ideas he attacks?

Bellow is being just a little too cavalier in so readily disposing of a central theme of modernist literature. Surely, as it was manifested in the work of writers like Joyce, Flaubert, Eliot and Baudelaire, the sense of alienation expressed a profound and even exhilarating response to the reality of industrial society. (An imagining of despair can be as bracing as a demand for joy can be ruthless.) And does not the sense of alienation, if treated not as a mere literary convenience but as a galling social fact—does this not continue to speak truthfully to significant conditions in our life?

I raise these matters because Bellow, as a serious writer, must want his readers to consider them not merely in but also beyond the setting of his novel. When, however, one does consider them strictly in the context of *Herzog*, certain critical issues present themselves. There is a discrepancy between what the book actually is—brilliant but narrow in situation and scope—and the sweeping intentions that lie behind it; or in other words, between the dramatic texture and the thematic purpose. In the end one feels that *Herzog* is too hermetic a work, the result of a technique which encloses us rigidly in the troubles of a man during his phase of withdrawal from the world. The material is absorbing in its own right; it is handled with great skill; but in relation to the intended theme, it all seems a little puny.

Bellow has conceived of the book as a stroke against the glorification of the sick self, but the novel we have—as picture, image, honest exposure—remains largely caught up with the thrashings of the sick self. One wants from Bellow a novel that will not be confined to a single besieged consciousness but instead will negotiate the kind of leap into the world which he proclaims, to savor the world's freshness and struggle against its recalcitrance, perhaps even to enter "politics in the Aristotelian sense."

Meanwhile, critics and readers, let us be grateful.

Herzog

Frank Kermode*

There is one famous compliment to a novelist that nobody is ever going to offer Saul Bellow, and that is to say that his books are the product of a sensibility so fine that no idea could violate it. It seems doubtful whether any interesting writer, even James, really fits that formula, in any case, if you think that is the condition the art should aspire to, Bellow is not your man. Yet for many people he is the man. In America, where more and more the hypotheses of literary historians tread the heels of literature, Bellow has already been snugly fitted into neat intelligible patterns. He is the big novelist who emerged at the precise conjunction of race, milieu and moment—when, as Leslie Fiedler puts it, 'the Jews for the first time move into the centre of American culture' as the group best-equipped to act as an urban, Europe-centred elite. Augie March is Huck Finn Chicago-Jewish-style, still, in Mr. Fiedler's dialect, in search of a primal innocence, but above all an urban Jew, with the appropriate worries, failures and aspirations. Or, according to Norman Podhoretz, Bellow in 1953 came through with *Augie March* at just the right moment to encapsulate and typify the new revisionist liberalism, moving away from the Left at the same conscientious pace as *Partisan Review*.

Aside even from these professionally large and resonant explanations, much has been written about Bellow, and this is not surprising. When all the reservations have been made he is so good that anybody can see it with half an eye; only severe doctrinal adhesion prevents the recognition that he is a far more interesting writer than Mailer. One remarkable thing about him is that along the way he has conjured out of the air new talents, powers he apparently did not have, even *in posse*, when he started in the Forties. With this bonus he is more gifted than the gifted young, including the handsomely endowed Philip Roth. Furthermore, he is, for all the glitter of ideas, accessible, easier to get to than John Hawkes, further out in the open than Malamud. Thus he made everybody flock to read him without sacrificing intellectual seriousness, and without growing plump enough to be caught in the meshes of the critics' hypotheses.

Bellow's career has some curious aspects. He has never lacked support. *Dangling Man* brought him respect, nearly 20 years ago, not only in America

*Reprinted from *New Statesman*, Feb. 5, 1965, pp. 200–01.

but here. Rereading it now, one finds it a little rigid, worthy but off-putting, a book one does not wish longer. I suppose that at the time, in a different and on the whole duller literary epoch, the intelligence with which the wretched but hard-thinking hero was placed, his eloquent and intellectually respectable introspection, were what won perceptive praise. Now the diagrams of alienation seem too square, the prose somewhat inelastic; it is hard to find in it the vivacity and inventive power one associates with Bellow. Perhaps it might be said that the austerity of the book gives it a kind of fidelity to its moment. Anyway, *The Victim*, though it had some of this rigour, and some of this period quality, was more various and flexible. But the big change, the *détente*, came only in the early Fifties, with *The Adventures of Augie March*.

It would be easy to run through the rollcall of this book's deficiencies, but the point is that Bellow had found his new form. Perhaps it struck him that the tragic stance of classic alienation, and even the existence of intellectuals, looked funny in this new world. They became a source of gags, and the hero turned picaro. Simultaneously with this new circumstance, Bellow became profusely inventive, exhibited a sense of the true comedy of intellect, which is painful as well as funny. There was some lamenting about what he gave up—the effects which arise from a firm management of structure, for example; it seemed that he thought these appropriate only to the short novel, and this guess was apparently confirmed when he next wrote a very good novella, *Seize the Day*, and went on to another inventive sprawl in *Henderson the Rain King*.

At least one ingredient is common to all the novels: the hero is, in Alfred Kazin's phrase, 'burdened by a speculative quest'. They all have the same humble need (however little this humility comes through in their conduct) to sort out human destiny by sorting out their own. In a world of chaotic particulars, where the only speculations which draw any support are bogus, vulgarised or corrupt, the speculative quest turns into a sequence of extravagantly funny or pathetic gestures, and the happiest ending that can be hoped for is that of *Seize the Day*, when Tommy Wilhelm, a middle-aged flop, winds up weeping at the funeral of somebody he doesn't know.

The great merit, and at the same time the great difficulty, of such writing is that it does try to get into fiction the farcical excitements of thinking as distinct from behaving. To do this straight seems almost impossible, or, if you think it works in *La Nausée*, unrepeatable. Bellow gets round the problem in the same way every time. The speculative interest is never put straight in. In *Seize the Day* the wise sayings come from the fraudulent Tamkin; in *Henderson* fantasy bears the freight of speculation. The new book is full of furious thinking, and Herzog, the hero, does most of it, but not 'straight'. The first sentence of the book says: 'If I am out of my mind, it's all right with me.'

Herzog is in the line of the fat novels, but has more structure than the others. The hero is a very well-read Chicago Jew on the point of a breakdown. Most of his thinking is done in letters, the kind of letter you might frenetically compose, if you had enough in your head, in the early stages of a sleepless night. 'Dear Herr Nietzsche, May I ask you a question from the floor?' 'Dear Doktor

Professor Heidegger, I should like to know what you mean by the expression "the fall into the quotidian." When did this fall occur? Where were we standing when it happened?' 'Dear General Eisenhower . . .' The letters, in a sense, do the work of Tamkin. As a way out of the difficulty, which was to show an intellectual operating in the world, they seem to me to have the exceptional merit of turning the technical trick and then, because sparingly used and full of wit, to become delightful in themselves.

Herzog is an authority on everything from Romantic theology to fish-scales, but all this equipment is of interest only as useful in the speculative quest. After all his adventures he may wind up where we find him at the start of the book, in his weird derelict Vermont country house in a state of peaceful choicelessness. But the main business of the novel is Herzog, under stress, trying to sort out Herzog. He can in various ways tell us all about himself: a genuine old Jewish type that digs emotion, but grown at this moment—his second marriage ludicrously broken—narcissistic, masochistic, anachronistic. His friends a sort of traitors, a bunch of real grotesques (one of them gives the kiss of life to a monkey dying of tuberculosis), seem to be engaged in 'a collective project' to destroy his vanity and push him 'down in the mire of post-Renaissance, post-humanistic, post-Cartesian dissolution, next door to the Void.'

Out of the goings on that ensue there begins to emerge an interesting design. Herzog, forced into sacrifice anyway, sees that what he has to sacrifice himself to is the truth, and we watch him both consciously trying to do this and unconsciously doing it. Under the pressure of his 'reality instructors' he moves hastily about, colliding with the world from which he is dissociated; in the subway he writes letters about negative entropy, and emerges to observe 'an escaped balloon fleeing like a sperm, black and quick into the orange dust of the west . . .' (This is not only powerful and versatile, it concretely presents the dissociation between things as they are and Herzog's speculations.) He is on the way to see a splendidly undemanding sexpot, whom he enjoys with the same comic metaphysical detachment from sense. The truth about sacrifice can't be got to by that route, nor by fast useless journeys, made by Herzog with 'all the dead and mad' in his company or custody, nor by surveying 'the story of my life—how I rose from humble origins to complete disaster'. When the answers eventually come, they come both from without and within.

The long climactic passage of this novel, which is about Herzog's trip to Chicago to see his daughter, is the first piece in which Bellow has improved on *Seize the Day*, a book it somewhat resembles. It has many layers, and a diagram would be misleading, especially if it sounded conventional or banal; but Herzog pays an important visit to an old, still Yiddish aunt, and carries off a gun he had once seen ineffectively flourished by his father. By this agency he gets his chance to come, though imperfectly, to terms with indignity and suffering, and that is a step in the necessary direction. As he had informed General Eisenhower in a particularly abstruse letter, the forces that make us human are history, memory, and a knowledge of death. A day in a New York courtroom had taught him more—for example about how high he stood in the scale of affluent misery; and he feels this more keenly when in a prison cell himself, knowing that this is not the place for him to do time; he belongs to the privileged classes who do it on the street. Finally, as in *Seize the Day*, the decisive message comes from the wisdom of a crank: you can't live until you know death; practise lying in a coffin, know it while you still live; then live. So, as far as it can be done in a self-hating civilisation, in an emotional language corrupted by all the fraudulent modern talk of crisis, apocalypse, desperation, Herzog touches bottom and finds health.

Bellow must be sick of hearing about his deficiencies, especially about his failure to invent women. There isn't a conventionally well-written woman in *Herzog*, though the hero's second wife is convincing as the inhabitant of a bad dream, a figure of fun who then bursts nightmarishly into the police station to press Herzog down to the bottom. The other girls, Herzog's mistresses, are about as real as Smollett's but little more is needed. This is a slightly caricatured world, male, Jewish, comic and pathetic, temporarily crazy too, so that the men friends are no less grotesque than the wife, and the remnants of Herzog's childhood are endearing emblems rather than original experiences profoundly evoked. This is the world refracted through the ageing Bellow hero; bricks and mortar, cab-drivers, what might be seen from the corner of an abstracted eye, are idiomatic, accurate; dialogue also can have accuracy as well as comic energy. But the nearer the foreground, the nearer the main interest, they come, the more distorted the characters tend to look.

Still, it is plausibly the view from Herzog's disciplinary coffin. So although the book has clear limitations, they are a long way off. And why should we be surprised that Americans make much of such powers of invention and intellect, such comic energy, so genuine a speculative quest? Wouldn't we?

Man in Culture

Irvin Stock[*]

A remarkable feature of Saul Bellow's career is that it is a kind of model of organic growth, his novels both alike and different, like a human being getting older. Their differences have been easier to see first—an intellectual's journal, a tight Kafkaesque nightmare, a loose, expansive, high-spirited picaresque tale, an African adventure story, and so on. But the novels are profoundly alike too, because from the start Bellow has had the luck to know what he most deeply cherishes, and he has clung to that knowledge against all the batterings of experience and all the seductions of intellectual sophistication. Each of his novels has asked: How can I hold onto the feeling, acquired in my (Jewish) childhood, that I am a precious soul and that life is full of beautiful promise? How can I hold onto this feeling when both experience and thought in our time seem to have turned it into a joke, and maturity seems to mean precisely the ability to see the joke?

Bellow's protagonists (each, however vividly individualized, a version of himself) have always fought against such maturity. To accept the idea that we are nothing special, and that the "nobility" that thrills us in history books is no longer among our possibilities—this, for Bellow, has always meant "to die," while "to live"—the phrases recur almost obsessively—has meant to be stirred to joyous activity by a faith that inspires, the faith that the self we imagine in our happiest moments can be real. ("Imagination is a force of nature," said Dahfu in *Henderson the Rain King.* "It converts to actual. It sustains. It alters. It redeems.") What that life-giving faith asserts is that we do have a "separate destiny" (Joseph, in *Dangling Man*); that "the eternal . . . bonded onto us . . . calls out for its share" (Henderson); that we can be "marvelous" (Herzog). It is the faith of the early Romantics—Blake, Wordsworth, Keats—whose ideas in fact suffuse Bellow's novels.

To this point, however, another must be added. Bellow is unique among American novelists not only because he has always clung to an unfashionably sunny faith, the faith of the child, but because he has been at the same time more heavily burdened with adult knowledge and thought than any American novelist since Melville. And in all his stories knowledge and thought tend to mock that faith, sometimes defeating it, sometimes merely complicating it.

[*]Reprinted from *Commentary,* 49 (1970), 89–94 and revised by the author for its appearance in this book.

One way to get at what is new in *Mr. Sammler's Planet* would be to say that in it the Romantic faith of Bellow's earlier novels might appear, at first glance, to have been abandoned. The book seems to be, in large part, an attack on a generation of Americans which is trying to stay "alive" in Bellow's own sense of the word—to have a separate destiny, to be marvelous, just as his former heroes have done. Some readers have said that the Romantic Bellow has here turned suddenly "neo-classic," and others, less kind, have called the book ungenerous and reactionary.

In my opinion, however, Bellow has done something far more interesting in *Mr. Sammler's Planet* than reverse himself. He has, it is true, moved from where he used to be: instead of the predictable repetition of old stances to which novelists incapable of growth tend to sink, he has tried, with unusual directness, to give expression to the new experience of a new time. But the fact is that the changes in emphasis which this novel dramatizes are changes required for Bellow to remain loyal, in this new time, to what has mattered most to him from the start. Today's rebellious young are indeed loud in proclaiming Bellow's own sense that each individual is precious and deserves a chance for rich fulfillments. But it is an old story that a good cause may be in danger from its own champions, and what Bellow is now trying to show is how the most prevalent ways of asserting that belief are actually, for reasons that lie deep in the recent development of Western culture, ways of caricaturing it, vulgarizing it. Now we have to grant, of course, that this is the work of a middle-aged man, and that Bellow's protagonist is his oldest yet, a man in his seventies. But it doesn't have to follow after all that it must therefore be less in touch with reality than the work of his youth. The distinction of *Mr. Sammler's Planet* is precisely that it is an embodiment, beautifully adequate to its subject, of the wisdom of Bellow's middle age.

To offer this new perspective, and to judge from it the new age, Bellow has created a protagonist different from his others, as well as like them, in appropriate ways. Artur Sammler is a Polish Jew who was spoiled by well-to-do parents as a child, and who, as a young man, fell in love with English reasonableness and good manners (he was a friend of H. G. Wells)—in short, he was shaped, like earlier Bellow heroes, to expect good things of himself and others. But later there came a moment when he crawled naked and half-blinded out of a mass grave of Nazi victims, leaving there the corpse of his wife. And soon after this he, in his turn, killed a German soldier he had disarmed and stripped—killed him deliberately, and with intense pleasure. For the rest of his life he struggles against the message then delivered to him, "that reality was a terrible thing, and the final truth about mankind overwhelming and crushing."

It is a message renewed, of course, again and again, not only among the bloated corpses Sammler saw as an elderly journalist in the Sinai desert in 1967, but equally on New York's upper Broadway, where it seems "the implicit local orthodoxy." But he fights it. Mainly it is "a vulgar and cowardly conclusion, rejected . . . with all his heart." Now he is living in New York on the charity of a rich doctor nephew, uncomfortable at what he sees around him, but hesitant to judge, increasingly fed up with "explanations"—to make "distinctions" is what he prefers—his favorite reading the work of Meister Eckhart, the medieval German mystic for whom the comfort of God requires that we abandon the false comfort offered us by His creatures. Yet others keep turning to Sammler as himself a source of mysterious comfort (even while his old-fashioned good manners make them smile): he remains hopelessly involved, through love as well as duty, with those same creatures. And the private vocation he has turned to in the leisure of old age is the search for "short views," a phrase of Sidney Smith's which, as Sammler uses it, means condensed conclusions about "some essence of experience," and which keeps recurring as the new hunger of his mind.

Sammler's, then, is the ripest intelligence Bellow has ever invented, a man educated not only by books, for he has learned at first hand the chief lessons of our time. And though the novel resembles *Herzog*, in that its story comes to us entirely through its hero's idiosyncratic Jewish responses and his wide-ranging memories and reflection, what makes it quite different is that it is actually just the sort of "condensation" a Mr. Sammler would have ordered. Action, memories, reflections are not here an image of the turbulence of life, but always in league with each other and building forward, each of the six chapters clearly a unit in a theme's development. The story is, in fact, an account of a series of confrontations between the elderly humanist and a group of characters chosen to represent the current *Zeitgeist*. And these confrontations are given increasing urgency and point by a classic philosophic challenge that soon begins to haunt them all—that is, by Sammler's struggle, through the tale's few days, to find some "word" to bring his dying nephew that might oppose the negation of death. (The nephew, rich in part with Mafia abortion money, has been no angel. But Sammler recognizes in him a man "assigned" to feel, especially for others—to reach out, please, help, as if the world were a family. And for this he loves him.)

There is, first of all, the new sexual morality, represented by Angela, the dying man's daughter, who has been set free by her beauty and her father's wealth for a "Roman" paganism of sexual behavior. *She* calls "perverse" not the "erotic business in Acapulco" that occurred when she and her fiance played switch with some beach acquaintances, but his sudden jealousy afterward. Her brother Wallace is equally familiar—"a high-I.Q. moron," who "finds out how to put things together . . . as he goes along," as in "action-painting," and whose one persistent motive seems to be to show his father that he can make it on his own, and that he can't—for his brilliant beginnings always end in failure that looks deliberately courted. Wallace's resemblance to Augie March, who also refused to let himself be pinned down or to risk, by accepting some limiting job or function, "a disappointed life," is symptomatic of Bellow's changed perspective. Augie, though he had his troubles, also had his author's sympathy. Wallace, unwilling to accept limits or models of being imposed by others, and yet incapable of respecting for long those chosen by himself, is clearly a failure and a waste.

Then there is Feffer, a Columbia University student who represents the type who does "make it." He is a clever promoter for whom ends justify means and liberal sentiments are quite enough for a good conscience. Feffer cons Sammler into lecturing on Bloomsbury to a Columbia crowd gathered to hear about Sorel on violence, an affair that ends in what is at this moment in history a familiar disaster. A "thick-bearded, but possibly young" member of the New Left, offended by an irony quoted from Orwell, stops the talk with, "Hey! Old Man! . . . That's a lot of shit!" and some remarks about Sammler's "dry balls."

Finally, there is Sammler's son-in-law Eisen, an Israeli avant-garde painter and sculptor, in whom we are shown what is now happening both to Jews and to artists. Like Sammler, he is a survivor of the Holocaust, but he is one who has willingly, even happily, embraced the cynical lesson that Sammler struggles to resist. As an artist, he paints living people as corpses: by this gimmick of a death-oriented outrageousness he gives to creative impotence a hectic pseudo-potency. As a Jew, he crushes skulls, when it seems reasonable to do so, without any crippling tremors of doubt or remorse. "You were a Partisan," he says, when the old man, in a scene I will sketch in a moment, protests in horror that he might have gained his end less bloodily. "You had a gun. So don't you know? . . . If in—in. No? If out—out. Yes? No? So answer." In Eisen the traditional allegiances of both Jew and artist—to life, to man—have been abandoned. And he now goes after personal development and distinction—an American "*karyera*"—with the greedy single-mindedness of the ethically "liberated."

The book is strewn with Mr. Sammler's reflections on what all these confrontations imply—on the "individuality boom" that has resulted from the increase of freedom and the dread of "futurelessness"; on the drive to be "real" that has merely replaced traditional human models with "dimestore" models out of recent literature and Hollywood; on the resort to madness in order to demonstrate availability for "higher purposes," which purposes "do not necessarily appear"; on the "non-negotiable" demands for instant gratification made by people who, refusing to admit any limitations on the possible, are doomed to humiliating misery and dangerous rages. But the opening chapter's presentation of what is happening to Mr. Sammler's planet is completed by the introduction of two characters who, though they also represent the new age, are types of the human he can respect. First, there is a tall, gorgeously dressed black pickpocket. Having caught Sammler watching him in action, the black follows the frightened old man into his hotel lobby, presses him to a wall, and displays, in significant silence, his massive penis. Immediately after this warning, Sammler finds in his room a manuscript work on "The Future of the Moon," stolen for him by his half-mad daughter from an Indian scientist, Dr. V. Govinda Lal. Reading its first line, "How long will this earth remain the only home of man?" he closes the chapter with the silent cry, "How long? Or Lord, you bet! Wasn't it the time—the very hour to go? . . . To blow this great blue, white, green planet, or to be blown from it."

The values represented by the black man—lawlessness, sexual potency, self-delight—may well have influenced mid-20th century youth. But as the story proceeds, Sammler becomes aware that the black is, in fact, like Sammler himself, an outsider and the new generation's victim. The pickpocket stole because "he took the slackness and cowardice of the world for granted." Puma-like, *eine Natur* (Goethe's respectful phrase), he was mad, if at all, "with an idea of noblesse." Indeed, Feffer, hearing about him, is thrilled, as by a "sudden glory." But Feffer's response to the "glory" is to photograph the thief in action for magazine exploitation. And when the black struggles with him for the camera and Sammler asks Eisen to help, that new-type Jewish artist coolly smashes the black's face with a bag of his crazy sculpture. It is the black who gets Sammler's passionate sympathy, the others his horrified rage.

As for Lal, Bellow has created in him a genuinely brilliant man of science, and, improbable though it may seem, the twenty-nine pages of philosophic dialogue which follow his meeting with Sammler are a moving and exciting fictional climax. (And yet, why so improbable? For such men to meet, recognize each other's quality, and, winning over the normal inner and outer obstacles, share their deepest thought, can be an experience as thrilling as love.) Lal, for whom nature, "more than an engineer, is an artist," is no mere opposite to Sammler; yet they differ on one point that relates to the novel's center. Lal is ready to call it quits on man's long struggle to make a home on this planet. For him space travel is not only the inevitable next step demanded by the human imagination. As an Indian, "supersensitive to a surplus of humanity"—that is, already familiar with the future—he believes that refusal to make the voyages elsewhere which are growing possible would turn this crowded planet into a prison, and bring the human species, now "eating itself up," closer than ever to leaping into Kingdom Come. Moreover, amid the rigors of space and under the leadership of technicians endowed with their own kind of nobility, he believes that man may yet be disciplined into recovering lost virtues.

Sammler's response is no simple disagreement. In fact, much of what he says is an anguished attempt to understand what has caused "the shrinking scope for the great powers of nature in the individual, the abundant and gener-ous powers." But he feels that there is "also an instinct against leaping into Kingdom Come. . . . The spirit knows that its continued growth is the real end of existence." And crowded and disappointing though it is, his own planet is still, for him, a home he cannot—will not—give up. Why not? His answer to this question—what he has to offer in place of a defeatist departure into space or Kingdom Come—constitutes the point of the book.

Mainly, of course, the answer is himself. But, as I have suggested, it is dramatized in his struggle to find some "word" which will comfort his nephew in the hour of his death. The struggle is real, its desperateness is genuinely evoked, especially in the mounting excitement that precedes the end: in that scene of blood when Eisen's killer-reasoning "sinks his heart," and then in his final confrontation in the hospital with Gruner's sexy daughter. Risking her rage, he tries to get Angela to feel what is now wanted—to put aside for once her own demands and grievances, to go to her father, say something, make some sign, at least, that will show she is sorry her behavior, of which he has heard, has caused him pain. But Angela, bold enough in other areas, naturally recoils from a scene so "hokey." ("You want an old-time deathbed scene. . . . But how could I—It goes against everything. You're talking to the wrong person. . . . What is there to say!") A few seconds later Sammler himself, standing alone beside his nephew's body, utters his "word" in the silent heartbroken prayer that ends the novel:

> Remember, God [Sammler prays], the soul of Elya Gruner, who, as willingly as possible and as well as he was able, and even in suffocation and even as death was coming, was eager, even childishly perhaps . . . to do what was required of him. At his best this man was much kinder than at my very best I have ever been or could ever be. He was aware that he must meet, and he did meet—through all the confusion and degraded clowning of this life through which we are speeding—he did meet the terms of his contract. The terms which, in his inmost heart, every man knows. As I know mine. As all know. For that is the truth of it—that we all know, God, that we know, we know, we know.

Here, then, is the new emphasis to which Bellow has been led by the new age (and his own new age). The mere assertion of individuality, the "non-negotiable" demand for one's own way, the leaps to ecstasy or "significance" that bypass duties and commitments to others—such behavior debases the self it seeks to glorify. It is only by loyalty to the "human bond," to the "contract" implicit in our humanity, that we can safeguard our sense of the self's value.

Indeed, as Sammler becomes aware during a moment of horror, to find oneself with *no other* to turn to in a time of need is "death," is to be "not himself . . . someone between the human and not-human states, between content and void, meaning and not-meaning, between this world and no world. Flying, freed from gravitation, light with release and dread, doubting his destination, fearing there was nothing to receive him." For Sammler, a man who believes in God, even our sense of ultimate destinations and receptions depends on that "contract." The term implies a faith not merely in the fact of a "human bond," but also in our obligation to create it for each other. By looks, by signs, by words, we make this planet a home for each other, we make a web of relationships and meanings that reach even beyond the individual life and reduce even the terror of the unknown future.

But if Bellow has tried to body forth the idea of a "contract," he also makes clear that idea's terrible vulnerability. For Sammler, the young who cry "Shit!" to their elders do have a case. He is aware, for instance, that the old attitudes toward sex were not a success, and that Angela's sexuality may well, as she cleverly observes, be the fulfilment of her father's repressed wishes. Even Eisen's killer-reasoning was once—or so it seemed—Sammler's own.

The truth is that Sammler's final "word" is no comfortable triumph. At best, it is a battle won in a war that will never end. Or more exactly, it is an assertion of faith, and faith is half the mere will that thing be so and so, asserted against the undying possibility that they may not be. But—we don't know everything. To swallow current "explanations" as the whole truth is to submit slavishly to ignoble reduction. There is in life an inexhaustible wealth of possibilities, and therefore freedom. In that freedom, intuitions of decency may be entitled to respect. (Bellow had already said something like this in *The Victim*. "Choose dignity," declared the sage Schlossberg. "Nobody knows enough to turn it down.") If nothing in culture is born out of unmixed conditions or causes, yet graces do emerge out of the mixture, ideas of human decency which, though they may be "compromised," may also be our chief safeguards against the brutes. To spit on such ideas in all relations because they have been alibis for evil in some may be itself a brute's way of justifying brutishness.

The novel has been called one-sided, its cast of characters not fully representative. There is some truth in this. We need other views of the time to place beside Bellow's. And yet the fact that there is more to say surely does not invalidate a work that attempts to describe a salient tendency. No novelist need be required to report everything. Moreover, since the intellectual's consensus of the moment is all on the side of the "idealistic," demanding young, it is good to have around a man like Bellow, for whom, as for his Sammler, "the place of honor is outside." Who but the outsider in any age is likely to expose what its fashionable idealism conceals?

To have explored a novel's meanings, however, is only partly to account for its power. And the question of this writer's power as an artist is especially interesting because he would seem to be laboring under a handicap. Saul Bellow is pre-eminently the novelist of man-in-culture, man swimming in an ocean of ideas in which he often feels near to being swamped ("there are times," says Sammler, "in which one lies under and feels the awful weight of cumulative consciousness. . . . Not at all funny"); and, as we are often told, ideas in art can be deadening. But the odd fact is that in Bellow's work the ideas themselves are a source of fictional vitality: they are part of the fun and feeling. There are several reasons for this. One is that Bellow has a gift, reminiscent of Wordsworth, for evoking in his sentence rhythms, as well as in his words, the *experience* of thought, the drama of its emergence out of the life of the whole man. Another, related to the first, is that the experience of thought rises in his novels out of a thickly detailed physical world that both provokes it and helps to give it expression. Then, even more important, Bellow is the kind of writer who knows, as Sammler put it, "Once take a stand, draw a baseline, and contraries assail you. . . . All positions are mocked by their opposites." The ideas which underlie his characters and plots are therefore more likely to safeguard than to violate the mysteries of reality.

But there is a deeper reason for the emotional power of Bellow's thought, and for the uniquely intimate response he elicits from some of us. It is that he is concerned above all with *man*-in-culture, man swimming for his life among ideas, wincing at or delighting in them, and challenging them always to answer the naive, irrepressible demands of the feeling heart. He carries amid the richest complexities of modern consciousness the claims and standards of our ordinary humanity. It is perhaps here, more than in his idiom or his subject matter, that his Jewishness may be located: that he writes as a champion of the human, of humaneness; he writes out of that tenderness for the hard-pressed human creature which has traditionally been the Jew's strength, and his weakness. In fact, *Mr. Sammler's Planet* is a beautiful defense of our common humanity against all the bogus idealism as well as the frank savagery that nowadays rejects it as "corn."

Saul Bellow at 60:
A Turn to the Mystical

John W. Aldridge[*]

On June 10 of this year Saul Bellow became 60, an age when most American novelists have ceased to live in expectation of doing important new work and many have given themselves up to producing menopausal recapitulations of their important old work. Bellow on turning 60 has done neither. He has marked the occasion by publishing a novel, his eighth, that contains abundant evidence of the continued expansion and deepening of his creative powers. It is richer in texture and implication than anything he has written since *The Adventures of Augie March,* and it may well be the most distinguished novel he has so far produced.

Bellow not only has endured but also has for some time prevailed as one of the two or three major novelists of his generation. And he has done so largely because he is a man of enormous intellectual vitality as well as talent, and because he has always been willing, like Mailer, to risk his career by venturing, with each new book, beyond the imaginative territories he has previously explored and consolidated. Where most writers take possession of their subjects, along with the technical means to engage them, fairly early in life and then proceed gradually to exhaust them, Bellow from the beginning has maintained a much more flexible and dynamic relation with the materials of his art, and he has brought to their service an intellectual culture far more extensive than that of his American contemporaries. Ideas for him are not only a primary basis of subject matter. Nor are they—as so much of our literature seems to imply—antithetical to the expression of honest feeling and the actualities of "real" life. Rather, they serve to broaden and intensify his perception of those actualities, and they help him to dramatize what he sees as the vital connections, so complexly explored in all his novels, between secular experience and the transcendences of history, morality, philosophy, and religion.

Bellow also has the capacity—very nearly as rare among our novelists as the power of abstract thought—to experiment with a variety of novelistic techniques in which to cast his continuously evolving conception of his materials. From time to time, and often within the limits of a single book, he has made brilliant use of the effects of naturalist realism, the comedy of manners, black humor, the mystery novel, the picaresque, psychological, and philosophical

[*]Reprinted from *Saturday Review,* Sept. 6, 1975, pp. 22–25.

novel, and literary satire (in *Henderson the Rain King,* partly a parody of the mythic narrative of descent into the heart of darkness), and his virtuosity has been reinforced by his very considerable knowledge of American and European literature, philosophy, and psychology. Jung, Wilhelm Reich, Sartre, Dostoevski, Dickens, Melville, Whitman, and Mark Twain have all been prominent influences on Bellow, but as is the case with most major artists, he has not so much imitated as transmuted certain of their features to fit the requirements of his imagination. His indebtednesses, however, are often obvious, and sometimes they are flagrant. For example, his first novel, *Dangling Man,* appears to have been strongly influenced by Sartre's *Nausea,* and the protagonist bears a close resemblance—as do, for that matter, so many characters in post-modern fiction—to Dostoevski's Underground Man. *The Victim* is also derivative, Bellow himself once admitted, of Dostoevski: in terms of sheer plot, it is virtually a retelling of *The Eternal Husband. The Adventures of Augie March,* the third and most ambitious of Bellow's early novels, is a mélange of styles, characters, dramatic episodes, and literary echoes, and as it represents a radical departure from the tight, highly formalized works with which he began his career, so it marks at least a temporary turning away from European in favor of native American influences—Whitman, Twain, Dreiser, and just possibly Melville.

Augie March was and remains Bellow's great transitional work, an expression of manic energy and high comedic talent that he had not previously been able to release, a kind of fiction sufficiently open and flexible to allow him for the first time to do absolutely anything he chose, in which he was freed rather than inhibited by the technical requirements of his medium. Ever since, Bellow has been experimenting with new arrangements and combinations of forms and styles, different angles of approach to materials that were all essentially present in *Augie March* but that, in his subsequent novels, needed to be processed according to the dictates of his maturing perceptions of experience. *Henderson the Rain King* is basically a mock-heroic rendering of Augie's quest for self-knowledge. Henderson's flight into Africa, where he becomes a buffoon fertility god among primitive tribes and finally believes or *decides* to believe that he has discovered himself, burlesques Augie's flight from the various "reality instructors" who want to educate him in their distorted vision of the world.

With *Herzog,* in the writer of unmailed letters to prominent people, the Underground Man reappears. The sufferer who seeks after goodness and wisdom is once again the farcical martyr persecuted by malevolent would-be teachers, and in the end he breaks out into freedom and peace or, depending on one's interpretation of the closing scenes, he capitulates to his situation and to himself as he is, saying, "I am pretty well satisfied to be, to be just as it is willed, for as long as I may remain in occupancy . . ."—a note of complacent resignation, which, as I once wrote, seems falsely imposed and which calls into question the authenticity of the novel's narrative voice.

Finally, in *Mr. Sammler's Planet,* the novel just preceding *Humboldt's Gift,* the sufferer, now an old man bewildered and put upon by the anarchy of life in the contemporary city, searches for some understanding of the ultimate purpose of human existence, some knowledge that will enable him to accept the fact of his nephew's and his own imminent death as well as, conceivably, the eventual extinction of human life on earth. In a fashion that becomes increasingly evident in Bellow's later protagonists, Mr. Sammler moves from self-preoccupation and secular intellectuality closer and closer to mysticism, seeking what one critic has called "the Tolstoyan moment," the instant of apocalyptic perception in which the patterns unifying the cosmos and linking man to the cosmos become visible and comprehensible.

However dissimilar Bellow's novels may be in other respects, they all tell essentially the same story. They are all informed by what can only be called a desperately affirmative view of human experience and possibility, a view too complicated to be reducible to a philosophical proposition, too dialectical and contradictory to be taken as dogma, creed, or panacea. Its central feature is, in fact, ambiguity, a recognition of elements which may be forever irreconcilable, of questions which must be pondered and explored, but for which answers will probably never be found, at least not by the merely human creatures who seek them. Bellow on several occasions has expressed his strong disagreement with the idea of cultural nihilism and alienation which pervades so much of modern literature and which he believes has its source far more *in* literature than in the actual life it purports to reflect. As he said in his Library of Congress address in 1963:

"Writers have inherited a tone of bitterness from the great poems and novels of this century, many of which lament the passing of a more stable and beautiful age demolished by the barbarous intrusion of an industrial and metropolitan society of masses or proles who will, after many upheavals, be tamed by bureaucracies and oligarchies in brave new worlds, human anthills. . . . There are modern novelists who take all this for granted as fully proven and implicit in the human condition and who complain as steadily as they write, viewing modern life with a bitterness to which they themselves have not established clear title, and it is this unearned bitterness I speak of."

Herzog, in one of his unmailed letters to his friend Shapiro, angrily denounces "the commonplaces of the Wasteland outlook, the cheap mental stimulants of Alienation, the cant and rant of pipsqueaks about Inauthenticity and forlornness. I can't accept this foolish dreariness. We are talking about the whole life of mankind. The subject is too great, too deep for such weakness, cowardice—too deep, too great, Shapiro."

Clearly, Bellow wishes to offer in his fiction a view of modern life that will be alternative to "the commonplaces of the Wasteland outlook," for he has said elsewhere that "a man should have at least sufficient power to overcome ignominy and to complete his own life. His suffering, feebleness, servitude, then have a meaning," and it is the writer's duty to affirm that meaning, to "reveal the greatness of man." This Bellow has steadily tried to achieve. He has celebrated life with remarkable vigor, and he has created some of the most compassionate portraits of the human condition—even in its thoroughly detestable manifestations—to be found anywhere in modern literature. Yet the ultimate revelation of the greatness of man has eluded him, partly because it is much easier artistically to represent evil than to find the terms for the convincing display of virtue, but mostly because Bellow has been thwarted by the very complexity and ambiguity of his view of man.

His problem is that as a writer of great perceptiveness and intellectual honesty he cannot help being aware and reflecting his awareness of all those elements in modern life to which the only sane response is despair and which have produced the climate of pessimism, alienation, and generalized forlornness he finds so oppressive. His moral impulse is to affirm life in some perhaps transcendental way that will be commensurate with his sincere belief in human possibility. But the observable facts of life as it exists at the present time not only afford no proof of that possibility but also seem to work actively to nullify it. Bellow has thus found himself in a position of *wishing* to believe amid conditions that do not provide adequate objective justifications for belief, and the consequence for his fiction is that it has tended to break apart into two kinds of dramatic statement which may be developed concurrently but which cannot be plausibly reconciled. On the one hand, there is material—usually of a speculative, philosophical, or mystical nature—which expresses Bellow's faith that man can attain self-understanding and transformation, that he can overcome the limitations of his individuality, and come into some recognition of his place in the social and cosmic order. On the other hand, there is the far more abundant and vital material that portrays man's cruelty, duplicity, venality, his maniacal self-obsessiveness, his hateful determination to exploit others in any way he can in order to prosper in a world where material value is the only value, success is measured by the standards of the con game, and the reigning morality is a cynicism that Bellow aptly calls "deceit without guilt."

It may be because Bellow cannot bring into single dramatic focus his optimism about man and his pessimism about the conditions of life that his characters so often seem schizophrenic and the endings of his novels disappointingly equivocal. His protagonists are men of goodwill and high hopes who make their way through a hellish wasteland in which they are forced to suffer every imaginable kind of humiliation and injustice. Yet at the end, in spite of everything, they are still seekers and believers. Martyred and persecuted though they may be, they remain pure and hopeful, still expecting transformation and revelation—perhaps in quiet confidence like Herzog, "well satisfied to be . . . just as it is willed," or like Augie, laughing at nature because "it thinks it can win over us and the power of hope," or like Henderson, who, during a stopover in Newfoundland, gets out of the airplane that is bringing him home from Africa and, believing he has at last begun to find his life, runs in ecstasy, an orphaned child in his arms, "over the pure white lining of the gray Arctic silence." These are all endings that represent cessations of narrative action but not conclusions, pauses in flight but not the attainment of thematic destination.

In *Humboldt's Gift* Bellow has still not found a way of successfully reconciling these contradictory attitudes and the two kinds of material in which they are expressed. But he does manage to cope with them more effectively than he has been able to do in any of his previous novels. The protagonist, Charles Citrine, confirms one's impression that Bellow's views of the nature of human existence are becoming increasingly mystical and may eventually find a formally religious framework. Citrine is a student of anthroposophy, a doctrine which maintains that through self-discipline cognitional experience of the spiritual world can be achieved, and his meditations on such a possibility become a significant yet unobtrusive leitmotiv of the world. But the critical point is that Bellow treats them throughout as meditations only. They are not required to bear a major thematic weight as are the speculative materials in the earlier novels. Therefore, Bellow's inability to reconcile them with his secular materials does not become problematical, since Citrine merely retreats from time to time into his meditations and at best only holds out hope that they may eventually lead him to a perception of spiritual truth.

This is to say that for the first time in this novel Bellow has been able to objectify his own wishful optimism and to accept it for just that, declining now to try to give it more crucial thematic importance than it can justifiably be given. Citrine emerges as, in other respects, a typical Bellow protagonist, but one who has a mystical turn of mind. He may be another seeker after cosmic understanding, but that role is de-emphasized because he is first and foremost a suffering victim whose journey through the purgatory of humiliation and betrayal is easily separable from his spiritual pilgrimage. He is therefore placed, with a minimum of distracting metaphysical encumbrances, at the center of the kind of action Bellow has always been able to dramatize with the greatest effectiveness, the action of relentlessly secular existence, and that is surely an important reason why Citrine comes to seem the most convincingly drawn of Bellow's major characters.

As the author of several works of popular biography and a successful Broadway play, Citrine is prosperous and well known but has reached an impasse in his life and career. His work has gone stale. He has been through a divorce, and is being hounded by his ex-wife, who, he is convinced, is determined to ruin him financially. He has lawyers who seem to be trying to assist her in this effort in every way they can, and a few friends who may or may not be any more trustworthy. His beautiful mistress is pressuring him to marry her, but since she seriously doubts that he is a man of responsibility, she takes the precaution of sleeping from time to time with a wealthy undertaker.

Because of these and other problems Citrine has withdrawn more and more into himself, spending days at a time alone in his apartment meditating on such matters as the fate of the soul after death and the possibilities of reincarnation. He is also obsessed with the memory of the dead poet Von Humboldt Fleischer, his closest friend and the literary mentor of his youth, a creative force of immense size, but a talent destroyed by neglect, eccentricity, paranoia, and alcohol. Fleischer has died alone in poverty and obscurity, and Citrine ponders his life trying to understand its significance, wishing he had been a better friend to Fleischer, regretting that he cannot carry on his work or in some way redeem his reputation.

Then all sorts of dreadful things begin to happen to Citrine and, in the fashion of contemporary black literature of the absurd, they simply happen at the behest of whatever agencies of capricious fatality govern the universe. One of Citrine's friends, troubled by his isolated existence, insists that he take part in a poker game where he will have a chance to meet people who belong to the real world. During the game Citrine drinks too much, babbles about his personal problems, fails to notice that he is being cheated by some of the players, and writes a check to cover his losses. When, the next day, he stops payment on the check, he is threatened by a small-time Mafia figure named Cantabile, who takes revenge by arranging to have Citrine's $18,000 Mercedes 280-SL clubbed to ruin in the street. Cantabile then forces Citrine to make an apology before witnesses for defaulting on the debt, and when Citrine offers him cash, he humiliates Citrine further by again forcing him to accompany him, this time to the top story of a skyscraper under construction. There, on a swaying catwalk high above the city, Cantabile takes the $50 bills Citrine has given him, folds them into paper airplanes, and sails them off into the wind.

These persecutions, as it turns out, are merely initiatory. A short time later a district judge decides that Citrine must pay his ex-wife an amount of money that will virtually wipe him out, and then orders him to post a bond of $200,000. Nevertheless, Citrine goes off on a long planned trip to Europe, where he expects to be joined by his mistress. But while waiting for her in Madrid, he learns that she has gone to Italy and married the undertaker—the betrayal having evidently been carefully plotted from the moment it became apparent that Citrine was no longer a good financial prospect. Left alone in Madrid, he resumes his meditations on the occult and experiments in trying to communicate with the spirits of the dead, in particular with Fleischer. The experiments fail, but in a remarkable way. Fleischer finally does communicate with Citrine and passes on to him his gift or legacy, the nature of which had perhaps best be left undisclosed. The proceeds from it will not make Citrine rich, but they will help him begin life again, and he supposes it will be a radically different kind of life, a cessation of struggle, extravagance, self-loathing, and boredom, an attempt to "listen in secret to the sound of the truth that God puts into us."

Described in this way, the action in its details may seem trivial or merely ludicrous. It is surely not redeemed by the metaphysical dimension, nor is the ending altogether satisfactory. But the power of the novel derives in the Jamesean sense from the quality and intensity of the felt life contained within it, the brilliant evocation of the social world, and the incredible sensitivity of its characterizations. It is here rather than in his philosophical assertions that Bellow expresses most forcefully his belief in life and the greatness of man. If he has so far failed to achieve a synthesis of his metaphysical and his secular materials, the failure may, after all, be fortunate. For we expect a novelist to be a chronicler and not a visionary, an observer and analyst rather than a seer. In searching for and never quite discovering the secret cohering principle of human existence, Bellow has given us a portrait of existence that may contain as much understanding as we can bear.

ESSAYS

Common Needs,
Common Preoccupations
AN INTERVIEW WITH SAUL BELLOW

Jo Brans*

Saul Bellow, the author of eleven books, among them *The Adventures of Augie March, Herzog, Mr. Sammler's Planet,* and *Humboldt's Gift,* received the Nobel Prize for Literature in 1976.

Jo Brans is a member of the faculty of the Department of English at Southern Methodist University. She interviewed Bellow when he visited Dallas in November, 1976, to speak at SMU's Literary Festival.

BRANS: You said recently that you began to write books because you love literature. And I thought that was the best answer to the question of "why" that anybody had given. But it seemed to be a strange answer. You didn't say anything about expressing yourself or revealing your feelings. None of that Rousseau stuff.

BELLOW: If I thought the project was about myself I would value it less. It isn't really about myself. What I have discovered over the years is that although it began with me, it is an activity that affects other people, and that I have the knack of expressing some of their unexpressed thoughts and feelings. For instance, for many years I had fantasies in which I wrote letters to people. Then I thought, oh, what an odd thing. Wouldn't it be amusing if I wrote a book about a man who, going out of his mind, is writing letters to everybody. And then I discovered that hundreds of thousands of people were doing just that—always had been doing that.

BRANS: Writing mental letters?

BELLOW: Yes. And so this was some evidence to me that I enjoyed some "clairvoyant powers." I had had that before, from my very first book. When I published *Dangling Man,* many people wrote me and said that they found their own situation in this. And then I began to realize that I had some feeling for where the nerves lay. That the enterprise was not really about me, that I was on loan to myself, as it were, and that I was doing something that expressed common needs, common preoccupations. If it were just about myself I don't think that it would have meant so very much to me, because I haven't all that much use for myself—myself, as such, my own ego, pride of accomplishment, or what you like. I think I had not an abnormal amount of such pride, but a relatively low amount. I would have been satisfied with a far more modest

*Reprinted from *Southwest Review,* 62 (1977), 1–19.

success. I never wanted to uncork the genie, or raise the lid of Pandora's box. I began to see some years ago that it was a Pandora's box.

BRANS: You mean your success? Or the connection that you made with people?

BELLOW: No, the connection was important, but the success was something else again, because the success meant that I was supplying a need, a public need—of a cultural kind. And that I was expected to act the culture figure, to be a public utility, an unpaid functionary, something between a congressman and a clergyman. And I saw that people felt they had a right to bring to me everything that troubled them in this province.

BRANS: That's what Sammler says about himself—that he is a priest or a psychologist.

BELLOW: Yes, you begin to feel that way pretty soon.

BRANS: When you say clairvoyant, do you mean that somehow intuitively or mystically you speak for other people? That somehow you are a kind of scapegoat figure as a writer and you bear the burden of other people, and you write about that? You have sometimes quoted Whitman, that the poet in America must create archetypes of Americans. Are you creating archetypes that come from all the people?

BELLOW: Well, I used the word clairvoyant. I might have chosen simpler, less mysterious language and said that because I'm concerned with what affects so many people, I have trained myself in an attitude of mind which provides just that sort of material. It may not be clairvoyance, but I have sometimes definitely sensed that it's a little more than a natural process. Something beyond positivistic, rationalistic common sense, or the clear light of day.

BRANS: That seems a curious thing for you to say, when your books are so full of ideas.

BELLOW: Well, not all ideas are clear and rational. And not all ideas belong to the modern idea system of scientific provability, or whatever you want to call it.

BRANS: I'm sympathetic to that. I know things all the time that I don't think through rationally, that are not even available to rational thought. But it seems really remarkable to me for a writer somehow to feel that he speaks for all kinds of people with whom he's never come in contact.

BELLOW: I think it's true, though. And I don't like to question the sources of my own ideas and feelings too closely. That is to say, I avoid the assumption that I know the origin of my own thoughts and feelings. I've become aware of a conflict between the modern university education I received and those things that I really felt in my soul most deeply. I've trusted those more and more.— You see, I'm not even supposed to have a soul.

BRANS: Who says you can't have a soul?

BELLOW: The soul is out of bounds if you have the sort of education I had. I got my bachelor's degree as an anthropologist. And I read Marx and Bertrand Russell and Morris R. Cohen; I read the logical positivists. I read Freud and Adler and the Gestalt psychologists and the rest. And I know how a modern man is supposed to think. The hero of my last book says, "If you put a test before me I can get a high mark, but it's only head culture." The fact is there are other deeper motives in a human being, which I don't like to call unconscious, because that's a term preempted by psychoanalysis, but I say to myself, "I have always behaved in such a way that I cannot escape the conclusion that I believe things I'm not consciously aware of believing. That I have hopes I can't justify. And that I have affections I can't explain by the modern system in which I was trained." Then you come to the point of choice. Do you believe the psychoanalytic explanation of your deeper motives? Or do you simply say, "These are my deeper motives, I don't care what psychoanalysis has to say about them." I've made the second choice. I don't care any longer whether my ideas square with the modern canon, which I have taken to calling the canon of head culture. I know that people live by something far deeper than head culture; they couldn't live if they didn't. They couldn't survive if they didn't. What a woman does for her children, what a man does for his family, what people most tenaciously cling to, these things are not adequately explained by Oedipus complexes, libidos, class struggle, or existential individualism—whatever you like. Now, I know that psychoanalysis has found a natural preserve for poets and artists called the unconscious. A writer is supposed to go there and dig around like a truffle hound. He comes back with a truffle, a delicacy for the cultural world. The poet is a wonderful Caliban, the analyst is the Prospero who knows how to put his discoveries to a higher purpose. Well, I don't believe that. I don't believe that we go and dig in the unconscious and come back with new truffles from the libidinous unknown. That's not the way it really is.

BRANS: How do you think it really is? If you act on what you get from this part of yourself . . .

BELLOW: There are persistent ideas, the truth of which we recognize when we meet them in literature. You read Tolstoy—it's not uncommon that a character of Tolstoy will hear an inner voice. We all know what that is. We immediately recognize it. We know how the soul of a child speaks to the child. We've experienced it ourselves, only there's no room for it in the new mental world that we've constructed, which is less and less a world and more and more a prison, it seems to me. But we know all these things when people talk to us about them. Our immortal hopes we know. We understand what they are. We don't dismiss them out of hand. And it's not just because of ancient superstition, it's because there is some unacknowledged information that we have. It's about time we simply dealt with it directly and without being so evasive.

BRANS: Now you're being Rousseau. You use this "we" so bravely. Aren't you making the assumption that what you think is really what everybody thinks? Isn't that a sort of Rousseau claim: I know my heart, so I know men?

BELLOW: "Je sens mon coeur, et je connais les hommes." Well, there's a good deal to it.

BRANS: How do you know that I'm not completely unlike you, and that you can talk about we all you want, but what you really mean is I?

BELLOW: I sense that when I say these things you don't actively disagree with me. At least, you're agnostic enough not to dispute them immediately. You'll think matters over.

BRANS: No, I'm not an agnostic at all. You know that I agree with you—I'm playing, I guess. Tell me about your teaching. What has been the importance of your teaching to your writing? You taught Tolstoy last year, didn't you?

BELLOW: Yes, and Conrad.

BRANS: Do you feel as frustrated about teaching as I do sometimes? What do you think about it? You teach graduate students all the time, who presumably feel lucky to be there, and who are dedicated to ideas—to what you have to say to them.

BELLOW: I suppose so. In Chicago it's very hard to find people to talk literature to. You find them at the university, and that's the long and the short of the thing. There is no literary culture in the United States. There are no colleagues to discuss novels with. Most of the critical articles that you read in magazines or newspapers are scandalous. And there is no community, so you talk to young people who know something. It's a great comfort. And, after all, why should one lock these things within one's bosom? I can't even talk to my wife about them. She's a mathematician. She's wonderful—she knows all kinds of things, but she doesn't know this, just as I don't know pure mathematics.

BRANS: But you both are using symbols, symbol systems.

BELLOW: Yes, but I'm dealing in broad human facts to which all human beings have access. Only an elite has access to what she does. I think there are only twenty people in the world who actually understand her theorems—this eliminates most mathematicians.

BRANS: So she really has to keep it locked within her bosom, whether she wants to or not.

BELLOW: Yes, it's hard for her—hard for her to live with a man who doesn't understand these things. I know that. We have other kinds of understanding, but her situation with me is not very different from my situation with most people in Chicago—mechanics, secretaries, lawyers, dentists, engineers, criminals, stockbrokers, or hoodlums. I can meet with them, we can find common ground, there's a lot we can talk about. But we don't talk about what matters most. Neither they nor I can do that.

BRANS: Can you talk to your students about that?

BELLOW: Not directly. I have to talk to them about *The Red and the Black*, which is what I am doing this term, but one can put a lot of things into that, and they understand.

BRANS: So in your teaching, then, you find this common ground where you can meet, and where you can really exchange experiences safely.

BELLOW: I think that the university contains all that there is left in this country, or indeed in most countries, of a literary culture.

BRANS: Maybe what we do in classrooms in a university is really our religion.

BELLOW: No, I wouldn't go so far as that. It's not my religion. But it really is the only avenue I have for expressing certain feelings and thoughts—or for talking shop, which can be important if you're deprived of it. I never much liked talking shop, but occasionally one does like to discuss one's trade.

BRANS: And this gives you a chance to do that.

BELLOW: I do it indirectly. I never talk about myself, and I never talk to students about what I'm writing, or what I'm thinking about my own work. But that I can obliquely touch upon some of these questions gives me nearly the kind of gratification I'm looking for. That's what it's meant to me all these years. Perhaps students learn something from it too.

BRANS: Yet you've been very critical of academics. Isn't there a contradiction here?

BELLOW: I'm critical of academics who take masterpieces and turn them into discourse in the modern intellectual style. I'm against that, of course. I am not for the redescription of *Moby Dick* by Marxists and existentialists and Christian symbolists, respectively. What does that do for *Moby Dick* or for me? It doesn't do anything. It only results in the making of more books—King Solomon has already warned us against that in Ecclesiastes.

BRANS: You make me very uncomfortable because I don't know exactly where you draw the line. And when I was coming to talk to you today I felt that somehow I might be doing some kind of disservice to your books by asking you questions about them. I thought, I'm supposed to take these books that mean a great deal to me—I'm supposed to understand what they mean. If I ask direct questions about them, maybe it's sacrilege.

BELLOW: I'm well prepared to defend myself against these incursions, if that's what they are. But there's no reason why people shouldn't talk about books. There is a prerequisite, though, which is that they should be deeply stirred by the books. They should love them or hate them. But not try to convert them into . . .

BRANS: Theory?

BELLOW: Yes. Or chatter. There's no need to babble about these things. They *can* be talked about. But so much of literary criticism is babbling.

BRANS: I'm not sure I understand exactly what you mean by babbling. Do you mean using special terminology? Or talking about little things and ignoring big ones?

BELLOW: Critics often translate important books—write them again, as it were, in the fashionable intellectual jargon. And then the books are no longer themselves. They have been borrowed by Culture, with a capital C. There are two things here that we must clearly distinguish. One is the work of art with its direct effect on people. The other is a work of art as a cultural commodity, as a piece of society's property in Culture. In the second form, art becomes a fertilizer for the cultivation of languages, vocabularies, intellectual styles, ornaments, degrees, honors, prizes, and all the rest of that. That's Culture with a capital C. That's what I'm talking about. And this is what always happens. Our model for it is the Christian religion, which started with faith and ended with churches.

BRANS: Are you afraid you will become a Culture object?

BELLOW: I think we must all be on guard against it. I don't want to become a support of the new clergy. Why should I? It's none of my business!

BRANS: You think sometimes that you might be drawn into writing for these people?

BELLOW: You're on the right track. The public has changed. It now includes more people who have gone to college. Until recently contemporary literature was not part of the curriculum. If you were a lawyer with a good education, or an engineer, or a physician, or a clergyman, it was assumed that you could read a novel. You didn't need ten manuals in order to read it. There is a process of mystification associated with this, you see.

BRANS: Do you think writers are tempted to contribute deliberately to this process of mystification?

BELLOW: I feel no such temptation. But many modern writers do. They reflect the rise of the intellectual level of the public. There is a public of professional intellectuals for whom poets and novelists perform a function. Take somebody like Joyce, especially in *Finnegans Wake*. He is writing for a small public of intellectuals—of highly skilled readers, people who know the history of modern literature and are amused by puzzles. The same thing is true of Thomas Mann. Of Eliot. Of all the small public writers.

BRANS: Is this what Stendhal called his happy few?

BELLOW: The happy few in Stendhal were people of spirit and energy and genius and passion and imagination and all the rest of that. They weren't necessarily intellectuals.

BRANS: Not the literary intelligentsia?

BELLOW: In the modern sense, you see. But Joyce was trying to please a certain kind of public, to which he himself belonged. These were scholars, or amateur scholars—people who liked mental games, people who would not be put off by a multitude of references to Homer or to Vico or Thomas Aquinas, or Irish history; and this reflects a change in the public and the writer's relation to that public. I don't blame writers for this; I'm simply pointing to the fact that modern art has a far larger intellectual burden than it ever had. And at certain points it really becomes an exercise in the history of the art itself, so that it's for people who know that history. I'm not against an elite literature, mind you. That's not really what I'm talking about. What I'm talking about is the amount of modern intellectual freight in literature and painting. One can find this agreeable, but you can't say that it is literature in the older sense.

BRANS: Which was intended for the man in the street?

BELLOW: Yes, at least the novel was.

BRANS: Do you see yourself, then, as writing for that man in the street?

BELLOW: I don't know him well enough to write for him in that direct way. But I have a good deal of feeling for him. I know that at bottom I'm just the same kind of human being. There are cultural differences, but I know they are only that. They may not be differences of the heart. I don't like the snobbery implicit in the idea of the "mass man" developed by Ortega, his German predecessors, and his recent successors.

BRANS: This mindless creature who goes around cultivating his body. You don't think he exists?

BELLOW: In some respects. I don't think that it fully characterizes anyone.

BRANS: I really could argue with you. What about people who go habitually to singles bars, that sort of thing? Instant Dionysus.

BELLOW: Yes, well, they are standardized in their quest for joy or diversion. But how do we know what their souls suffer in abreaction from this? We don't know. Do we really think that in their secret human agonies over what they do, they are still standardized? We don't know that.

BRANS: But surely if their sufferings are real there should be some way of finding something—something more particular.

BELLOW: It would be nice if they had a language for it. A wonderful liberation. Unfortunately "education" and the mass media fill them up with formulas.

BRANS: You don't want to write for a literary intelligentsia. And your books sell beautifully. Do you think of yourself as somehow serving all of those people?

BELLOW: No, I write as I do because I am what I am. I can't really help myself.

BRANS: You're not trying to teach people how to live?

BELLOW: No.

BRANS: But your books seem so much as if you have the answers. Before I met you I thought, "Here's a man who has the answers, and if I can just ask him the right questions, then he'll give me the right answers." And I wondered if maybe you had that sense of yourself at all? And when you began talking about clairvoyance, I thought that's what you meant, partly. So you don't see yourself as a teacher of the masses.

BELLOW: Not necessarily. . . . Although when I think about it, I do believe that I have something of importance to transmit. Just how to name it, I don't know. But I think of myself as speaking to an inviolate part of other people, around which there is a sort of nearly sacred perimeter, a significant space, if you like, a place where the human being really has removed to, with all his most important spiritual possessions. Yes, that I do think about. I'm not very clear about it, but I don't have to be because I'm not a philosopher. All I have to do is feel it, and that I do feel.

BRANS: That you're talking to someone other than the social being?

BELLOW: Yes, I'm talking to human beings who have certain permanent attributes—that there is something in them—as in myself. I've never doubted it. I don't think of myself as different in that way. On the contrary, I think of myself as ordinary in many ways. But when I say ordinary, I don't mean what people commonly mean by ordinary. I mean something extraordinary which is in every human being. At the moment there is no place for this extraordinary universal possession. It's rushed out of sight by material preoccupations (which I have too), by fear, by fashion, which is the child of fear. But I really do think that I am talking to a part of people that I know is there and that they know is there. Though my books may not make sense to many readers. Perhaps the sound of my voice communicates this sense of things.

BRANS: I've been curious about that. I've wondered why people bought *Herzog* so enthusiastically, because it's hard to believe that most people feel quite as fragmented or as confused as Herzog, and yet the book has sold millions of copies. So evidently there is something . . .

BELLOW: I think they recognized certain things in it. The theme of divorce, the feeling of being shut out, their humanity denied by the arbitrary acts of those who are very close to them, evicted, deprived of a connection that they thought they had. And in Moses Herzog a kind of self-critical comic sense, an amused objectivity toward himself, almost amounting to courage.

BRANS: The straw hat, and the striped jacket, and the whole bit?

BELLOW: Yes, putting up a resistance to these crushing antagonists. Even if it's only a comic resistance.

BRANS: That's the best kind. But I don't think it is only comic. Do you? It ends with Herzog sitting out in the sun, the flowers, the candles, the whole thing. The whole thing about grace. Do you think your life is touched with grace?

BELLOW: Not exceptionally. But I think of Herzog in a different way. I think of him as a man who, in the agony of suffering, finds himself to be his own most penetrating critic. And he reexamines his life, as it were, by reenacting all the roles he took seriously. And when he has gone through all the reenactments, he's back at the original point.

BRANS: That's wonderful! I never thought of that. Ok, reenactment of what?

BELLOW: The professor, the son, the brother, the lover, the father, the husband, the avenger, the intellectual—all of it. It's an attempt really to divest himself of all of the personae . . .

BRANS: The social selves?

BELLOW: That's right. And when he has dismissed these personae, there comes a pause.

BRANS: But that's grace—"Thou movest me." Or is Herzog just like a cat, accepting the life of the universe, or something?

BELLOW: It's better than his trying to invent everything for himself, or accepting human inventions, the collective errors, by which he's lived. He's decided to go through a process of jettisoning or lightening. That's how I saw the book when I was writing it. And I wrote it with passion, because I believed in it with a passion. I thought, "Enough of this."

BRANS: Then, is Madeleine necessary to him because she causes all these things? Is she like Proust's *madeleine*, the thing that makes you think, remember all the past—reenact the past?

BELLOW: Oh, he loved her deeply. She wounded him horribly, and he is trying to live with the wound. And he's also very angry, of course, and critical.

BRANS: And he's wrong about her, isn't he? I mean, she's not what he said she was, is she?

BELLOW: No, she's both better and worse than he said she was. But of course he's at war and he can't be fair. But he loves her, and he loves the child, and he feels that she's replaced him with Valentine, a liar, a phony, and there's something of the phony in her, to which the phony Valentine appeals.

BRANS: But he's such a loser! You know, no woman can take such a loser. At a point, you just have to get away from somebody like that.

BELLOW: Well, it isn't that he's a loser. It's that he's so chaotic; no woman can stand so much disorder. It's not the losing at all, it's the chaos, and the complexity of life which would tire a woman out, just trying to follow it. This complexity is intolerable, I agree.

BRANS: Right. You mean simple losing would be ok, but complicated losing not so good. But tell me about Humboldt—he's even more complex. I tried first of all to fit Humboldt into John Berryman. But of course biographically he's very close to Delmore Schwartz.

BELLOW: Yes.

BRANS: And I began to see that he probably wasn't either of those men exactly.

BELLOW: No, he's not.

BRANS: There seem to be stories about both of them in the character. The thing I remember is something about pushing the big girl downstairs that you wrote about Berryman. And that sounded like Humboldt chasing the girl through her apartment. But you're saying something about the artist and what the writer has to expect in that book.

BELLOW: American society likes its artists and writers, certainly, it's proud of them, it rewards them, but it doesn't know what the hell they're all about—and there's a sort of vulgar cheerfulness in its relation to them. Some of the writers share this same vulgar cheerfulness. They make something of it, at times. Think of Allen Ginsberg's line, "America, I'm putting my queer shoulder to the wheel."

BRANS: You mean writers feel responsible.

BELLOW: It isn't just that they feel responsible. They feel attached. Attachment. Piety. Even when they think it awful. When Humboldt feels his talent leaving him, he begins to clown. He's putting his poet's shoulder to the wheel. We too are America's children. It's this part that Citrine finds Humboldt guilty of playing.

BRANS: You mean the artist-in-residence?

BELLOW: That's right, when there's a slackening of the talent, then there come all these other games that the poet invents.

BRANS: Like the whole con thing about going to Princeton.

BELLOW: Exactly. Or the automobile, or the farm, or the relations with women.

BRANS: Which are often the things that sell books of poetry. Don't you think that's true?

BELLOW: That's right. But there's something really promotional, exhibitionistic, and impure about it. And Charlie knows that, you see.

BRANS: But Charlie is successful.

BELLOW: Charlie is not really successful. Charlie is a man who, by having success, has excused himself from success. Charlie is like Julien Sorel in *The Red and the Black*. When he gets to the top of society, there's nothing to do but shoot Madame de Rênal and get his head cut off.

BRANS: He doesn't care any more.

BELLOW: Of course not.

BRANS: I like that.

BELLOW: That's exactly the Charlie position in the book. That's why he'd rather hang around with card players and bums and tramps.

BRANS: Does he think they're more genuine?

BELLOW: It isn't that he thinks they're more genuine. No, everybody's equally genuine or false. It's just he thinks they express the ludicrousness of the position.

BRANS: The games are all out in the open.

BELLOW: That's right.

BRANS: Charlie resembles you a lot in the outward aspects. I think of a matador executing dazzling veronicas, with the cape very close to the real human body. Tell me how not to see Citrine as Bellow.

BELLOW: I would have to suffer from dissociation of personality to be all these people in the books. I can't possibly be all of them. I lend a character, out of pure friendship, whatever he needs, that's all.

BRANS: The amazing thing about Charlie is all the love he has, for these bums, and for the people in his past, for almost everyone.

BELLOW: True. Nobody has noticed the amount of affection in that book. The critics are unaware of that sort of quality in a book.

BRANS: He loves his past, in a way that seems so accurate. I can't remember anything that happened to me yesterday. Things just leave me all the time. But I can remember everything about the past. I can remember precisely a certain day in Mississippi when I was fifteen. And this is the sort of thing I think your books bring so vividly to life. I don't mean they're all recollection. I think you're creating them. But you focus on these things that seem important to me but that most people, or at least most current writers, don't care about. Do you think that somehow the ability to remember or to create memory is important for a novelist?

BELLOW: In my own case these memories serve to resurrect feelings which, at the time, I didn't want to have. I had them. They were very powerful. But they were too much for me to deal with, and I covered them over with cynicism or wit or whatever. And now I realize how much emotion was invested in them, and I bring them back.

BRANS: You mean in loving your family?

BELLOW: Yes.

BRANS: Did you feel at the same time that they were really not you, and that you were trapped in this family?

BELLOW: No. I always had a great piety about my life. I always thought my life—I didn't think about it as my life when I was a kid—I thought it the most extraordinary, brilliant thing in the whole history of the universe that we should all be together. And there was so much unusable love that in the end it turned against itself and became a kind of chilliness, and for many years it stayed that way. The Marxist attitude toward the family, the modern attitude toward mothers, or fathers, or . . .

BRANS: Mothers can't do any good. There's no way!

BELLOW: And all the rest of it. And then I realized that I was simply fooling myself. That it has really been a feast of love for me which I couldn't persuade the others to share. They weren't aware of it in me. Mostly not. Sometimes they were.

BRANS: Do you really think it would have made them uncomfortable? You say that, sometimes, in the novels. Citrine, for example, feels that Julius is uncomfortable with the love that Charlie has to give him—that it really is superfluous or shouldn't be expressed. It might be there, but it shouldn't be shown in any sort of overt way.

BELLOW: Yes, because Julius has made his way in life as a tough business operator.

BRANS: Why do you so often have your heroes the brothers of all those tough-minded businessmen who've made lots of money?

BELLOW: Because they're all over the place. After all, I am a historian. Every novelist is a historian, a chronicler of his time. Of course I write about business types.

BRANS: People making lots of money? Being successful?

BELLOW: Well, it's the history of the United States, in a way. Here we sit in Dallas. Isn't it the history of Texas?

BRANS: Can we talk about *Sammler*?

BELLOW: Sure.

BRANS: That was the first one of your books that I read. I think it came out in the *Atlantic*. As I began reading it, I was absolutely dumbfounded.

BELLOW: Why?

BRANS: I thought it was a real accusation. I thought I was supposed to take all this stuff about the mass man to heart.

BELLOW: No, not really. I'll tell you how I saw it. There's enough European in me to be able to look at America as a foreigner.

BRANS: Is that true? You really still feel close enough to Europe?

BELLOW: Yes, I do, through my family. My parents were immigrants. They spoke Russian. In 1920 their table talk was still about the Czar, the war, the Revolution.

BRANS: Well, I thought *Sammler* was just a gripy old man's opinion of the world, when I first read it. Then I read it again, and I began to see that you had a distance from Sammler, and that he was not your spokesman. At least I imagined that he was far grouchier than you would have been. And I finally decided that the book was a limited affirmation of America. And that what people like Angela had was a kind of energy, a kind of creativity, that Sammler could only grudgingly recognize.

BELLOW: *Sammler* would have been a better book if I had dealt openly with some of my feelings, instead of filtering them through him.

BRANS: You mean everything had to come out with a kind of bias because of him?

BELLOW: Not a bias in the ordinary sense. But he is a Lazarus—a man back from the dead.

BRANS: You were talking earlier about these experiences, these feelings that we all have, and you think there are certain of those experiences that Sammler no longer has. Is he disenfranchised somehow?

BELLOW: Well, I think he's cold, because he's known the grave.

BRANS: I think *Sammler* is a wonderful book. I don't have any reservations about it. Once I discovered that Sammler wasn't the voice of God, or something, then I was comfortable enough with it. It was only when I thought that he had all the answers that I was . . .

BELLOW: Oh, he doesn't have the answers. If he had had all the answers he would have been the religious man he wished to be. In reading Meister Eckhardt he was feeling his way. He was only beginning to acknowledge the first stirrings of religion.

BRANS: He was terribly bound to being a human creature, in spite of all his mysticism and so forth.

BELLOW: Yes, but then you see it was really a sort of an exotic report on life in the United States; it was not condemnatory.

BRANS: It was misread, then.

BELLOW: Of course it was misread. We started out earlier by talking about criticism. One of the troubles with criticism is that it's simply linear, if you know what I mean—sketchy. The novelist never feels he's got anything until he has it in all the density of actual experience. Then he looks at a piece of criticism, and all he sees is the single outline of thought. It's not the same thing. And you can't deal with a phenomenon that way. So he never really trusts criticism, because it lacks the essential density.

BRANS: Well, the critic has to make a point. He has to take a line, and then he has to develop the line. I haven't written much, but from what I've written I know that you feel all these things rushing in upon you from the book, and yet you can't, for your own sanity's sake, try to say all there is to say about the book, and what you finally want to keep saying is, "Go read it. Go read this novel, and you'll see what I mean."

BELLOW: Or, "Don't go read it."

BRANS: Do you think of yourself as a survivor, like Sammler or Citrine?

BELLOW: No, I think of myself as horribly deprived of people whom I loved and who are dead.

BRANS: You know, I really loved John Berryman. I never even knew him, but I believed in him, in Henry. I hate to face what he became at the end. But you must have known that bad side of Berryman. I'm sure he called you late at night, and all that . . . the terrors.

BELLOW: I know, but he was full of feeling. . . . He was a real man. John and I were very close in spirit as writers, I think. He knew it, and we would sometimes talk about it. He wrote a little piece once after *The Adventures of Augie March* came out, in which he said that this book had cleared the way for him to do certain things. Maybe it was so. But he loved literature. That is rare even among writers. John gave himself to it, heart and soul.

BRANS: Why was he such a disaster, though? Why did his life have to be such chaos? Your life is not like that. You've controlled your life.

BELLOW: Yes, I know. Oh, I didn't have to face the kinds of things he faced—the suicide of a father—coming out on the porch and seeing his dead father in the morning.

BRANS: Don't you think at a certain point you just grow out of that? Or you move away from that? You take control of yourself.

BELLOW: Well, he lacked control.

BRANS: But in his poetry he had fine control.

BELLOW: Yes, in his poetry he had the control. In his life there was none at all. Then because he decayed physically he knew he must die soon. He was really sick. He had no liver any more, he lacked muscular coordination. He was getting dirty. And it was getting to be pretty pukey. And he knew it. His pride suffered from it. And he probably said, well, enough. He was a derelict, in hospitals. And he just stopped it.

BRANS: It seemed to me a deprivation for the rest of us that he should do that. I felt really angry because he'd do it.

BELLOW: Well, he thought he was on the Wagon, and he thought he was straight with his wife, and he thought he was out of the woods, and all of that Boy Scout optimism of somebody who feels, "At last, I'm on the right path." And then he went off completely, got drunk again—horribly drunk. Disappeared for days, and found himself in bed with some strange girl.

BRANS: But you see, I don't buy this "found himself" thing: I mean, he got there. He did it.

BELLOW: Yes, but in disgust with himself. Of course he did it. He had no further use for himself. And I believe he thought he didn't want to write, that he had done it all.

BRANS: The death of the poet. Like Humboldt. But Rinaldo Cantabile survives. Now there's a name! I can't say it without rejoicing that you thought of it. Why a musical name for a thug?

BELLOW: Well, I know the common people in Chicago; the bums, or whatever you like, in Chicago all have these unfathomed cultural and intellectual ambitions, and they don't know what to do about them really. They bring the greatest enthusiasm and devotion to these things, but at the same time they're clumsy, stupid, arrogant, ambitious.

BRANS: You mean like Rinaldo, who thinks he's going for the big time, and then somehow it all. . . . I never have enjoyed anything as much as when Citrine bests him. It was so marvelous. I was so afraid that somehow he was going to be in service to Rinaldo forever.

BELLOW: Oh, no.

BRANS: And Rinaldo really gets put down. But he's a splendid character. Tell me, you're a daring writer: why haven't you ever used a modern woman as your protagonist? I don't agree with some of your critics who say that you don't understand women, and that you have only a Schopenhauerean attitude toward women.

BELLOW: Well, I don't. No, unfortunately I just struck the women's movement at a bad time.

BRANS: But why haven't you ever written from the point of view of a woman? Why do you always have to have Madeleine as interpreted by Herzog, and Renata as interpreted by Citrine?

BELLOW: Well, I sometimes think of doing it; I just never got around to it. I was working out problems that couldn't be worked out that way. The only thing I ever wrote about a woman directly was a story called "Leaving the Yellow House." About Hattie. I loved her. But of course you could say she's an older woman. She's an old lady.

BRANS: But your women do seem to be around mostly just to stick on band-aids at opportune times, or they leave when things get rough. There's this attitude toward women. I think it's because the women always are filtered, or falsified, through the minds of the heroes.

BELLOW: Maybe. But I thought there were some rather nice women in this last book. I thought Demmie Vonghel was an awfully nice woman.

BRANS: Oh, she's fine. I loved Demmie.

BELLOW: She's a real sort of American—you know—young lady.

BRANS: But she dies. And then there's Renata. I imagine all the men who talk to you about your books like Renata. I really don't like Renata very much.

BELLOW: Well, Renata is a delight. She's not supposed to be a marvelous "woman," only a grand female.

BRANS: What was all this stuff about her marrying death—what's his name? Flonzaley? Why didn't Citrine get the girl? I think Citrine should—it's American for Citrine to get the girl.

BELLOW: I think it's American for a swinging girl like that to make the best match she can.

BRANS: With a mortician?

BELLOW: Oh, well, that's just poking fun at poor Charlie, not at Renata. I was not poking fun at Renata.

BRANS: I like to think that Demmie is what you really think women are. And Renata is just a sort of . . .

BELLOW: Renata is the nympholeptic dream of elderly gents like Charlie Citrine, who still want to be accepted as virile and desirable, as a wonderful man for a beautiful woman to have.

BRANS: Why couldn't you have told the story of Charlie Citrine, say, from Demmie's point of view? I'm just asking that as a possibity. Could Demmie have told that story?

BELLOW: Yes, she could. I could have done it, too.

BRANS: Yes, she's a fully realized character. You could have talked from her. There are passages in there where she speaks . . . You know, she has the wonderful ability just suddenly to haul off and knock Charlie in the chops.

BELLOW: Yes.

BRANS: But you've never tried this, really?

BELLOW: No, I think I could. I know I could, as a matter of fact. All this stuff about my prejudices is just nonsense. I probably have certain prejudices. I mean, never believe what a man says about his own prejudices. Because he doesn't know. That's why they're prejudices. But . . . I do have the kindliest, closest feelings to certain women. I always have had, and it just hasn't come out that way, that's all.

BRANS: I think it has come out that way. I really think that people who read your books with any attention know that. It's just that you do always have this kind of Schopenhauerean female figure, standing there in all of her curves.

BELLOW: Take somebody like Ramona in *Herzog*. Now Ramona is nice, an awfully nice girl. She just happens to be realistically portrayed, and this is what people can't take. She is the good-hearted (and she is good-hearted), giving, charitable, but ideological female. She is an ideologist. She makes speeches. She thinks she knows what's best for Moses.

BRANS: But it seems that at the end of the book he's pretty much disposed toward her point of view. He's waiting for her, after all.

BELLOW: He's going to forgive her all this ideological stuff. It is a matter of forgiving, because he has no use for it. He's gotten rid of his own. And why should he consent to listen to hers?

BRANS: But her ideology is all about love, and renewing the spirit through the flesh.

BELLOW: He doesn't believe that!

BRANS: He doesn't? At all? Well, then he really doesn't find the solution. He's just sort of at a way station, is that the idea?

BELLOW: Well, he's come to a point of rest, which is saying a lot for anybody these days.

BRANS: But it won't last.

BELLOW: No, he's going to have to assume roles again, and deal with people again. He's just come to a well-earned interregnum. Don't grudge poor Moses *that*.

BRANS: Do you equate those two things? Assuming roles and seeing people?

BELLOW: Well, you have to deal with them. You have to make allowances for them. You have to make allowances for their vanities and their weaknesses and so on, even though at bottom they're really ok. But there are so many vain struggles, and there's so much wrangling, and so much nonsense. Most of what passes between human beings, except in their finest moments, is nonsensical.

And it gets more nonsensical all the time. The more books we read about conduct, self-regulation . . .

BRANS: What books?

BELLOW: I'm thinking about those deep books, those heavy works which tell you what to do at every moment of your life. Americans seem to be unable to live without prescriptions.

The Rhetoric of Bellow's Short Fiction

I

In an uncommonly self-deprecatory passage, introducing his own short fiction, Norman Mailer compares the art of the short story writer to that of the jeweler. "He stays in his shop, he polishes those jewels, he collects craft, lore, confirms gossip, assays jeweler's rouge, looks to steal the tricks of the arcane, and generally disports like a medieval alchemist who's got a little furnace, a small retort, a cave, a handful of fool's gold, and a mad monk's will. With such qualifications, one in a hundred becomes an extraordinary writer, but on the other hand, the worst of this guild makes a life from kissing spiders."[1] It is a descriptive act, with its ironic and begrudging admiration for a talent which Mailer has in short measure, which might easily seem to suggest Bellow. Everybody knows that Bellow is no polisher of jewels. Everybody who cares about Bellow knows that *Seize the Day* and *Dangling Man* are comparatively small and tight but that, in general, Bellow's talent needs space, consequently producing a series of expansive books for which the jeweler's metaphor is quite inappropriate.

Yet Bellow's short fiction carries an uncommon power and integrity. One who has read "Looking for Mr. Green" never forgets it. And I, for one, testify that even so minor a fiction as "A Sermon by Dr. Pep," never collected, never re-printed, hardly noticed by Bellow's critics, hangs in the mind with a curious kind of tenacity. The authority of the short fiction has something to do, of course, with the way in which it extends, in small, the characteristic thematic interests of Bellow, with his customary intensity and his customary intelligence. But the authority of the short fiction has something to do, also, with the highly individual way in which it is made. Not classic modernist stories, not "experimental" in any recognizeable sense, they are, moreover, not like anybody else's.

The classic modernist short fiction concentrates time, image, mind, and sensibility in the interests of evoking plateaus of insight, states of self-knowledge, epiphanic moments. Short fiction since the great modernists has tended to

[*]This essay was written specifically for this volume and appears here for the first time by permission of the author.

emphasize the ludic, the fabulous, and the linguistic, making reflective inventions, aware of their own artifice. Bellow's short fictions, unlike either, concentrate rhetoric. Not exploitations of the possibilities latent in language qua language, certainly not explorations of the limits of language and the claims of silence, they are exploitations of speech used for effect, or, just as often, speech intended for effect which is ineffectual. That is why their structures are often perplexing, or unconventional: because those structures often turn not upon event, or revelation, or insight, but upon social utterance. And that is why their import is sometimes elusive: because the center of that import is in the intertaction of speaker and listener.

Only a portion of Bellow's short fiction has seemed to him worthy of reprinting. Undoubtedly some of it is apprentice work. But those early fictions, several not available in collected form, indicate the nature of the whole body of his short fiction. A remarkable number of the stories in the years 1941 to the publication of *Mosby's Memoirs and Other Stories* in 1968 are monologues. Some of them, "Two Morning Monologues," "A Sermon by Dr. Pep," and the "Address by Gooley MacDowell to the Hasbeens Club of Chicago" are pure, sustained monologue, not dramatic monologues in the Browning sense, for there is little sense of audience, no drama, no ironic invitation to see through the speakers. Neither are they first-person stories, in which a "speaker" is imaged to tell his own story. There is no sequence of events. There is only the voice. Even certain early stories, such as "The Trip to Galena," which are not monologues, still tend toward that form, easily two thirds of that story, for example, being a spoken explanation, occasionally interrupted by the listener, of the central character's dilemma. Clearly, from the start, Bellow indicates a fascination with voice, virtually a wish to define man in terms of talk, *homo loquens*.

Of the later fictions that sustain the primacy of voice without allowing it the exclusivity of those early monologues, "Looking for Mr. Green" is an example. Its structure is not built upon images heavy with symbolic import, nor upon interior states of mind; its structure is built upon questions, basically the same question, and the answers, lies, and evasions which they evoke:

> "Are you the janitor?"
> "What do you want?"
> "I'm looking for a man who's supposed to be living here. Green."
> "What Green?" . . .
> "Does anybody here know how I can deliver a check to Mr. Tulliver Green?"
> "Green?" . . .
> "Does Tulliver Green live here? I'm from the relief."
> The man narrowed the opening and spoke to someone at his back.
> "Does he live here?"
> "Uh–uh. No." . . .
> "Is this where Mr. Green lives?"
> But she was still talking to herself and did not hear him.
> "Is this Mr. Green's house?"
> At last she turned her furious drunken glance on him. "What do you want?"[2]

The story is a wonderfully evocative rendering of the underside of Chicago, a brilliant parable of urban anonymity, class and racial hostility, the interaction of institution and individual, the shared paranoia of the contemporary world. But the central, irreducible element which is the means to this larger significance is Grebe asking, asking.

"A Sermon by Dr. Pep" shares almost nothing with "Looking for Mr. Green," except that both are Chicago stories and both structure themselves upon rhetorical acts.[3] Dr. Pep's audience is addressed as "dear friends" but there is no sense of whether the audience exists. It is entirely possible that no one is listening. Yet Dr. Pep is relentlessly rhetorical, modulating between his philosophy of food and animal life, disease and health on the one hand and confidential anecdotes of his personal life on the other, hectoring, pleading, asking questions which he is about to answer, guessing aloud what some of his audience is thinking, dropping names, authorities, old friends, asking for more time, working for the single tear of pathos, anticipating disagreement, seeking assent, clarifying the seriousness of his address, imploring his audience to remember, choosing sides, naming enemies, wondering aloud, seeking a shared admiration. He confounds his audience with allusions they could not possibly recognize and a philosophy which he may or may not recognize is crankish and recondite; he also makes love to his audience with his words. But there is no audience, or if there is, Bellow prefers not to show it. Which is to say that "Looking for Mr. Green" and "A Sermon by Dr. Pep" present a paradigmatic display of Bellow's rhetorical technique. The appeals to the audience, in both of these quite different stories, are the very center of the fiction. The characteristic action, that is, is someone seeking to speak in such a way as to elicit the desired response. Yet in both, the response is elusive, or evasive, or mendacious, or altogether absent. And that, in the most radical and irreducible sense, is what Bellow's short fiction is "about": the wish to persuade, the act of attempting to persuade, and the sense that that persuasive attempt is, at least, problematic, at most, utterly ineffectual. It goes without saying that large questions, social, cultural, and metaphysical, are implicit in that basic impasse.

I suggest a third example of the principle I am attempting to articulate. "A Father to Be" is a small, unpretentious story, most memorable for Bellow's insights into the small humiliations, ritual castrations, if one likes, of a modern husband, more precisely husband-to-be.[4] The low-grade domestic tensions and the urban, upper-middle-class world of the story make it seem not much different from countless art stories of the post-war period. So does its most potent moment of illumination, in which Rogin sees a thoroughly uninteresting fellow passenger on the subway and fancies him to be the image of his future son grown middle-aged. What makes the story seem unusual is its structure, since it moves from point to point by a route that is not, like the conventional epiphany story, intelligible after the fact in terms of the nature of the epiphany. Some of the events of the story, in fact, seem to have little to do with the interior progress of Rogin: Rogin overhearing a conversation between two friends, one of whom confesses himself to be a considerable alcoholic, Rogin being shampooed by his fiancee as the story closes. The trouble is that the reader is likely to look for a system either of events or illuminations that provide the structural spine of the story. And what Bellow provides, instead, is a system of rhetoric, a curious chain of socio-linguistic interchanges (or pseudo-socio-linguistic interchanges, since Rogin is fond of addressing himself with questions and exclamations, the full range of rhetoric, so that what Bellow reveals of Rogin's inner life reads very like an animated conversation between two people).

Anterior to the action of the story, Rogin has had a telephone conversation with his fiancee, which he recalls and reports, a problematic conversation in which, although she has bought some roast beef at a delicatessen, she asks Rogin to buy some more and although he has given her spending money, she has given it to her cousin, who is "extremely wealthy," to pay the cleaning woman. No classic account of the principles of rhetoric can describe that opening interchange because what Bellow does is to catch, with extraordinary economy, the difficulty of responding to slightly unreasonable requests that come from somebody one cannot see but whose voice one can hear. Rogin moves into a reflection on Joan's extravagance, in which the emphasis falls upon his failure to complain, and from there to a larger level of reflection, which takes the form, typically, not of interior monologue but of highly animated speech. "Superimposition is the universal law. Who is free? No one is free. Who has no burdens? Everyone is under pressure." *His* answers to *his* questions change his mood; his own inner rhetoric has persuaded him to be happy, observant, at one with the world of the delicatessen. The storekeeper speaks sharply to a Puerto Rican employee, and it is that exchange that draws Rogin into their world. Even choosing food at the counter becomes a rhetorical exercise, with Rogin's typical inner dialogue and a missed irony in his exchange with the clerk. The overheard conversation in the subway is less significant for what it tells Rogin than for the mode of its rhetoric—two shapeless men, one confessing an intimacy that is obvious before its revelation, with Rogin as accidental listener over the noise of the subway, at once feeling and understanding, also detached and uncaring.

So it goes. His epiphanic encounter with his imagined son grown old is, once again, not rendered as revery but as inner dialogue. And when he finally arrives at Joan's apartment, she addresses him with her own special rhetorical appeal. " 'Oh, my baby. You're covered with snow. Why didn't you wear your hat? It's all over its little head'—her favorite third-person endearment." Finally, shampooed—humbled, emasculated, baptised—Rogin responds with the verbal gestures that end the story. " 'You always have such wonderful ideas, Joan. You know? You have a kind of instinct, a regular gift.' " "About" many things, the story is centrally about talking: conversing on the telephone, listening to strangers on the subway, ordering gherkins at a delicatessen counter, greeting a fiancee, asserting oneself and abasing oneself with words.

Finally I suggest "The Gonzaga Manuscripts" as another example of the self delineated by social speech.[5] The story attempts a subject which James once did with such authority and insight that comparison is inevitable. In *The Aspern Papers*, the quest of an American for the manuscripts of a poet whom he adores involves some typically Jamesian conflicts of class, style, and nationality. But what James's story finally asks is what such a quest ought to cost, in terms of the searcher's moral character. No such interest engages Bellow. The passion of

Charles Feiler, the scholar in quest of the Gonzaga Manuscripts, is convincing enough but quite unambiguous and nonproblematic. The work of Gonzaga represents, for him, poetic excellence and clarity of vision, more than that, a kind of positive force in a negativistic culture. What the story turns upon is not at all the compromises he is willing to make to see the manuscripts; no compromises are suggested. It turns rather upon the responses that people who knew the poet make to his requests. It is, again, a story about asking questions and getting answers, bad answers, misleading answers, banal answers, answers that defile the memory of the poet. Characteristically, before he asks anyone else about the whereabouts of the manuscripts, Feiler asks himself if his quest matters. It is the one question he asks which receives a brisk, satisfying, wholly humane answer. It does matter. To recover the manuscripts is to bring that much of Gonzaga to the world, which is, for Feiler, an act of salvation, the world being badly in need of the act of faith that the poems represent.

Feiler has an encounter with a particularly repulsive British woman who baits him for his American-ness. It is a curious diversion from his purpose, which, as he sees it, only strengthens his resolve. His next encounter is with a Miss Ungar, a literate, educated woman, whose function is to provide an exchange of dollars for pesetas, should the opportunity arise to buy the manuscripts. " 'Have you ever heard of a poet named Gonzaga?' " he asks. " 'Gonzaga? I must have. But I don't think I ever read him.' " she replies. He responds with a burst of naive confidence. Guzman del Nido, Gonzaga's friend, military comrade, and literary executor is his next encounter. And, once again, the exchange between the two is more important to the cumulative power of the story than Feiler's motives, more important than del Nido's state of mind, more important than the Gonzaga manuscripts. Del Nido, it turns out, is crass, vulgar, and uncomprehending. "It's natural," Feiler muses, after the encounter, "to suppose, because a man is great, that the people around him must have known how to respond to greatness, but when these people turn out to be no better than Guzman del Nido you wonder what response greatness really needs." During the course of the interview with del Nido, by the way, questions of Feiler's American-ness similarly arise, with the customary impasse in communication, the usual condescension, the ritual offenses. Del Nido tells a joke, with an American punch line, which gets a small laugh; and Feiler tells another, which nobody laughs at. Feiler, by that time, has summed up the interview, in rhetorical terms, knowing, by now, what question gets what answer. "Clarence at once sensed that del Nido would make him look foolish if he could, with his fine irony and his fine Spanish manners. Del Nido was the sort of man who cut everyone down to size."

The Povlo family, whom Feiler interviews next, prove to be "a family of laughers. They laughed when they spoke and when you answered." It surely occurs to the reader at this point that indiscriminate laughter is as symptomatic of rhetorical impasse as those witless jokes of a few pages before at which nobody laughs. The international misunderstandings throughout the story develop into a riot of offenses, misconceptions, and linguistic tangles: Feiler mistaken for an Englishman, a dog with a Scottish name, Luis attempting to speak a few idiotic words of English, another character speaking a line of French, and a series of jocular references to the atomic bomb. From here the story works toward its conclusion, its culminating misunderstanding, and as that last failure to find the poems develops, Feiler has yet another exchange that must remind the reader of those several parallel exchanges before it. Alvarez-Povlo has taken Feiler for a financier; Feiler replies that he has come in quest of Gonzaga's poems. And Alvarez-Povlo replies: " 'Manuel? The soldier? The little fellow? The one that was her lover in nineteen twenty-eight? He was killed in Morocco.' "

Like those stories I have described before, the primary unit of "The Gonzaga Manuscripts" is not the event or the moment of consciousness but the speech act. In each of the four stories, elements are introduced which tend to make communication unusually difficult: in "A Sermon by Dr. Pep" the very presence of an audience is problematic; in "Looking for Mr. Green," the respondents are uniformly hostile and evasive; in "A Father to Be," the subtle play of power which Rogin's fiancee exerts over him affects every communication between them; and in "The Gonzaga Manuscripts," the characters are prevented from responding satisfactorily to Feiler both because of national misunderstandings and because of their parochial obtuseness. Except for "A Sermon by Dr. Pep," which is entirely public, the main characters in the other three stories all display an inner life which is not meditative or associative but which is, rather, inner speech. And in all four of the stories, the act of speech carries with it an investment of self which is extraordinary.

II

The implications of so rhetorical a fiction seem to me three. First, such a fiction necessarily devises its own range of verbal effects, its own grammar, as it were, of rhetoric. To some extent, to be sure, this grammar is derivative of earlier writers, Chekhov for example, for whom the appeal to another's attention is significant, or others, Kafka for example, for whom the question badly answered is central, or still others, a long tradition from Cervantes, through Diderot, Richardson, Dostoevsky, Conrad, and a substantial group of Bellow's contemporaries, for whom a passage of unmediated monologue is the best means to the presentation of self. Still, to a considerable extent, Bellow's range of rhetorical appeals is his own.

Secondly, such a fiction implies the invention of a grammar of either response or resistance. Once again, both Chekhov and Kafka clearly imply the difficulties of being heard, being listened to, being understood, and being properly answered. And the reader of Dickens, Mann, countless others, understands the barriers to communication that age, class, profession, and temperament provide. But here, too, Bellow finds his own way of laying out the problematics of making connections by public speech.

Thirdly, such a fiction implies certain valuations of the human community. In one sense, reasoning from Bellow, man is most fully human when he is speaking for effect, his mind, craft, and sense of others most fully engaged. At the same time, it is as easy to argue that if the center of human affairs is rhetoric, then all the world's a stage and all of us are merely role players. The idea of rhetoric inevitably carries both a pejorative and an honorific sense. It is a duality that the characters themselves imply. Bellow's characters are rhetorical because that is their nature, and the situations in which they find themselves compel them to be rhetorical. Consequently there is an obsessive, compulsive, repetitive aspect to them that undermines their dignity and makes them appear, to varying degrees, slightly comic. Yet their rhetoric is, finally, in the service of anxieties and desires that are more nearly existential, or spiritual, than social and persuasive. Consequently their rhetoric enobles them, allowing them to present themselves, as characters in short fiction rarely do, as being passionately involved with the deepest questions of their humanness.

I suggest the beginnings of a grammar.

1. The compulsive list: "Money owing, rent postponed, hole in your glove, one egg, cheap tobacco." ("Two Morning Monologues")[6]

2. The series of rhetorical fragments, suggestive of urgency or anxiety: "Presently I understood. The black market. This was not then reprehensible. Postwar Europe was like that. Refugees, adventurers, G.I.s. Even the Comte de la M-C. Europe still shuddering from the blows it had received. Governments new, uncertain, infirm. No reason to respect their authority." ("Mosby's Memoirs")[7]

3. Interior questions presented serially: "To whom should she leave it? Her brothers? Not they. Nephews? One was a submarine commander. The other was a bachelor in the State Department. Then began the roll call of cousins. Merton? He owned an estate in Connecticut. Anna? She had a face like a hot-water bottle." ("Leaving the Yellow House")[8]

4. The fragmentary afterthought: "They dug and saved. Mrs. Isaac Braun wore no cosmetics. Except a touch of lipstick when going out in public. No mink coats. A comfortable Hudson seal, yes." ("The Old System")[9]

5. The summary epithet: "And she vetoed all the young women, her judgments severe without limit. 'A false dog,' 'Candied Poison.' 'An open ditch. A sewer. A born whore!' " . . . "Aunt Rose said he was a minor hoodlum, a slugger. . . . This hired killer, this second Lepke of Murder, Inc." ("The Old System")

6. The summary epithet used ironically: "that friend of liberty Franklin Delano Roosevelt . . . that *genius* of diplomacy, Mr. Cordell Hull." ("Mosby's Memoirs")

7. The arch circumlocution: " 'She's a very handsome woman and my guess would be she has plenty of other opportunities even if Felipe does play the oldest bull with her.' " " 'The oldest bull; that's good!' " ("The Mexican General")[10]

8. The demonstrably bad joke at which nobody laughs: " 'Two dogs meet in the street. Old friends. One says, "Hello." The other answers, "Cock-a-doodle-do!" "What does that mean? What's this cock-a-doodle-do stuff?" "Oh," says he, "I've been studying foreign languages.' "

"Dead silence. No one laughed." ("The Gonzaga Manuscripts")

9. The self-conscious shift of dictional levels: " 'It was supposed to be preliminary to worthwhile, in expectation of the important. If that's too high-flown, I was bored.' " ("The Trip to Galena")[11]

10. The rhetorical question whose answer is implicit: " 'Is that something to surprise us?' " ("Address by Gooley MacDowell")[12]

11. The rhetorical question for which no answer is implicit or appropriate: " 'Or also what things happened, seeming neither intrinsic nor even called-for: what have these done to you, what have they made of you?' " ("Address by Gooley MacDowell")

12. Miming: " 'Do as I tell you,' he said."

" 'That's exactly how he would say it. You imitate him marvelously,' said Paco." ("The Mexican General")

13. The imputed response: "Now, friends, some of you will be thinking of the rule of nature and will ask my opinion, for instance, of the tame cat eating her way wag-headed into a mackerel with her nice needles." ("A Sermon by Dr. Pep")

14. The self-address: "*I was never one single thing anyway*, she thought. *Never my own. I was only loaned to myself.*" ("Leaving the Yellow House")

15. The inner address that analyzes somebody else's rhetoric: "The girls called Pop Dick Tracy, but Dick Tracy was a good guy. Whom could Pop convince?" ("A Silver Dish")[13]

16. The compulsive insult, non-specific in its address: " 'They send me out college workers in silk pants to talk me out of what I got comin'. Are they better'n me? Who told them? Fire them. Let 'em go and get married, and then you won't have to cut electric from people's budget!' " ("Looking for Mr. Green")

17. The formulaic appeal to conventional wisdom: " 'You're a teacher, aren't you. Five years in college. The best. Alright, you can't get a teacher job? the market is flooded? go get another job for a while. ("Two Morning Monologues")

Not much is gained by extending such a grammar since there is a kind of infinite plenitude in Bellow's rhetorical modes. Another area of Bellow's rhetorical virtuosity, however, is almost unanalyzeable but needs to be noticed, and that is the way in which some of his narrative diction and some of his speakers display a subtle sense of their orientation which is sometimes merely American urban, sometimes Jewish, but is almost never the "Yinglish" of more deliberately Jewish writers. It is, of course, the word order that makes the difference in this sentence from "The Old System": "A vision of mankind Braun was having as he sat over his coffee Saturday afternoon." With this, from "A Silver Dish," on the other hand, it is less easy to say where, exactly, its special rhythm comes from: "How, against a contemporary background, do you mourn an octogenarian father, nearly blind, his heart enlarged, his lungs filling with fluid, who creeps, stumbles, gives off the odors, the moldiness or gassiness of old men. I *mean*! As Woody put it, be realistic." The point, in any case, is obvious enough, that Bellow's rather modest body of short fiction contains its own range of technical forms, imitative of the full range of passionate, persuasive speech, and that, at times, those rhetorical forms carry with them, often with the very slightest variations from standard speech patterns, a rhythmic sense of who the speakers are.

I have suggested that, along with its rhetorical appeals, the short fiction also necessarily contains a range of either response or resistance. A response ordinarily derives from a perceived kinship. In "Looking for Mr. Green," Grebe and his supervisor Raynor achieve a kind of union at the point at which they confess themselves to be former students of Latin, now, incongruously, working for a relief agency, and exchange a few formulaic words of Latin. Scampi and Weyl in "The Trip to Galena," Mosby and Lustgarten in "Mosby's Memoirs" grope for some common sensibility, Doppelgängers, that image of which Bellow is so fond, polar opposites yet able, at moments, to listen and understand, even implicitly to confess themselves brothers. Kinship in the conventional sense, that is, family, helps to achieve a rhetorical union in Bellow. But in "A Silver Dish," "Leaving the Yellow House," and "The Old System," blood relatives understand each other all too well, so that the communication, once made, is inevitably discounted.

What prevents the rhetoric from taking its proper effect is the usual generational or stylistic gap, as it is with innumerable other writers from Dickens to the present time. Fathers do not understand sons; orthodox Jews do not understand liberal or nominal Jews. But, as with the rhetorical appeals, Bellow provides a quite remarkable spectrum of barriers to communication, so that the image one carries away from his short fiction is rather like the image one carries away from Dickens, of characters posturing, protesting, confessing, explaining, insulting, all to some space slightly beyond the face of the person they are addressing. Consider a naive and well-meaning American speaking to arch, condescending Spaniards. Consider an orator at Bug-house Square, Chicago, speaking to an audience, no audience, we do not know. Consider a fiance speaking to his fiancee, he being confident and successful in the world, cowed and humiliated by her, neither of them finally knowing each other. Consider an official white, speaking to ghetto blacks.

Moreover, consider the range of mechanisms that interfere with speech. The lapses into other languages are numerous, and significant. There are moments of Spanish, French, German, Latin, and Yiddish. And there are allusions which the respondent of the speech could not possibly recognize, references to books, public personages of faded fame, direct quotations from eccentric sources, nodding recognitions of areas of learning which must seem, to the listener, to be strange and arcane. And there are the mechanisms that inhibit rhetorical union: the law, the telephone, the conventions of the stranger knocking at the door, the anonymity of mass transit, the interposition of medicine and organic failure, American cars. Finally, there are those unbridgeable gulfs of spirit, between those characters who are obsessively in quest of something, or driven to confession, or hysterically assertive of their own sense of the contours of experience and those others who are tied to their dailiness.

Finally, I suggest that the short fiction, taken together, presents its own image of the human condition. It is not exactly the image of the longer fiction. Critics of Bellow, for a long time now, have called attention to his "defense of man," the extent to which he takes the full measure of the despair and nihilism of the contemporary condition, the dualities of madness and sanity, sickness and health, darkness and light, and then erects against it possibilities of action and dignity. His Nobel Prize acceptance speech asserts as much, a defense of that human spirit that lies beyond intellectual vogue, beyond things, and beyond illusion. Yet it is hard, in the short fictions, to find that assertion of human dignity, not, God knows, that the short fictions are some kind of Americanized Beckett, virtuoso versions of the end. It is that, given their time and space, they are prevented from "working out." Mosby doesn't get his memoirs written, although he understands what he lacks; Feiler doesn't get his manuscripts, although he knows why he can't. It is rather more knowledge of the impediments than assertion of self that comes to the protagonists of the short fiction. Which is to say, truistically, that the short fiction presents the short view of experience, the long fiction the long. Any given chapter of *The Victim* shows Leventhal asserting, lamenting, explaining, caring, and suffering. But it does not show Leventhal finally discovering his wholeness. That is something that takes two hundred fifty pages. Not twenty.

There is an old Jewish joke in which a speaker asks, "Do you know something peculiar about you Jews? that if somebody asks you a question, you answer with another question?" The other speaker replies, "We do?" It is a slight and mildly amusing joke, but it somehow carries with it the sense of Bellow's short fiction which I have described: its feeling for the problematics of intrapersonal speech, its attempt to define large areas of human nature by displaying modes of discourse, and its assertion that there is a way of looking at the world in which every question, whether it is merely a request for information or a metaphysical lament, has implicit in it another question.

Notes

1. *The Short Fiction of Norman Mailer* (New York: Dell, 1967), p. 9.

2. *Mosby's Memoirs and Other Stories* (New York: Viking, 1968), pp. 85–109.

3. *Partisan Review*, 16 (1949), 455–62.

4. *Mosby's Memoirs*, pp. 143–55.

5. *Mosby's Memoirs*, pp. 111–42.

6. *Partisan Review*, 8 (1941), 230–36.

7. *Mosby's Memoirs*, pp. 157–84.

8. *Mosby's Memoirs*, pp. 3–42.

9. *Mosby's Memoirs*, pp. 43–83.

10. *Partisan Review*, 9 (1942), 178–94.

11. *Partisan Review*, 17 (1950), 779–94.

12. *Hudson Review*, 14 (1951), 222–27.

13. *The New Yorker*, Sept. 25, 1978, pp. 40–62.

Brueghel and Augie March

Jeffrey Meyers[*]

In chapter ten of *The Adventures of Augie March* (1953) Augie describes Padilla's technique of stealing books and remembers an old, singular, beautiful Netherlands picture I once saw in an Italian gallery, of a wise old man walking in empty fields, pensive, while a thief behind cuts the string of his purse. The old man, in black, thinking probably of God's city, nevertheless has a foolish length of nose and is much too satisfied with his dream. But the peculiarity of the thief is that he is enclosed in a glass ball, and on the glass ball there is a surmounting cross, and it looks like the emperor's symbol of rule. Meaning that it is earthly power that steals while the ridiculous wise are in a dream about this world and the next, and perhaps missing this one, they will have nothing, neither this nor the next, so there is a sharp pain of satire in this amusing thing, and even the painted field does not have too much charm; it is a flat place.[1]

Pieter Brueghel's *The Misanthrope* (1568) is more significant in the novel than this brief paragraph suggests, for like Augie's various jobs it is a "Rosetta stone, so to speak," of his life. Brueghel's painting forms a symbolic center of meaning in the complex and variegated book and expresses some of its dominant themes: the earthly pilgrimage, the relation of character to fate, the pessimism about human misery, the conflict between acceptance and rejection of the world, and the idealistic longing for rustic simplicity. An understanding of why Bellow was attracted to this painting and how he used it in *Augie March* will clarify the themes and illuminate the meaning of the novel.

Bellow's aesthetic analogy, like his allusion to Henri Rousseau's *The Sleeping Gypsy* of 1897 (p. 520), emphasizes the inherent relationship of literature and painting, extends the potentialities of fiction to include the representational characteristics of the visual arts and concentrates the themes of his episodic novel into an immediate image. By reproducing the painting visually, by describing it verbally, by interpreting it iconographically, by looking at it with the same attention as Bellow did, we can attempt to see what he saw and to make an ideal correspondence between his visual image while writing and the one in our minds while reading.[2]

A number of important writers have been attracted to and influenced by Brueghel. Joshua Reynolds's discussion of *The Massacre of the Innocents* emphasizes Brueghel's modernity and aptly compares his originality and profun-

[*]Reprinted from *American Literature*, 49 (1977), 113–19.

N. 12067 Napoli, Gallerie Nazionali di Capodimonte—Il misantrope (Brueghel, Pieter). Photograph by F.lli Alinari, Firenze, Italia.

dity to the poetry of Donne: "This painter was totally ignorant of all the mechanical art of making a picture; but there is here a great quantity of thinking, a representation of variety of distress, enough for twenty modern pictures. In this respect he is like Donne, as distinguished from the modern versifiers, who carry no weight of thought."[3] Goethe also found in Brueghel's paintings "the serious character of the sixteenth century,"[4] the age of Luther and the Reformation. And Baudelaire, whose "Les Aveugles" (1861) was inspired by *The Parable of the Blind,* was fascinated by the fantastic, hallucinatory and diabolic qualities of Brueghel's art, which seemed to reflect his own preoccupations:

> In the fantasic pictures of Brueghel the Droll the full power of hallucination is revealed to us. But what artist could produce such monstrously paradoxical works if he had not been driven from the outset by some unknown force? . . . How could a human intelligence contain so many marvels and devilries? how could it beget and describe so many terrifying extravagances? . . . I challenge anyone to explain the diabolic and diverting farrago of Brueghel the Droll otherwise than by a kind of special, Satanic grace.[5]

The sophisticated connoisseur Aldous Huxley, who believed that Brueghel's greatness was not fully recognized, praised his technique, content, intellect, honesty, perception, and philosophy: "He is highly competent aesthetically; he has plenty to say; his mind is curious, interesting and powerful; and he has no false pretensions, is entirely honest. . . . He was the first landscape painter of his century, the acutest student of manners, and the wonderfully skillful pictorial expounder or suggester of a view of life."[6] Brueghel's paintings have had a significant influence on modern poetry and have directly inspired Auden's "Musées des Beaux Arts" (1940), Williams's *Pictures from Brueghel* (1962), Nemerov's "Hope" and "Brueghel: The Triumph of Time," and Joseph Langland's "The Fall of Icarus: Brueghel" and "Hunters in the Snow: Brueghel" (1963). Fritz Grossmann's summary of the richly contradictory characteristics of Brueghel, whose reputation has reached its zenith in the twentieth century, suggests the attractive ambiguity of both the man and the artist:

> The man has been thought to have been a peasant and a townsman, an orthodox Catholic and a Libertine, a humanist, a laughing and a pessimist philosopher; the artist appeared as a follower of Bosch and a continuator of the Flemish tradition, the last of the Primitives, a Mannerist in contact with Italian art, an illustrator, a genre painter, a landscape artist, a realist, a painter consciously transforming reality and adapting it to his formal ideal.[7]

The Misanthrope, in the Naples Gallerie Nazionali di Capodimonte, is a literary painting that tells a story and has an inscription that clarifies the meaning of the allegory. Brueghel's painting, like Bellow's novel, is a masterpiece of naturalistic observation; and is both realistic and symbolical, dramatic and reflective. In the painting a wide-eyed, round-faced, crouching barefoot thief, dressed in ragged lilac clothing and enclosed in a glass orb surmounted by a cross, which symbolizes the Christian world, stares brazenly out of the picture with an idiotic expression as he cuts the bright red purse that hangs by a cord from the waist of the Misanthrope. The tall, gloomy wanderer, whose upright cone-shaped figure contrasts with the crouching round thief, wears a long deep-blue cape and tasseled monkish cowl that covers his eyes. He has a long nose, tightly closed thin lips, reddish face and pointed silver beard. He walks with his hands clasped before him, lost in meditation, and is unaware of the three sharp caltrops which are dangerously strewn in his path. In the background of the flat Flemish landscape, with its farmhouse and windmill, a faithful shepherd tends his peaceful flock. He represents the ideal of a bucolic life, and the contrast of man's folly and nature's purity.

The same enclosed thief appears in Brueghel's *Netherlandish Proverbs* (1559) and illustrates the maxim: "You have to stoop low to get along in the world." And the Flemish inscription at the bottom of the *tondo* painting explains the Misanthrope's gloom: "Because the world is so faithless I wear mourning." The cutpurse disturbs the quiet of the landscape, mars the meditations of the Misanthrope and expresses Brueghel's pessimistic view of mankind. This pessimism was probably intensified by contemporary political events for in 1568, the year of the painting, the Spanish Duke of Alba, a religious fanatic and ruthless absolutist who was determined to crush the attempt of the Netherlands to gain religious toleration and political self-government, arrived in Brussels with 20,000 soldiers to begin his brutal regency.

The paradoxical quality of Brueghel's art, noted by Baudelaire, is manifest in this painting, for the Misanthrope has renounced the sinful world but has not renounced the world's sin. His bulging purse reveals that he has not freed himself from hypocrisy and avarice, and he is threatened with the punishment of spikey crosses. He is enclosed by the circular painting as the thief is by the circular orb and cannot escape the robbery of the perfidious world.

Bellow offers an interpretation as well as a description of the satiric and amusing painting. Though the old man is thinking of St. Augustine's City of God, he is both foolish and self-satisfied. Like Padilla, a gifted crook who takes pride in his technique, the cutpurse (who symbolizes earthly power) steals while the ridiculous wise man dreams about the next world, misses this one and gets nothing in either world. This singular, beautiful picture raises for Augie, who drifts aimlessly and passively through his picaresque peregrinations, the central question of the novel: what to do with his life.

Like the cutpurse, Augie is a thief who robs a department store and a leather goods shop and is caught stealing books. But like Padilla, Augie is not a real crook, "not interested in it, so nobody can make a fate of it for me"; and he rejects the acquiescence in worldly corruption and the multifarious swindles of Simon, Einhorn, and Mintouchian. These men, like his other mentors— Grandma Lausch, Mrs. Renling, Mimi Villars, Lucy Magnus, Thea Fenchel, and Bateshaw—all want to force him "to stoop low in order to get along in the world" and to exchange his tattered rags for elegant clothes (Augie experiences sartorial transformations first with Mrs. Renling, then with Simon and finally with Thea). But Augie, as Einhorn truly observes, has "opposition," and he tries to tell Thea that "I had looked all my life for the right thing to do, for a fate good enough, that I have opposed people in what they wanted to make of me, but now that I was in love with her I understood much better what I myself wanted" (p. 333).

But when Thea, like Simon and Lucy, is "faithless," Augie, "eternally looking for a way out" and pondering whether he was "a man of hope or foolishness," retreats from the world into himself and continues the "circlings" of his earthly pilgrimage—oblivious of the spikey dangers that await him. For he cannot escape torpedoes at sea, Basteshaw's murderous mania, Mintouchian's corruption, or Stella's betrayal. His character is indeed his fate; for he is born to be victimized and is unable to set his "feet on a path of life and stop looking over the field." Augie is confused by his "bewilderment of choices," yearns for both the active and the contemplative life, and can neither accept nor renounce the world. The pessimistic figure of the mourning Misanthrope reflects Augie's compromised idealism and represents the "rock-depth of heavy trouble, where, I guess, the greater part of human beings have always spent most of their silent time" (p. 98).[8]

The peaceful shepherd in the background of the paintings, safely removed from the corruption of the world and harmoniously integrated with the natural landscape, symbolizes a way of life that Augie longs for but can never achieve. His dream is to marry a loving wife, get "a piece of property and settle down on it" and do a little farming and beekeeping. But Bellow's ironic tone suggests that the pastoral ideal of "March's farm and academy," "this private green place like one of those Walden or Innisfree wattle jobs under the kind sun" is not possible for the "Chicago born" Augie, as it (briefly) was for Thoreau and Yeats.[9]

Brueghel's painting portrays three distinct ways of dealing with the hostile world: joining in its corruption, making a partial renunciation, and retreating to a bucolic ideal. Augie ponders all three alternatives without committing himself to any of them, and like the "ridiculous wise" old man has neither worldly wealth nor spiritual purity. Though Augie is battered by rough forces and disappointed in life, he remains a "laughing creature, forever rising up" and resists the pessimism of Brueghel's *Misanthrope*.

Notes

1. Saul Bellow, *The Adventures of Augie March* (New York, 1971), p. 200.

2. See my book *Painting and the Novel* (New York, 1975).

3. Sir Joshua Reynolds, *"Journey to Flanders and Holland in the Year 1781,"* in *Works*, ed. Edmund Malone, 3rd ed. (London, 1801), II, 408. Johnson's discussion of the Metaphysical poets in his "Life of Cowley" (1779) probably drew Reynolds's attention to John Donne.

4. J. W. von Goethe, *"Landschaftliche Malerei"* (1832) in *Werke*, XII (Hamburg, 1953), 219.

5. Charles Baudelaire, "Some Foreign Caricaturists" (1857), *The Mirror of Art*, trans. and ed. Jonathan Mayne (New York, 1956), pp. 189–90.

6. Aldous Huxley, "Brueghel" (1927), *On Art and Artists* (New York, 1962), pp. 207, 209.

7. Fritz Grossmann, *Pieter Brueghel: Complete Edition of the Paintings*, 3rd ed. (New York, 1973), p. 50.

8. This idea is similar to Thoreau's assertion in the first chapter of *Walden:* "The mass of men lead lives of quiet desperation."

9. The urban hero of West's *Miss Lonelyhearts* (1933) also fails in his desperate attempt to escape to a country idyll.

Reichianism in *Seize the Day*

Eusebio Rodrigues[*]

In his tribute to Isaac Rosenfeld, Saul Bellow casually mentions the fact that Reichianism had absorbed them both for a time but does not elaborate on the nature of this absorption. His friend (who died in 1956, the year *Seize the Day* was published) was apparently a charmingly eccentric Reichian: he would calculate the amount of character armor people wore, and had even put together a homemade orgone accumulator to produce better tomatoes and to treat the headaches of his friends.[1] Bellow's own involvement was of a deeper kind, that of a writer who takes what he needs for his own artistic purposes and strategies. By 1964, when *Herzog* was published, Bellow had for the most part shed Reichianism from his creative system. In *Henderson the Rain King* (1959), Bellow, in complete control of his fictional material, fully charged the novel with Reichianism. He used the mode of fantastic farce to cast a magical spell over its Reichian constituents, playing around with them, poking fun at them, taking them seriously when it suited his fictional needs, and finally, making them into powerful, but almost invisible, presences in the novel.[2] The compelling force that Reichianism came to exert on his imagination, however, had already begun to emerge in *Seize the Day*.

Seize the Day (1956) is as powerfully charged with Reichianism as *Henderson the Rain King*, but there are significant differences in the Reichian material used and in the artistic control of this material. The deliberate restriction of fictional space and time (in contrast to the amplitude of *Henderson*) and the need to pack other thematic concerns into this compact and complex novella did not allow Bellow enough room to maneuver its Reichian elements with complete ease. Further, the continuous shifting of narrative perspectives (in contrast to the first person singular of Henderson, who tells his tale with immense gusto) created problems of aesthetic distance. Most of the events are routed through Wilhelm's point of view which, at times, slides into the first person singular. Behind Wilhelm stands the narrator who is aware of the predicament of his protagonist. At other moments Wilhelm is seen through the eyes of the minor characters in the novella. This at times abrupt shifting of narrative angles creates problems for the reader who has to maintain the ironic distance necessary to smile wryly at a comic slob, and then suddenly adopt the stance of one who has to look with sympathy at a passive sufferer living through

[*]This essay appears for the first time in this volume, and is published by permission of the author.

a terrible day. Bellow presents Tommy Wilhelm as a clown-victim, but found it difficult to blend both elements into complete fictional harmony. Wilhelm is more victim than clown, and the novel insists on a compassionate understanding of his psychic plight.[3]

Tommy Wilhelm is a dramatic illustration of how human character structure is molded and distorted by a society that is patriarchal, death-dealing, money-oriented and barren. Reich, who combined the insights of a sociologist with those of a psychologist, insists that the vast majority of human beings suffer from a character neurosis because of inner tensions generated by the conflict between natural human demands and the brutal pressures exerted by the world of business, money, and power. The so-called civilized and seemingly cultured human being has a three-tiered character structure. The deepest layer consists of man's natural sociality, his enjoyment of work, and his innate capacity for love. When these impulses are almost overwhelmed, a second layer forms where all the inhibited drives of greed, lust, envy, and sadism (the Freudian tier) congregate and harden. The outer layer is a mask of politeness, self-control, and artificial sociality.

The three layers of Tommy Wilhelm are apparent as he lives through his tragic day. He tries to assume the mask of success, but is a failure as an actor, being merely an extra. In contrast, the denizens of the Hotel Gloriana and the gamblers at the stock exchange are all consummate actors who wear perfect masks. The German manager of the brokerage office, for example, is a model of correctness, and always appears to be "silvery, cool, level, long-profiled, experienced, indifferent, observant."[4] Wilhelm tries hard to be sociable, polite and charming. But his second layer, suggested by the gruff voice within him, expresses the anger and resentment concealed behind his social mask. His outer layer greets Mr. Perls politely, but his second layer asks: " 'Who is this damn frazzle-faced herring with his dyed hair and his fish teeth and this drippy mustache?' " (p. 31)

What differentiates Tommy Wilhelm from the other inhabitants of the glamorous, empty world that is Upper Broadway (with its hotels and supermodern cafeterias, dental laboratories, reducing parlors, beauty parlors, funeral homes, all dedicated to the business of pampering the body and putting up a show) is the fact that his core layer has not been stifled but is still alive, though it has been greatly damaged. It is from this layer that he receives mysterious promptings. It is from these depths that he gets an obscure message which suggests that the real, the highest business of his life is "to carry his peculiar burden, to feel shame and impotence, to taste these quelled tears" (p. 56). This small, feeble voice that emanates from the very center of Wilhelm's soul is an embodiment of the central premise in Reichian theory, the presence of orgone energy. Unlike the clamorous, insistent, passionate voice (a comic dramatization of the existence of orgone energy) that arises from Henderson's heart, Wilhelm's voice whimpers, weeps, and complains. Both protagonists, somatically speaking, are huge, and in both the vital force is trapped and does not circulate freely. The psychological difference between the two, however, is tremendous. Henderson is an impulsive man of action who ventures into the jungles of Africa in frantic search of psychic health. Tommy Wilhelm is a masochist who suffers from the fear of bursting: he will not and cannot allow his pent-up energy to discharge itself.

Tommy Wilhelm embodies a form of armoring that constitutes the masochistic character.[5] In 1932, Reich published an essay that set forth his preliminary clinical investigations of masochism.[6] This article signaled Reich's break with Freud and refuted the Freudian explanation of masochism as the expression of a hypothetical death instinct. Reich demonstrated that the masochistic drive towards suffering was not an inevitable result of the biological will to suffer, but a product of the disastrous impact of social conditions on the biopsychic apparatus.

According to Reich, masochism is the result and the expression of an inner tension that cannot be discharged. To illustrate the masochistic dilemma Reich made use of a vivid image, the biopsychic apparatus seen as an armored bladder:

> *How would a bladder behave if it were blown up with air from the inside, and could not burst?* Let us assume that its membrane would be tensile, but could not be torn. This picture of the human character as an armor around the living nucleus was highly relevant. The bladder, if it could express itself in its state of insoluble tension, would complain. In its helplessness, it would look for the causes of its suffering on *the outside,* and would be reproachful. It would ask to be pricked open. It would provoke its surroundings until it had achieved its aim as it conceived this. *What it could not bring about spontaneously from the inside, it would passively, helplessly, expect from the outside.* (*DO,* p. 213)

Typical masochistic character traits, according to Reich, are:

> Subjectively, a chronic sensation of *suffering* which appears objectively as a *tendency to complain;* chronic tendencies to *self-damage* and *self-depreciation* ("moral masochism") and a compulsion to *torture others* which makes the patient suffer no less than the object. All masochistic characters show specifically *awkward, atactic behavior* in their manners and in their intercourse with others, often so marked as to give the impression of mental deficiency. (*CA,* p. 219)

Bellow translates these masochistic character traits and forms of behavior into vivid, concrete, and at times oddly comic detail. Wilhelm is a gigantic human bladder, a Rouault tragic clown at times, at other times a pathetic buffoon. He has a nodding Buddha head and an obscenely huge belly. He walks, observes the narrator, "like a tower in motion" (p. 74). Dr. Adler sees with disgust that his son is "either hoisting his pants up and down by the pockets or jittering with his feet. A regular mountain of tics, he's getting to be" (p. 28). Wilhelm's laments and complaints assume grotesque forms. In the restaurant he eats the remains of his father's breakfast (signifying that he needs some form of sustenance from his father) and then sits "gigantically in a state of arrest" (p. 42). This clown-victim then grasps his own broad throat and proceeds to choke himself to demonstrate by an act of self-sabotage how his wife strangles him at long distance. He is sloppy in his personal habits, and his car and apartment are greasy and filthy. He hurls names at himself in self-depreciation. He calls himself an ass, an idiot, a wild boar, a dumb mule, a hippopotamus. Tommy Wilhelm, like a hippopotamus, wallows in his own sufferings.

The person to whom Wilhelm has returned for relief from his sufferings is his father who psychically stands for the frustrating reality Wilhelm identifies with. It was Dr. Adler, the immediate and forceful representative of the tyrannical world of money and success, who initially damaged his son's psyche. Reich regarded the patriarchal family as a fortress of modern social order and as a factory for tyrannical ideologies and conservative structures. Tamkin terms Dr. Adler "a fine old patriarch of a father" (p. 62) and refers to the parent-child relationship as "the eternal same story" (p. 61). More than an Oedipal battleground, the family was the domestic arena where the masochistic damage began and where the anchoring of the social order within the individual took place: "The first and most important place of reproduction of the social order is the patriarchal family which creates in children a character structure which makes them amenable to the later influences of an authoritarian order" (CA, p. xxiii).

Bellow does not dramatize (again, perhaps, because of lack of time and space) the psychodynamics of Wilhelm's masochism, but he does provide the reader with some hints. Tommy Wilhelm deliberately returns after twenty long years to the source of his conflicts. " 'I expect *help!*' " he cries out loudly and frantically at the breakfast table (p. 53). " 'When I suffer—you aren't even sorry. That's because you have no affection for me, and you don't want any part of me,' " he complains bitterly (p. 54). "*Dear Dad, Please carry me this month, Yours, W.*" is his childish plea on the note he slips into an envelope together with his unpaid hotel bill (p. 74). And yet, with his pill taking, his dirty habits, his whining pleas for help, he invariably irritates his father and provokes him to fury.

These provocative pleas offer a clue to the genesis of Wilhelm's masochism. Reich focuses on deep disappointment in love during childhood as the root-origin of masochism. The provocative tactics of a masochist are directed against those persons who were loved intensely and who either actually disappointed or did not gratify the child's love:

> "You must love me, I shall force you to; or else, I'm going to annoy you." The masochistic torturing, the masochistic complaint, provocation and suffering, all explain themselves on the basis of the frustration, fantasied or actual, of a demand for love which is excessive and cannot be gratified. This mechanism is *specific* for the masochistic character and no other form of neurosis. (CA, p. 225)

There is no traumatic Freudian moment when the rejection that damaged Wilhelm's psyche occurred. Instead, Bellow suggests that there had been a series of critical conflicts during Wilhelm's childhood and adolescence. Wilhelm's dissatisfaction always reaches its intensest when he discusses family matters with his father. He is nostalgic about a "warm family life" (p. 26), but is unsure about the reality of his father's kindliness to him as a child. He complains that his father had starved him of affection. Dr. Adler was at the office, or the hospital, or out lecturing. "He expected me to look out for myself and never gave me much thought," broods Wilhelm (p. 14). Bellow focuses on the period when Wilhelm commits his first mistake by going to Hollywood. He is vaguely aware of the masochistic nature of this mistake: "Like, he sometimes thought, I was going to pick up a weapon and strike myself a blow with it" (p. 17). His father's attitude had been one of cold indifference. Wilhelm had quarreled with his mother who had tried to stop him. Four years later she died and, as Wilhelm reminds his father, their family life came to an end. Dr. Adler freed himself from the shackles of his family, but his son has not been able to break away. An umbilical cord of memories still binds him to his mother. And now, at forty-four, Wilhelm demands from his father the love and help he was denied as a child. He is aware of his own childish demands: "It's time I stopped feeling like a kid toward him, a small son" (p. 11).

The sufferings of Wilhelm spring from the continuous tension within him. But the methods he uses to insist on his father's love are doomed to fail. For these demands, in the form of provocation and spite, increase both his fears of losing love and his feelings of guilt, for it is the beloved father who is being tortured. Wilhelm suffers from the peculiar masochistic dilemma: the more he tries to get out of his situation of suffering, the more he gets involved in it. Tamkin diagnoses Wilhelm's condition correctly when he tells him there is lots of guilt in him and warns him not to be dedicated to suffering.

The details that Bellow provides about Wilhelm's psycho-physical condition at forty-four assume a clear Reichian pattern. When he was a young man, before his first mistake, Wilhelm's body bespoke his health: "Wilhelm had the color of a Golden Grimes apple when he was well, and then his thick blond hair had been vigorous and his wide shoulders unwarped; he was leaner in the jaws, his eyes fresher and wider; his legs were then still awkward but he was impressively handsome" (p. 17). His present disfigured armored condition needs to be treated and dissolved. Reich divides the human body into seven armored segments—ocular, oral, neck, chest, diaphragmatic, abdominal, and pelvic. In *Seize the Day*, Bellow refers to the four upper armor rings of Wilhelm's bodily system.[7]

Wilhelm's problems are directly visible and emotionally expressed in these four regions. Bellow disguises the Reichian symptoms in unobtrusive modes of behavior which appear to be quite natural to Wilhelm. The symptoms to look for in the head or neck are: a slight indication of the facial expression of a suckling infant, a wrinkling of the forehead, a hasty, jerky way of talking, a certain way of holding the head to one side, of shaking it, etc. After recalling how he had disappointed his mother, Wilhelm drinks his coke as if he were a baby at a bottle: "He swallowed hard at the Coke bottle and coughed over it, but he ignored his coughing, for he was still thinking, his eyes upcast and his lips closed behind his hand" (p. 15). On his forehead there is "a wide wrinkle like a comprehensive bracket sign" (p. 6). His movements are jerky; he constantly keeps nodding his large head, and he stammers and talks in staccato bursts and in exclamation marks. His troubles are indeed inscribed on his anxious face.

It is in the region of the chest, the central part of the muscular armor, according to Reich, that Wilhelm experiences severe pains. His breathing is highly irregular: he either pants like a dog, or else draws and holds a long breath in an effort to control his feelings. He retracts his heavy shoulders (biophysical extensions of the chest segment) and draws his hands up into his sleeves, gestures that denote the attitude of holding back. More significant, he suffers from a continuous feeling of strangulation, choking and congestion all through the day.[8] When his problems assert themselves, and when he thinks about his father, the energy within kicks at his armor and his body proclaims its pain: "He pressed his lips together, and his tongue went soft; it pained him far at the back, in the cords and the throat, and a knot of ill formed in his chest" (p. 14). After the angry exchange with his father at the breakfast table, Wilhelm suppresses his rage and he feels the tightening pressures of his armor: "He was horribly worked up; his neck and shoulders, his entire chest ached as though they had been tightly tied with ropes" (pp. 55–56). Any inhibited aggressive impulse, according to Reich, directs the energy towards the musculature of the peripheral extremities where it becomes manifest. With sly humor, Bellow suggests that even Wilhelm's hair registers the expansion of this energy: it "twists in flaming shapes upward" (p. 50) and rises "dense and tall" (p. 53) when he is angry. The energy manifests itself clearly in the warm, panting laugh (the oral segment) that issues from him throughout the day,[9] and is also seen in his wide, gray circular eyes that are so oddly expressive (the ocular segment).[10] It displays itself at moments when Wilhelm controls the rage that boils furiously within him: "His face flamed and paled and swelled and his breath was laborious" (p. 48).

Bellow undertook the tremendously difficult feat of setting forth Wilhelm's psychic predicament and of presenting the therapeutic process that leads to the dissolution of his armored condition, all in the course of a morning through an afternoon. In order to achieve this fictional task Bellow created the mysterious and fascinating Dr. Tamkin, a protean figure who assumes a variety of roles that shift and dissolve as he swindles Wilhelm, educates him about the real business of life, and finally vanishes just before the moment of Wilhelm's rebirth. Tamkin has been termed a schnorrer, a zaddik, and a shaman,[11] but he himself claims to be a mental scientist, a psychological poet who has been treating Wilhelm for some time. His qualifications as a psychologist are, as Dr. Adler rightly suspects, highly dubious.

Bellow has never set down his views on psychologists and analysts, but is clearly ambivalent about them and about their therapeutic practices. *The Last Analysis* (published in 1966) is surely a spoof of Freudianism, though it is more than just that.[12] In an interview, Bellow has referred to his early interest in Freudianism, and to his later violent reaction against Freud, especially against his theory of the unconscious.[13] As a novelist who sets out to capture modes of behavior and individuality, Bellow obviously makes use of psychological insights, but he refuses to allow his creative imagination to be imprisoned by any one psychological system, even that of Wilhelm Reich.

Seize the Day is full of references, direct and oblique, to psychologists. The names Bellow has chosen for some of the minor characters have a strange origin: Adler, Perls, and Rappaport (a variant of Rapaport) are names of modern psychologists, but with the possible exception of Dr. Adler (who like his name-sake wants to safeguard the future), there is no real connection between the name and the character in the novella. Perhaps Bellow wanted to suggest that psychiatry has become, in the words of Dr. Adler, a "modern industry" and that twentieth-century urban man is so bombarded by competing forms of therapy that he cannot escape from them or distinguish what is true from what is false. Tamkin's hotel room is full of various kinds of books, among them the volumes of Korzybski, Aristotle, Freud, and W. H. Sheldon. Carol M. Sicherman has pointed to the ironic juxtaposition of Aristotle and the non-Aristotelian, Korzybski, and of Freud and the violently anti-Freudian Sheldon.[14] This jux-taposition of the trivial and the profound in Tamkin's collection parallels the mishmash of jargon and wisdom that pours out of his mouth. Mr. Perls is right when he characterizes Tamkin as both sane and crazy. Bellow deliberately does not allow the narrative angle to shift to Dr. Tamkin's point of view in order to create an aura of mystery about him.

Tamkin, "the confuser of the imagination" (p. 93), both attracts and repels Tommy Wilhelm. Irritated by the pretender, the "puffed-up little bogus and humbug" (p. 95), Wilhelm is drawn to the Tamkin who talks about the deeper things of life. The psychological jargon that Tamkin uses about spontaneous emotion, open receptors, and free impulses makes no impact on Wilhelm, who is also highly suspicious of the fantastic stories Tamkin spins out about his adventures and about the patients he has treated. The here-and-now exercises (Bellow parodies here the techniques of Gestalt therapy[15]) that Tamkin uses in order to demonstrate how Wilhelm should calm himself, have no effect, for Wilhelm is back in the past brooding about his wife.

Wilhelm feels profoundly moved only when Tamkin tosses out bits of advice and wisdom that touch his inner being. They happen to be fragments of Reichian insights which Tamkin has made part of his vocabulary and repertoire as a psychological conman, despite the fact that no books by Wilhelm Reich can be seen in his collection. Wilhelm is unmoved when Tamkin twice uses the word "background" (p. 66), a significant term in Gestalt theory, but is impressed when Tamkin uses the Reichian term, "plague" (pp. 63, 64). Tamkin's cryptic analysis of the crucial conflict of the two souls in the human breast—the pretender soul that loves money and success, and the real soul that merely needs love—appeals profoundly to Wilhelm because it describes (without using Reichian terminol-ogy) the truth about his own condition. In Tommy, the name he shifted to after his decision to go to Hollywood, he sees the pretender soul that still clings to fame, money, and success. His real self, uncontaminated by the pretender, was present when he was Wilky, the name his father used for him as a child. And, Wilhelm suspects, it existed in a purer state at the time when his grandfather called him Velvel, a name which in Hebrew means "wolf."

Tamkin's Reichianism is surreally clear in the strange poem he offers Wilhelm. The title of the poem, "Mechanism vs. Functionalism/Ism vs. Hism," springs straight out of the pages of Reich. The introduction to *Selected Writ-*

ings, which is an essay by Reich, announces that orgonomic functionalism is a way of exploring and dealing with the living, a method of bringing "the human animal again into harmony with his natural biology and with surrounding nature" (SW, p. 23). In opposition to functionalism is mechanist thinking which cannot understand the processes of nature.

The poem itself (a wonderful parody of romantic poetry in general and of Blake and Emerson in particular) is a mixture of claptrap (as Wilhelm immediately realizes) and wisdom. Despite its absurd surface, it proclaims the truth that man is part of nature and essentially great, if he would only open his eyes and discover his own nobility. Tamkin explicates the poem insisting that it applies to Wilhelm himself and to sick humanity. The poem is both a warning and a plea. The world of money and mechanism destroys the real soul, says Tamkin, echoing one of the fundamental tenets of Reichianism. Instead, suggests Tamkin, one should seize the day and surrender oneself to the processes of nature. Tamkin's advice is the climax of a course he has been giving Wilhelm on the great English poets, perhaps a kind of poetry therapy. All through the day Wilhelm, under the influence of Tamkin, recalls poems that moved him profoundly when he was an adolescent. He remembers lines from four poems—Shakespeare's seventy-third sonnet, Milton's *Lycidas*, Keats's *Endymion*, and Shelley's *Ode to the West Wind*—that voice the needs of his self and speak of natural human experiences, suffering, love, death and the healing influences of nature. Tamkin's voice sounds most genuine when it sketches out for Wilhelm in bright, rhythmic images the need to return to the natural world: " 'Nature only knows one thing, and that's the present. Present, present, eternal present, like a big, huge, giant wave—colossal, bright and beautiful, full of life and death, climbing into the sky, standing in the seas' " (p. 89).

Tommy Wilhelm's Reichian education is now almost complete, but his character armor has yet to be dissolved. Dr. Tamkin dispenses a kind of Reichian wisdom, but does not administer the Reichian form of therapy. Unlike King Dahfu, who uses an exotic Reichian agent, the lioness Atti, for the dramatic and spectacular treatment of Henderson, Tamkin was limited to the use of the talking cure for Wilhelm.[16] Bellow had therefore to invent a process of therapy that would lead to the cure of his protagonist. He put together a strange process, one involving self-therapy and self-awareness (Wilhelm, as his own therapist, is given Wilhelm Reich's first name), variations and parodies of Reichian therapy, and ordeals that lead to genuine suffering.

The dissolution of Wilhelm's character armor begins in the lobby of the Hotel Gloriana when Wilhelm senses the first stirrings of the energy within him, and becomes aware that his routine is about to break up and that "a huge trouble long presaged but till now formless was due" (p. 4). He feels a "knot of ill" form in his chest. All day long tears from deep within approach his eyes but he does not let them flow. Bellow allows his protagonist to indulge in a comico-serious form of self-therapy at the breakfast table. Wilhelm's choking of himself is comically grotesque, but it is also the Reichian "gag-reflex"[17] which induces the vomiting of emotions that are held back by neck armoring. The armor begins to loosen up as Wilhelm's energy mounts steadily to a climax. After the lard figures drop and he knows he is wiped out financially, Wilhelm realizes that his pretender soul no longer has any sustenance to feed itself. He senses his unshed tears rising, wave-like, and, the narrator tells us, he looked like a man about to drown. He is in a state of panic, but he steels himself lest he break down and cry. This effort "made a violent vertical pain go through his chest, like that caused by a pocket of air under the collar bones" (p. 104). The second ordeal ends when Tommy Wilhelm is finally and completely rejected by his father. His masochistic self now realizes that it has no prop on which it can shrug off its woes. Wilhelm tries desperately to suppress the murderous anger and fury within him and experiences these emotions in physical terms: " 'Dad, I just can't breathe. My chest is all up—I feel choked. I just simply can't catch my breath' " (p. 109).

Lacking a human agent who could act as a Reichian therapist, Bellow had to resort to a parody of a Reichian therapeutic device to stage the breakdown of Wilhelm's armored condition. Invented by Reich in 1940, the Orgone Energy Accumulator was a six-sided box that consisted of several layers of alternating organic and metallic material in which the patient sat and absorbed concentrated orgone energy. According to detractors of Reich, like Robinson and Rycroft,[18] it was shaped like a narrow telephone booth. It is in a telephone booth that Wilhelm's final ordeal takes place. With deliberate care Bellow sets down the details that indicate the furious upheaval within Wilhelm.

During the conversation with the hard and unyielding Margaret, Wilhelm at first breaks into a heavy sweat. As he reels under her verbal assaults, his voice (without his realizing it) begins to grow louder. It rises, the narrator tells us, and then, as Margaret notes, Wilhelm begins to rave and yell. His face expands and he feels suffocated as if he is about to burst. What he experiences in the booth is what he had demonstrated to his father, a form of strangulation that once again results in the "gag-reflex" and that now impels him this time to action: "He struck a blow upon the tin and wood and nails of the wall of the booth" (p. 114). By focusing on such unusual detail about the make-up of an ordinary telephone booth, Bellow forcefully suggests that the combination of metallic and organic material (the tin and the wood) transforms it into an orgone box, while the pointed reference to the wood and the nails makes it into a kind of cross. Bellow's "orgone box" is a parodic device, which has also to be regarded as an enclosure where Wilhelm, whose armor is in the process of breaking down and who is therefore porous, can be charged by the energy the box radiates. It is also a place where Wilhelm experiences excruciating pain and violent suffering which, in the words of Henderson, is a reliable burster of the spirit's sleep.

The energy now storms within Wilhelm so that he is driven to forceful action: "He struck the wall again, this time with his knuckles, and he had scarcely enough air in his lungs to speak in a whisper because his heart pushed upward with a frightful pressure. He got up and stamped his feet in the narrow enclosure" (p. 114). The breathless condition, the upward thrust of the heart, and the violent stamping of his feet indicate that a tremendous churning is taking place within Wilhelm. So enraged is he that he yells loudly, grinds his teeth, and tries to tear the telephone apparatus from the wall "with insane digging fingers" (p. 114) like an animal; an elderly woman is appalled by the distorted look on his face. The chest armor cannot be dissolved, according to Reich, without "liberating the emotions of raving rage, of intolerable longing and genuine crying" (CA, p. 379). Chest armoring usually occurs at the time of critical conflicts in a child's life. When this armor segment is dissolved, says Reich, traumatic memories of parental mistreatments and frustrations are summoned up.

Bellow offers a dramatic clue to the genesis of Wilhelm's chest armor by having Margaret refer to her husband's ravings as the howls of a wolf. " 'I won't stand to be howled at,' " says Margaret (p. 114). Wilhelm now senses the truth of what Tamkin had told him, that the lonely person feels impelled to howl from his city window like a wolf when he cannot bear his loneliness any longer, especially when night comes. Reich links the child's excessive demands for love with the fear of being left alone which the masochist experiences intensely in very early childhood. The name, Velvel, meaning wolf, which his grandfather called him, pointedly suggests the utter loneliness and lack of paternal love which Wilhelm now experiences and must have experienced as a child.

Bellow uses a funeral home to stage the final dissolution of Wilhelm's armored condition. Wilhelm rushes out on to Broadway, significantly abandoning all his change in the booth, and is carried by the pressure of a crowd into a funeral chapel. The beating of his heart is "anxious, thick, frightened," the narrator tells us, and adds, "but somehow also rich" (p. 114). Wilhelm's face once again expands, and his eyes are bright with instant tears. He begins to weep, softly at first, and then loudly and uncontrollably.

For the sight of the corpse decked out like an actor (Bellow packs many meanings into this symbol, which also stands for Dr. Adler) triggers a huge explosion within Tommy Wilhelm. An eruption takes place, the armor cracks completely, and tears, like lava, flow from the depths within: "The source of all tears had suddenly sprung open within him, black, deep, and hot, and they were pouring out and convulsed his body. . . . The great knot of ill and grief in his throat swelled upward and he gave in utterly and held his face and wept. He cried with all his heart" (p. 118). What Wilhelm experiences is the Reichian throat spasm, the final stage in the dissolution of his armor. In Reichian therapy the patient has to suffer a breakdown and experience the "ill-smelling, blocked off, sequestered realm of the self" (SW, p. 465) before he can arrive at health. The tears, the cries and the sobs that well out of Tommy Wilhelm are the form the energy within assumes as it struggles painfully out of its black prison.

The last paragraph of Seize the Day, a miracle of compression, flashes before us the moment of illumination and ecstacy that follows immediately after the breakdown:

> The flowers and lights fused ecstatically in Wilhelm's blind, wet eyes; the heavy sea-like music came up to his ears. It poured into him where he had hidden himself in the center of a crowd by the great and happy oblivion of tears. He heard it and sank deeper than sorrow, through torn sobs and cries toward the consummation of his heart's ultimate need. (p. 118)

Almost all the words and images in this paragraph, freighted with accumulated meaning, flow in unison to produce a feeling of transcendence. The *flowers* speak of the world of nature to which Wilhelm will now return. The *lights* are not those of the illuminated screen in the brokerage office, but the light of true knowledge. The *sea-like music* that pours into Wilhelm signifies his acceptance of the natural processes of life and death, which Tamkin had likened to a giant wave. The word *ecstatically* amplifies the ecstasy that Tamkin's poem promised Wilhelm would feel when he became aware of man's essential greatness. The *crowd* within which Wilhelm hides himself is the larger body of disfigured and lurid-looking people in the subway under Times Square whom he had loved and blessed as his brothers and sisters.

The tears that flow out of Tommy Wilhelm fuse with the primordial cosmic energy suggested by the sea-like music that pours into him to produce a vast oceanic feeling of submergence and drowning. All day long Wilhelm has had the sensations of a man about to drown. Reich tells us that masochists "cling to the rigid armoring of their movements and attitudes as a drowning person clings to a board" (*DO*, p. 229). Wilhelm finally lets go and experiences the Reichian vision of man emerging from the ocean of being and eternally returning to it. The waters of the earth roll over him as he becomes aware of the fundamental unity of man and nature. As he sinks beyond sorrow,[19] his experience becomes almost religious. Words like *consummation, ecstatically, lights* and *oblivion* conspire with each other and, aided by the slow, deliberate, majestic rhythms of the whole paragraph, compel the reader to participate in Wilhelm's moment of *samadhi* and transcendence. At this moment Wilhelm is neither clown nor victim. For the strange and rather informal therapeutic process Bellow put together has affected and transformed this clown-victim so that he becomes "the visionary sort of animal" (p. 39) who now knows why he exists. A Reichian parable of hope for modern urban man, *Seize the Day* ends at the moment when the doors of perception fling open, and Wilhelm realizes his heart's ultimate need, a feeling of brotherhood and a love for all mankind.

Notes

1. Isaac Rosenfeld, *An Age of Enormity*, ed. Theodore Solotaroff, foreword by Saul Bellow (Cleveland: World Publishing Co., 1962), p. 14.

2. This article is a companion piece to my "Reichianism in *Henderson the Rain King*," *Criticism*, 15 (1973), 212–33.

3. In an interview (Chirantan Kulshrestha, "A Conversation with Saul Bellow," Vol. 23, No. 4 and Vol. 24, No. 1, 1972, pp. 12–13), Bellow states that *Seize the Day* is "victim literature, very much like *The Victim* itself."

4. Saul Bellow, *Seize the Day* (New York: Viking Press, Viking Compass Edition, 1961), p. 60. Hereafter, page numbers will be cited in the text.

5. For a Freudian analysis of Tommy Wilhelm as masochist, see Daniel Weiss, "Caliban on Prospero: A Psychoanalytic Study on the Novel *Seize the Day* by Saul Bellow," in *Saul Bellow and the Critics*, ed. Irving Malin (New York: New York Univ. Press, 1967), 114–41.

6. Originally published as an article in the *Internat. Zeitschr. f. Psychoanalyse*, 18 (1932). "The Masochistic Character" is Chapter XI of *Character Analysis*. The works of Wilhelm Reich

mentioned in the text are: *Selected Writings: An Introduction to Orgonomy* (New York: Farrar, Straus and Giroux, 1970), cited in the text as *SW; Character Analysis*, Third, enlarged edition (New York: Farrar, Straus and Giroux, 1971), cited as *CA; The Discovery of the Orgone: The Function of the Orgasm* (New York: Noonday Press, 1970), cited as *DO.*

7. In *Henderson* Bellow takes into account all seven armor segments.

8. References to Wilhelm's chest pains and congestion can be found on pp. 14, 36, 43, 46, 56, 76, 89, 104, 109, 114, 118.

9. The references to Wilhelm's panting laugh are on pp. 9, 18, 20, 41, 65, 87.

10. Wilhelm's eyes are mentioned on pp. 12, 15, 17, 25, 31, 37, 81.

11. For Tamkin as schnorrer see Sarah B. Cohen, *Saul Bellow's Enigmatic Laughter* (Urbana: Univ. of Illinois Press, 1974), pp. 103–04. For Tamkin as zaddik see Ralph Ciancio, "The Achievement of Saul Bellow's *Seize the Day,*" *Literature and Theology,* eds. Thomas F. Staley and Lester E. Zimmerman (Tulsa, Oklahoma, 1969), pp. 70–71. For Tamkin as shaman see Lee J. Richmond, "The Maladroit, the Medico, and the Magician: Saul Bellow's *Seize the Day,*" *Twentieth Century Literature,* 19 (1961), 21–24.

12. In the Author's Note to *The Last Analysis* (New York: Viking Press, Compass Books Edition, 1966) Bellow states: "*The Last Analysis* is not simply a spoof of Freudian psychology, though certain analysts have touchily interpreted it as such."

13. "Literature and Culture: An Interview with Saul Bellow," *Salmagundi* 30 (1975), 19.

14. Carol M. Sicherman, "Bellow's *Seize the Day:* Reverberations and Hollow Sounds," *Studies in the Twentieth Century,* 15 (1975), 18.

15. See Cohen, p. 112.

16. According to Bellow, Dr. Tamkin is the most interesting character in the novella, one whom "he wishes he had done more with." See Joseph Epstein, "Saul Bellow of Chicago," *New York Times Book Review,* May 9, 1971, p. 12.

17. The gag-reflex is described on p. 375 of *CA:* "The armoring of the *third* segment is found mainly in the deep neck musculature. . . . One has only to imitate the attitude of holding back anger or crying to understand the emotional function of the armoring of the neck. . . . The movements of the Adam's apple show clearly how an anger or crying impulse, without the patient's being aware of it, is literally "swallowed down." This mechanism of suppressing emotions is very difficult to handle therapeutically. *One cannot get with one's hands at the larynx muscles as one can with the superficial neck muscles.* The best means of interrupting this "swallowing" of emotions is the elicitation of the *gag-reflex.* With this reflex, the wave of excitation in the esophagus runs counter to that occurring in the "swallowing" of rage or crying. If the gag-reflex develops fully or the patient even reaches the point of actually vomiting, the emotions which are held back by neck armoring are liberated." (Italics mine.) 'It is clear that Bellow got the idea of Wilhelm's self-strangulation from this passage.

18. That the orgone accumulator looked like a telephone booth is mentioned in Charles Rycroft, *Wilhelm Reich* (New York: Viking Press, 1972), p. 84, and in Paul A. Robinson, *The Freudian Left* (New York: Harper Colophon Books, 1969), p. 73.

19. In the original version of *Seize the Day (Partisan Review,* 23, [1956]) the final sentence of the novella is significantly different: "He heard it and sank deeper than sorrow, *and by the way that can only be found through the midst of sorrow,* through torn sobs and cries, he found the secret consummation of his heart's ultimate need" (Italics mine). The words italicized, omitted in the final version, suggest that Bellow had in mind the need for Wilhelm to undergo genuine suffering before he could be redeemed.

Herzog: The Making of a Novel

Daniel Fuchs*

I

Herzog is a triumph of tone, and had to be. When an oblique plot is complicated by an intricate consciousness, when, indeed, plot in the broadest sense involves the uncomplication of that consciousness, the narrative voice(s) must give the illusion of absolute pitch. I say illusion because, perfect as the voice appears in the narrative, this was an illusion which had to be achieved. No book of Bellow's came harder than *Herzog*, none gives us more insight into the process of artistic metamorphosis. With characteristically anti-Flaubertian animus, Bellow has remarked that "the main reason for rewriting is not to achieve a smooth surface, but to discover the inner truth of your characters."[1] A case in point, *Herzog* illustrates how in achieving one the other inevitably follows. That anxious, fulminating yet jaunty and even comic beginning, already part of general literary consciousness, seems inevitable, but it was not always that way.

The book deals with purportedly autobiographical material yet the sense of original crisis had to be recaptured. The earliest draft of *Herzog* begins with a scene which would be unthinkable in the novel. We are introduced to a Dr. Amram Herzog, Professor of Physics, who, familiarly enough, "for the last few days . . . had fallen under a spell, which he did not resist, and was writing letters to everyone under the sun" (B.16.1).[2] We are told that "most of these letters couldn't be sent, but that didn't seem to matter, he wrote them anyway." We can not imagine the final Herzog mailing letters. And if the tone seems all too casual in comparison with the novel, the dramatic context is even more casual. Professor Herzog, slightly potted, goes for a midnight swim with an equally drunk Miss Thurnwald. Both are soon naked. She swims, Herzog "rolled in the shallows." Lost and confused, Herzog can find neither his clothes nor Miss Thurnwald. "Suppose they had his trousers hanging from the mantelpiece in the living-room and were waiting for nude Herzog to enter? Or suppose even they had found the letters in his pocket and were reading them aloud?" Clearly, Herzog's letters in the final version are not in the same realm as bedroom (or livingroom) farce—or not this kind of bedroom farce. They return to the house,

*This essay appears here for the first time and is published by permission of the author.

she naked from the waist up, everyone there thinking Herzog guilty. In this dramatically awkward circumstance, the recognizable Herzog emerges: "The Professor was not thinking about her at all. He was absorbed in a deeper passion than any Miss Thurnwald, with her green eye shadow and her wagging breasts could arouse in him. He was writing letters by the score" (B.16.1). In another version Herzog is rather more chivalrous: "It was up to him to spare her the bestiality of a drunken lay" (B.18.11,72). Miss Thurnward herself is, variously, someone who used to sing at the Village Vanguard (B.18.5), who complains about the job competition with young, rich Cliffies (B.18.12). Meanwhile Herzog thinks of his letters. The two strands are incongruous.

There is additional artistically aimless detail. We are informed that this houseguest never went anywhere without a kosher salami, stuck as he has too often been with stingy hearts; and that he loved his breakfast (together with an elaborate description of same). This visit to the Treshansky summer place (the Vane house in *Herzog*) is altogether too relaxed. We see Herzog and Treshansky, a bio-chemist turned businessman, play four-handed Hayden and Schubert. When we are told Herzog is going back to Chelsea, not as the Treshansky's believe because of Miss Thurnwald but because he wants to be alone to write the letters which bring him out of his depression, we ask, what depression? Though Bellow has the later tone in mind it is not here adequately dramatized. The building up of an inner tension is here mandated, and this the revisions work toward.

Significantly, the scientist—although "too mixed, too irregular to be a true scientist" (B.16.1)—becomes an intellectual in the later versions; the relative detachment of the early versions gives over to a more appropriately passionate, self-ironic tonality. Our scientist tells us, "If I'm out of my mind it's all right with me. . . ." The narrator adds, "But he knew that he was all right and that he was not out of his mind" (B.16.1). The novel does not give such immediate balance and assurance.

One version gives us the trip to Libby's in a plethora of realistic detail. There is no mental turmoil, the meditation about the post-Cartesian Void and politics in the Aristotelian sense (*H*, pp.92–94) virtually non-existent (B.18.5). Other versions give us other uncertainties. In one we are given an elaborate description of Libby in her "ripeness" (B.18.18). This is mostly dropped in *Herzog*, where the first signs of age—"Death, the artist, very slow, putting in his first touches" (*H*, p.95)—are emphasized. There is some confusion as to what significance to give Libby. In the novel she is a good friend whom Herzog has helped to defuse her marital difficulties, partly, it is suggested, because she was sensual and attracted to Herzog. One early version puts things rather more explicitly. Herzog somewhat randomly feels that he should have married Libby and "he would, if anything happened (to her husband, Sissler), ask her to be his wife" (B.18.11). When, in the novel, Herzog imagines Sissler dead, he notes cryptically, "*Ideas that depopulate the world*" (*H*,p.95). It is less cryptic when one considers the manuscript. But this involvement with Libby is scarcely felt even in the manuscript and the visit is consistently relaxed. In the novel, by contrast, it is not until considerable dramatization of enervated consciousness that the trip to his friends is taken. The visit itself is tense and abrupt, an anticlimax to the inner movement. In his enlarged psychological present, Herzog hasn't got an hour for Libby, let alone a lifetime.

There is a similar tightening in the back to Chelsea section which is re-worked from a more or less straightforward realism to a tense, subjective lyricism. Much detail for its own sake is cast aside: a reference to some window boxes, to Puerto Rican groceries, a super's wife, an undertaker's chauffeur, a lady with two chihuahuas. The smell of dishrag and bugspray in Herzog's apartment are eliminated as is a reference to Herzog being aroused by a "thin, sad" cash register girl or later licking his green stamps. Here, as in *Henderson*, the establishment of an intimate personal voice had to be dug for, like an oilstrike. Indeed, Chelsea is scarcely mentioned in the novel. Instead we have intensification of the psychological world. Herzog comes home to a homeo-pathic cure. Inuring himself to the catastrophe, he rereads Portnoy's letter as his heart smolders about Mady and Val. Repetition of this experience helps bring a sane balance.

The placing of the letter is itself a stroke worth noticing. Even late man-uscripts (e.g.B.22.1) place the letter after the courtroom scene and just before his trip to Chicago. The trials, however, seem to be enough of a blow to get Herzog to fly to save his daughter. The Portnoy letter—with Junie locked in the car by Val as he and Mady argue—would be only an unneeded addition to the already intense vapours. Cast in the earlier part of the book (in B.22.4,111a) it is quite sufficient to maintain that edge of constant tension, that strain hovering near the bursting point, so necessary to the beginning chapters as they finally appear. The tension is brought to a fine head indeed by the style of the letter and Herzog's reception of it (added in B.22.1, when the letter was moved), by the contrast between his personality and its impersonality, heartbreak and university jargon, disintegration and preternatural calm. Geraldine Portnoy's diction—"significant encounter", "pregnant experiences", "tends to be au-thoritarian", "basically", "actually"—does not succeed in smothering Herzog's resentment in cotton batting. Some minor changes—the last line, for example, from "I don't think Madeleine is actually a bad mother" to "I don't think Madeleine is a bad mother actually"—do her genteel fairness and confidence to a maddening fare-thee-well.

One of the devices used to establish the dissonant, fragmentary rhythm of the dramatized consciousness in the novel is the recasting of epigram. Anxiety about his carelessness and passivity may direct Herzog's subversions: "Waste not the road to hell a watched pot a fool and his money. The meek shall inherit the hearse" (B.20.20,92). The novel generally presents this wit with more point and more art, giving us a sort of fortune cookie for neurotics or people in trouble. Herzog notes that this game is akin to free association and that "a psychiatrist might have made something of them" (B.16.1). Or perhaps a novel-ist. One early version has Herzog returning to Chelsea and finding notes on a piece of paper in a drawer: "*Marry in haste, lie down with dogs. An old pot gathers remorse.*" These nuggets of womanly bitterness "were written in a feminine progressive-school (printed and written) hand." Herzog "picks up the game" in masculine counter-anguish: "*A bitch in time breeds contempt. . . . Hitch your agony to a star*" (B.16.4). The sexual distinctions dissolve in the novel and the game becomes more elaborate. A clap scare Herzog has in the early version seems too broad, too low for the dignified disintegration of the final comedy and it, too, is deleted. More appropriately, Herzog makes ironic use of even biblical authority to unscramble himself. "*Answer a fool according to his folly lest he be wise in his own conceit. Answer not a fool according to his folly, lest thou be likened unto him. Choose one,* (H,p.3) adds the professorial Herzog. Apparently random, these epigrams intimately relate to the movement and tone of the book. *Herzog* moves from an attitude of severe judgment, even revenge, to a tolerance, an acceptance based on an integration of cultural and personal attitudes. *Choose one* suggests the difficulty of the choice which is ultimately made in favor of the latter. "*Death—die—live again—die again—live*" (H,p.3), while having nothing comic about it, is another apparent fragment which actually describes the movement of the book, a movement from death to life, resolving, as it were, the irresolution of the Wasteland pattern. "*Grief, Sir, is a species of idleness,* thinks Herzog (H,p.3), attempting quick Johnsonian dismissal of the postmodernistic gloom. Yet the haze does not lift easily and seems strangely hallowed in the aura it emits.

A number of small verbal changes and minor dramatic development add to the opening oppressiveness. For example, Herzog's "overstrained nerves" are not as tense as the later "overstrained galloping nerves" (B.23.4,10a;H,p.27), nor is "the train" as good in this context as "the confining train" (B.23.6,10a;H,p.27). His clothing purchase is, in later versions, complicated by a near blowup with the salesman (B.22.3;H,p.21) and, on the subway platform at Grand Central Station he sees, in later versions (not in B.18.18 or B.19.14), the "soft face and independent look" of a woman whose eyes "were bitch eyes, that was certain. . . . They expressed a sort of female arrogance which had an immediate sexual power over him." (H,p.34) Here again is one of many instances contributing to an overriding tone. When Herzog writes to Smithers about an idea for a new course, he says that "*people are dying—it is no metaphor—for lack of something real to carry home when day is done. See how willing they are to accept wildest nonsense*" (H,p.28). The grimness of the cultural description is consonant with the accounting of Herzog's personal condition.

Herzog's first described encounter with the outside world, the visit to Zelda in March, reflects the same tendency. A middle version has Herzog filing an epistolary complaint about the usual slander: "*You shouldn't have repeated to Juliana what I said about her. And you shouldn't have told me what she was saying. . . . Thanks to her my reputation in Chicago is near absolute zero. That I'm a wild beast, that I'm an idiot, impotent, insane. What can I say? What can I prove? Shall I carry affidavits from women?*" (B.18.8,38). Things are tense here but there is some sense of comic recovery. The more piercing version of the letter to Zelda is a later inclusion (not in B.18.18): "*As long as I was*

Mady's good friend, I was a delightful person. Suddenly, because Madeleine decided that she wanted out—suddenly, I was a mad dog. The police were warned about me and there was talk of committing me to an institution. I know that my friend and Mady's lawyer, Sandor Himmelstein, called Dr. Edvig to ask whether I was crazy enough to be put in Manteno or Elgin" (*H*,p.35). This is not a reaction to the usual slander but to the threat of enforced incarceration. Hysteria takes the place of the earlier semblance of balance. And Zelda is not merely a witness but an accomplice: *"You took Madeleine's word as to my mental condition and so did others. . . . But you knew what she was up to . . . and I know now that you helped your niece by having Herman take me away to the hockey game"* (*H*,p.35). If Herzog is paranoid here, he is a paranoid with enemies. His contempt for Zelda extends to a kind of physical disgust. Her dyed hair and purplish lids make Herzog exclaim, "Oh! . . . the things women apply to their own flesh. And we must go along, must look, listen, heed, breathe in" (*H*,p.35). Moreover, there is a cultural disgust: To Zelda's I'm-not-just-another-suburban-hausfrau appearance, Herzog responds, "Your kitchen is different . . . your cerebral palsy cannisters are different" (*H*,p.38). Betrayed, Herzog reflects that Zelda *"had a tremendous pleasure, double excitement, lying from an overflowing heart"* (*H*,p.38). The train at this point takes Herzog through a particularly depressing stretch, "Spanish Harlem, heavy, dark, and hot, and Queens far off to the right, a thick document of brick, veiled in atmospheric dirt" (*H*,p.41). In this darkness, Herzog rises to a brilliant bitterness: *"Will never understand what women want. What do they want? They eat green salad and drink human blood"* (*H*,p.41f.). The placement of this paraphrased Freudian epigram about the nature of woman shows us something about the nature of composition. In an early version we see Herzog imagining himself lecturing to students. He says in a Memo to Whittaker, "Listen, my dear boys, they are all the same of course, but they are considered weak and have the ethics of the weak." Herzog reflects on "the tendency of the social order to protect the weak. Their occasion for strength comes and then— watch out. (Wilhelm had a similar insight.) Their ambling, their lisping. In the restaurant they order green salad, but how often at home they drink human blood. . . . As usual he recoiled from his own excesses. Kindness he had known from women came rapidly to his mind" (B.16.1). A necessary addition, this last turn, but tenderness is not what is dramatically wanted. To be sure, the novel in the long view does make just this meliorative point—makes it again and again—but good will does not possess him at this stage of his tale.

In the much recast first chapters the most important device to emerge in revision is the letters, though they do not appear in this part of the novel first. Even in a fairly late draft (B.19.) there is nothing of the well known letter to Dr. Edvig. Almost everything is in dialogue. The new device helps to establish the effect of intense subjectivity, a counterpoint to the retrospective objectivity he tries to maintain. So, the relative calm of an earlier version of an Edvig session is broken by, *"you turn out to be a crook too! . . . I was near the point of breakdown"* (*H*,p.53). And the letter's cultural argument, the defense of charity, for example, against psychoanalytic and Calvinist reductiveness, is a dramatic ordering of hitherto not quite dramatized insights. In all, the scalding, accusatory tone, so appropriate to the essential grimness of the opening, is heightened by epistolary elaboration. The second and third chapters, then, end on a particularly intense psychological note (the Edvig letter, the Portnoy letter and Herzog's reaction to it). The letter to Edvig soars into an empyrean of staccato hysteria: "*You knew nothing. You know nothing. She snowed you completely. And you fell in love with her yourself, didn't you? Just as she planned. She wanted you to help her dump me. She would have done it in any case. She found you, however, a useful instrument. As for me, I was your patient*" (*H*,p.65). It is instructive to compare this rhythmic crescendo to an earlier, flat version of it. Herzog thinks of Edvig on the way to the courtroom (the first placement of these observations!): "I am out Juliana (Mady) is in. She remained your patient. I left town. It bothered me a lot" (B.17.5). As a character Edvig is perfect for the beginning. Not only is he part of the dupery of the divorce but, as we shall see, he represents a version of that modernistic outlook which, along with the divorce, is the other major cause of Herzog's gloom. How different is the tonality here from that of the note he writes Edvig after the murder scene: "*Dear Edvig. . . . You gave me good value for my money when you explained that neuroses might be graded by the inability to tolerate ambiguous situations. . . . Allow me modestly to claim that I am much better now at ambiguities*" (*H*,p.304).

We are here a long way from the accusation that Edvig fell in love with Mady himself. But the first chapters typically call for the exposition of mean motives. Sandor Himmelstein is another instance of the modern reductiveness. Herzog sees that Sandor's underlying assumption is that "you must sacrifice your poor, squawking, niggardly individuality—which may be nothing anyway (from an analytic viewpoint) but a persistent infantile megalomania, or (from a Marxian point of view) a stinking little bourgeois property—to historical necessity. And to truth. And truth is true only as it brings down more disgrace and dreariness upon human beings, so that if it shows anything except evil it is illusion, and not truth" (*H*,p.93). The earliest version of the Himmelstein scene contains none of this retrospective meditation on his significance, no letters, no place in that downer series of flashbacks which propels him to Libby's and back. It is unrelated to the trip to the Vineyard, taking place after not during the trip. In a scene between Brown (Herzog) and Raskin (Himmelstein) we are given a good deal of dialogue and much detail for its own sake. We see Raskin's ashtray with shards of cut tobacco, his foot in a neat leather loafer. As part of this kind of detail, Raskin (called Rubenstein a bit later) regales Herzog with divorce stories, such as the one about the widow who was making it with a young Italian sailor while her husband's coffin was below in the ship's hold. This seems to be Mintouchian country. In one version we are told that Rubenstein "doesn't recognize any such thing as adultery" (B.21.9,247) though Val was sleeping with his wife. Rubenstein's cynicism ought not to be so blatant, however, and Val must be saved for better things. In the novel Himmelstein

(Rubenstein) acts as if the world assumes what he assumes, as if Herzog has no recourse in justice and is naive to even think of a custody fight. The discussion of custody does take place even in the earliest version of the scene between them, yet much of the vividness in the dialogue (e.g. the description of Mady at Fritzl's), the bristling give and take (e.g. "Do you know what mass man is Himmelstein"? [H,p.86]) comes later. After seeing Raskin, Brown goes home where he is still with his child and puts in the storm windows. He appears to be a little late. Mady here is called Lola, because, perhaps, as the popular song of the time had it, whatever she wants she gets. Once upon a time, Brown was the little man little Lola wanted. The final version, then, casts the whole Himmelstein incident more clearly into Herzog's dramatized consciousness as part of his homeopathic cure.

The counterbalance, making positive sense of the experience, comes in later versions with some of the most quoted formulations coming last. Herzog's yearning for recovery into citizen heroism is well known: "The occupation of man is in duty, in use, in civility, in politics in the Aristotelian sense" (H,p.94). Nowhere in the earliest version, it appears in a later version as, "Tell me, Herzog, where is life real? Perhaps in use? In common (sic). In duty. In civility and patience" (B.16.10). In a still later version (B.22.4,106b) we get everything but "in politics in the Aristotelian sense"; finally, we get it all (B.23.4). Many of the idea letters follow a similar pattern of development. In their combativeness and insight they show us that Herzog is still very much alive and that intellect has its own emotional weight and can be instrumental is dispelling the personal gloom.

The letter to Shapiro is a case in point. A somewhat affected intellectual, Shapiro serves to elicit Herzog's contempt for culture without direction, mind without heart, a contempt which covers Mady by extension. Shapiro, out-WASPing the WASPS, says things like "join issue" and "I should not venture to assay the merit of the tendency without more mature consideration." He exhibits a cohabitation with gentility which Herzog finds ludicrous. If this sequence seems to be too much a matter of settling old scores, we recall that Herzog is described as merely sulking. In any case, he evens the score in the main part of the letter. Though one of the most important letters in the novel, the bulk of this part (H,pp.74–77) is a late inclusion (not appearing until B.22.3,87a,b,c). Here, in other words, we see that Herzog's intellectual formulations, so crucial to the fabric of the book, came rather late. Nor is this letter an exception. The greater part of the major idea-letters are late inclusions, which means that many of the most substantial parts of the book were conceived only after it had taken fairly definitive dramatic shape. This is not a question of aesthetic pattern. It is a question of a writer making definitive sense of his own experience. The very earliest versions, then, show no letter material; next come the letters of primarily personal grievance (e.g. Edvig) and, finally, the idea-letters (along with a heightening of the idea element in the straight dramatic parts). As in *Henderson*, the novel was not so much "found" as created. Herzog's most characteristic accent, his truest beseeching voice, was not at all present in the beginning, was not really present, one could argue, until near the end. There is no clearer illustration of Bellow's view that the function of writing is not the polished surface but the truth of your characters. In *Herzog,* as elsewhere in Bellow, the inner truth may be a mental truth, yet it is a mental truth and emotional truth at once. One's life is indistinguishable from one's perceptions. Bellow excels at dramatizing this integration, and the epistolary form enables him to do so with unexampled brilliance. It is, in point of polemic, not only the solution to a book, but to much of a lifetime of literary effort.

The letters are not only central to the book but central to Bellow's career. The argument against *"the full crisis of dissolution, . . . the filthy moment . . . when moral feeling dies, conscience disintegrates, and respect for liberty, law, public decency, all the rest, collapses in cowardice, decadence, blood"* (*H*,p.74) is *the* argument in Bellow's arsenal. It is the "axial lines" feeling made cultural, and, therefore, intrinsically dramatic in the thick of the constant polemicism of the present. The cast is familiar. Spengler, Eliot, Pound, Wyndham Lewis, Ortega (the Wasteland outlook), Sartre and Heidegger (Alienation, Inauthenticity, Forlornness), Burckhardt, Nietzsche (a merely aesthetic critique of modern history), the orthodoxy of modernism which often issued into cultural fascism and even political fascism. Herzog sees this clearly: *"To have assumed, for instance, that the deterioration of language and its debasement was tantamount to dehumanization led straight to cultural fascism."* Here, as elsewhere, Herzog rejects the dehumanization of ordinary life (though he seems to leave unchallenged the idea of the deterioration of language). The letter is "positive," a ray of light in the modernist gloom, a prediction of Herzog's recovery. This gloom within the gloom itself contributes to Herzog's psychological tension, but at one point well on into the composition of the novel, Bellow seems to have seen a clear connection between Herzog's life and the cultural predicament, one which resolves itself in the "murder" scene. His rejection of the Wasteland outlook permits him to endure his enemies while he saves his soul. His personal recovery goes hand and hand with his cultural assault. The novel takes this shape as it is being written.

The original letter to Shapiro (B.18.17), very brief, is a casual allusion to Herzog's review, which goes immediately to Herzog's being impressed with the connection between millenarianism and paranoia. The tone is polite. The nightmare edge is yet to come. Herzog does suffer a sense of loss and mentions Juliana (Mady) to him so that "you'll know how great my loss is." There is none of this friendliness, this gentility, in the final version. Although the traits of paranoia are described, clearly Mady's traits, Herzog harbors little resentment for Shapiro, even though he sounds like "The Decline and Fall of the Roman Empire" (B.18.17,21). With Shapiro, he "wanted to forgive and be forgiven, not to win." The novel, of course, despite some contrition about his inadequate review of Shapiro's book, gives us a full scale assault. Many small changes show this. "Shapiro was not good-humored although his face wore a good-humored look," is added later, and "His nose was sharp and angry" even later (not in B.18.11). "Natty but dignified" (B.18.17) becomes "He had a dumpy figure, but wore natty clothes" (*H*,p.69). Shapiro's tight, conservative necktie on that hot day is an addition, as is "That snarling, wild laugh of his, and the white froth foaming on his lips as he attacked everyone" (*H*,p.70). The sentences, no longer merely Gibbonesque, are "actually Germanic, and filled with incredible bombast" (*H*,p.70). The learned conversation" is elaborated into a comic catalogue of learned reference. Shapiro as *parvenu*, but not really as rich as his apple-peddling father, is added. When Shapiro declines the pickled herring (B.18.17) he says, "No, thanks. Delightful. But I have an ulcer." In *Herzog*, Shapiro calls it a "stomach condition" (*H*,p.73), to which Herzog adds, "He had ulcers. Vanity kept him from saying it; the psychosomatic implications were unflattering." There are comic bits to ease the tension—the weight of Shapiro's study, the fear of a hernia from it, the overweight charges, all late inclusions—but the sequence seems peculiarly unrelieved. It seems that the deracination, not to say phoneyness, which may be involved in the process of high acculturation oppresses him to an extreme. When Herzog says, "Culture—ideas—had taken the place of the Church in Mady's heart (a strange organ that must be!)," he means, presumably,[3] that Mady assumes attitudes as if they were garments, as does Shapiro, as does Val. And if one is wearing culture one will wear what is fashionable. Consequently, one will carry the Wasteland view. Hence, Herzog's attack on Shapiro's attitudinizing in the subsequently developed letter. The letter, then, like everything else considered so far, contributes to that down-to-the-bone agonizing which is at once the truest expression and final dramatic effect of Herzog's first day.

Focusing on the problem of nuclear contamination, the letter to Strawforth is a typical day-one transformation. Combining a grim theme with irrepressible flashes of humor (e.g. Dr. Teller's argument that the new fashion of tight pants, by raising body temperatures, could affect the gonads more than fallout), the somberness is again intensified in the revision to include the use of words like "contamination" and "poisoning," a place like Hiroshima, and a negative prophecy of Tocqueville's darkly interpreted (all revisions occurring in B.22.3). The Tocqueville inclusion is, to be sure, part of the general intellectual heightening, but Herzog's treatment of it is more than that. To Tocqueville's prediction that democracies would produce less crime, more private vice, Herzog adds that he might have said *"less private crime, more collective crime,"* implicating thereby the nuclear philosophy of risk. Without explicitly accusing, Herzog seems overcome by darkness: *"DeTocqueville considered the impulse toward well-being as one of the strongest impulses of a democratic society. He can't be blamed for underestimating the destructive powers generated by the same impulse"* (*H*,p.50). An even later inclusion is tonally more emphatic: "While in the parlors of indignation the right-thinking citizen brings his heart to a boil" (B.23.4,18).

After the doldrums of day one, other letters reflect a similar movement but are somewhat different tonally. The letter to Eisenhower is a case in point. Herzog's early manuscript thoughts about Eisenhower display a certain confidence. "The leader of huge armies, chief of state for eight years, can't be a fool, must have tremendous powers. Must" (B.18.18,128), notes Herzog long-ingly. But he also notes that "the mutual estrangement of public and private ends" is not dealt with by the report of the Committee on National Aims. The revision of this letter contains great skepticism as to the corporate executive makeup of this committee and greater skepticism about trying to communicate with Eisenhower altogether, a man who "hates long, complicated documents", who would "pay no attention" (*H*,p.161f) to Herzog's complex, moralistic ap-proach to civil order. The letter to Eisenhower moves from the theme of dimi-nution of selfhood in the Gross National Product to the expanded time industry has brought to private life. This private life, however, competing with technol-ogy and other quantitative measures and threats, is driven into "the inspired condition" to assert the reality of self. The ideational considerations here be-come too refined and original, and the second, newer half of the letter becomes the letter to Pulver. Thus, a further measure of Herzog's disenchantment is written into the book. Yet the letters in this part of the novel—after day one, before the murder scene—though still embattled, are not personally grim, are less strident tonally, more balanced, more positive intellectually. The letter to Pulver is one of the most important idea letters and this may be why Bellow saw fit, at first, to address it to President Ike. However, it is also one of the most subtle and such confidence was short-lived. The letter is in none of the early versions, first appearing in B.20.32. By B.22.2, it is essentially complete, except that the end, where Eisenhower is addressed, is crossed out. Herzog speaks to the vogue of negative transcendence, which includes, without his naming it, the new authority of the Marquis de Sade, as in Mailer's appropriation of romantic criminality in such works as "The White Negro" and *An American Dream* in which last there is a modern misuse of Dostoevsky. We have seen that a central thrust of Bellow's fiction is against " '*philosophical,*' '*gratuitous*' *crime and similar paths of horror*" (*H*,p.164). As he adds (B.22.4,191b) in a final tighten-ing, "*It never seems to occur to such 'criminals' that to behave with decency to another human being might also be 'gratuitous.' *" Such crime is the dead-end Romantic reaction to the threat of a quantified universe, a threat which Herzog feels as well; but he prefers to see himself as an instance of this "age of social comedy" (*H*,p.163), in which moral insight turns ironically in on itself. "*Good is easily done by machines of production and transportation. Can virtue compete?*" (*H*,p.164) It can and it can not, but we need not agree with Hof-mannsthal that a word like virtue can no longer be used. For Herzog, virtue exists. So does reason. He notes that in an age in which annihilation is no longer a metaphor, "*Good and Evil are real. The inspired condition is no longer a visionary matter. It is not reserved for gods, kings, poets, priests, shrines, but belongs to mankind and all of existence*" (*H*,p.165). To the Hulmian contempt for the present ("*we have fashioned a new utopian history, an idyll, comparing the present to an imaginary past, because we hate the world as it is*"), Herzog posits a vaguely Bergsonian "*evolutionary self-development . . . the discovery of qualities*" (*H*,p.163f.), which would transcend the special comedy. And in a very late revision (B.23.4,61), speaks as optimistically as an essentialist can: "*I* *am certain that there are human qualities still to be discovered"* (*H*,p.164). The Pulver letter is no lark, but it has a balanced, upbeat content and is not modified by personal bitterness. Herzog has been recalled to stability. This is attributable to Herzog's homeopathic, epistolary cure.

II

Herzog's regard for human qualities appears as well in his letter to Monsignor Hilton, whom he addresses seriously, as between one rabbinical temperament and another. Most of the letter does not appear until the manuscript is faily well on (B.20.8), which is in line with its idea tenor. Coming even later are some of the interconnected narrative sections, which contain a considerable elaboration of Mady's religious appearance, theatrical Catholicism (hence the special appeal of Monsignor Hilton), and neurotic quirks (e.g. her "voice rose sharply . . . some string had tightened and twisted in her breast, and her figure grew rigid. Her fingertips whitened as she pressed the edge of the table and glared at him, her lips thinning and the color darkening under the tubercular pallor of her makeup" (*H*,p.116)). The ideational core of the letter is something that a clergyman would easily understand, affirming as it does the ultimate inseparability of fact and value. Again he assaults the modernist mind through an attack on existential assumptions, *"what Heidegger calls the second Fall of Man into the quotidian or ordinary. No philosopher knows what the ordinary is, has not fallen into it deeply enough"* (*H*,p.106). In so saying, Herzog affirms the American faith in the ordinary, one which in different ways inspired the classic American writers Bellow feels close to—Whitman, Mark Twain and Dreiser.

As the culture weary Herzog laments, if Mady brought ideology into Herzog's life, Val (his first name, Valentine, speaks for itself; his second, originally Grenzabach—border brook—made some sense, now—Gersbach—it just sounds bad) brings it into everyone's, in a Dostoevskean sense. Herzog tells us that "as soon as he slams the door of his Continental he begins to talk like Karl Marx" (*H*,p.217, inserted B.22.5,256). This is the sort of satiric intellectual tightening which so often comes in late revision. Val is making what his parents would call a Golden Living blasting the affluent society. Much of the satiric heightening through Hebrew reference comes at about the middle of the revisions. Hence, Gersbach "lecturing at the Hadassah on Martin Buber", his prophetic eye like that of "a judge of Israel" (*H*,p.58f not in B.19.43) is not in early versions. Spouting "I and Thou," he sets his best friend up in a career of cuckoldry, more saintly than his victim since his suffering is greater. "Perhaps the worst part of this was the absence of hypocrisy," quips Herzog, as early as B.16.5. "Grenzbach is not Tartuffe. Tartuffe knew what he was doing." What is most damaging in Val is his weightlessness, a moral posturing without moral meaning. Bellow does not forget that moral weightlessness can support physical vitality, and many of Val's vital mannerisms—his pounding the table, dancing, stumping with the bride—are added late (B.22.4,119). His hair change, from "blue-black" to "flaming copper," comes early (B.16.6) and carries a similar significance. As for the wooden leg, Bellow shows that stock comic devices can be put to contemporary use.

Romona too is ideological, but she has a body so fine that no idea can violate it. Romona (her name, in an occasional early version Rosette, is reminiscent of the old, sweet love song) consoles, but hers are not the consolations of philosophy. Even in early versions Herzog worries that "Romona will take me over from sheer weakness" (B.8.12,11). Her Sag Harbour retreat is metaphor as well as geography, subliminal as well as on the map. Essentially "right" from the beginning, Romona picks up some attributes in the composition. In an early version Herzog says that he met a Sybil Weber at a lantern party at the Wadsworth Square mews. She walked with "some impudent swagger as if she had a dagger in her garter belt" (B.19.35,131), a quality later attributed to Romona in the boudoir. And in another early version it is Juliana (Mady) who "cooked shrimps (sic) and almonds" (B.18.18,159). It seems appropriate to associate Romona with all sensuous gratification, and Mady with none as far as Herzog is concerned. The dish itself undergoes a culinary metamorphosis from shrimp with almonds to shrimp with lemon sauce (B.20.40) to shrimp Arnaud. In one early version, Romona's kiss—Romona near her Garden of Eden—gives him a "taste of Eternal Sabbath" (B.17.6). But this is not quite the metaphor for Romona, any more than her *specialité* would be *gefülte* fish. Non-kosher, shrimp has the advantages of the forbidden. With Romona too, a final intellectual tightening—reference to Brown, Marcuse—is saved for late revisions (B.22.5,245). Beyond this specificity, her "meaning" is underscored in later versions. Her voice is a call to pleasure, "not simple pleasure but metaphysical, transcendent pleasure—pleasure which answered the riddle of human existence" (*H*,p.150). The summary statement rising to epigram comes in later revision: "Romona had passed through the hell of profligacy and attained the seriousness of pleasure. For when will we civilized beings become really serious? said Kierkegaard. Only when we have known hell through and through" (None of this in late B.20.20). This is a far more culturally elegant fate than the earlier, she "had been sleeping with everyone, a human turnstile" (B.20.40,188). Sic Transit Authority gloria mundi. In the revisions, Romona is given insight along with learning. "Unless you're having a bad time with a woman you can't be serious," she says (*H*,p.157,B.23.4,58). Herzog has, overall, an adequate reply to this but the idea lingers.

Sono can raise no such questions and therein, doubtless, lies her charm. Scrubbing Herzog down in the warm tub, she is everyman's return to the womb of the Orient. Pliant, secondary, amenable, "if he were a communist she would be one too," says an early draft (B.18.12,83). All this is very fine, thinks Herzog, but, alas, "I had to have a woman I could talk to" (B.18.12,84). Not a bad idea for a professor. Yet Sono is in her way faultless.[4] Curiously bringing to mind Romona's criticism of him, Herzog writes, "*To tell the truth, I never had it so good. But I lacked the strength of character to bear such joy*" (*H*,p.169). The last word is, however, his. As in Melville's *Typee* there is a Western resistance to uncomplication, stemming perhaps from the biblical—Herzog is Jewish here—idea that moral struggle is more real than pleasure. "When a man's breast feels like a cage from which all dark birds have flown—he is free, he is light. And he longs to have his vultures back again. He wants his customary struggles, his nameless, empty works, his anger, his afflictions and his sins" (H,p.169). So long as it has meaning, Herzog, in the Judeo-Christian tradition, is in love with his own suffering. Yet Sono was indeed right about Mady and there is a distinction between valuing your suffering and pursuing it. Is this last unAmerican? There is no Constitutional guarantee for "Life, Liberty and the Pursuit of Suffering." Is this yet another instance of the internationalization of American culture?[5]

What seems most disturbing to him about his relationship to Daisy, fast fading flower, was the meaninglessness of the suffering it entailed. In an early version he argues with his first wife about how suffering is not true but a vice when it just keeps coming with "no wisdom, no profit." Hospitalized with pneumonia (in Princeton), Herzog enlarges on his feeling by parodying Shelley: "I fall upon the thorns of life, I bleed. And then? The same. I fall upon the thorns of life, I bleed again. I learn nothing" (B.18.10,82). Herzog then explodes, rejecting Daisy's mothering and offer of home. He does not have the feeling of being alive with her, yet in one version he writes in a letter to Daisy, "I broke off and escaped, vengeance pursuing, and nearly died of guilt" (B.20.24,210). Such guilt is effectively expunged from the novel where he has overcome the trauma of separation. Herzog surely does have the feeling of being alive with Romona, but is aware of the Shelley syndrome there too. Kissing Romona goodbye at her Bower of Bliss or Garden of Eden on Lexington Avenue, "he had a taste of the life he might have led if he had been simply a loving creature." But the "inescapable Moses Elkanah Herzog" soon thinks, "I fall upon the thorns of life, I bleed. And then? I fall upon the thorns of life, I bleed. And what next? I get laid, I take a short holiday, but very soon after I fall upon those same thorns with gratification in pain, or suffering in joy—who knows what the mixture is! What good, what lasting good is there in me?" (H,p.206f.) Like the underground man, Herzog lives on terms of uneasy, masochistic coexistence with his own demanding consciousness. Like him, he will not forego this one "most advantageous advantage"[6] for anything. "Consciousness", say the underground man, "is the greatest misfortune for man, yet I know man loves it and would not give it up for any satisfaction."[7] Though bearing the weight of an hypertrophy of consciousness, he can paradoxically say, "I have more life in me than you" because of it. He has individuality, authenticity. Like the underground man who feels a miserable moral lack—"they won't let me, I can't be good"—Herzog yearns for a personal incarnation of the good. Unlike the underground man, he has the psychological and moral wherewithal to break out of solipsism. And unlike the underground man, who has failed in love and been stationary for sixteen years, he feels that he can move and act: "And what about all the good I have in my heart . . . this good is no phony. . . . He felt he must do something, something practical and useful and must do it at once" (H,p.207).

III

The dramatic center of the novel is the attempted "murder" with its prefatory courtroom scene. Dropping an elaborate description of Herzog's ablutions and breakfast and talk about the inflated art market, Bellow has the scenes come abruptly after Herzog's talk with lawyer Simkin. Truth comes in blows, says Bellow's Henderson, uttering a truth which extends well beyond the limits of that particular book. The courtroom scene shows us in the mad queen a more likely descendant of the underground man; he "was purer, loftier than any square, did not lie" (*H*,p.229). His flaunting manner illustrates, in the abstract language of the last revisions, "nastiness in the transcendent position" (*H*,p.229,B.23.4,84). What Herzog sees in the courtroom shatters his moral composure. He thinks of the old song, "There's flies on me, there's flies on you, but there ain't no flies on Jesus." Yet his Victorian upbringing and its acculturated moralism seem hollow, self-congratulatory. This was not always the case. In an early version the letter to Edvig appears as part of the courtroom sequence with Herzog saying that he happens "to be clear for the time from accusations though having many of the sores . . . of the soul as some of those locked in cells. . . . I've been too clever to be caught." In its problematic insularity this last phrase recalls Asa Leventhal's "I was lucky. I got away with it," from *The Victim*. This is a composure of sorts, capped by a desire for "the final radiance of final love" and blessed by the famous lines from Blake's "The Black Boy": "For we are placed on earth a little while to learn to bear the beams of love" (B.17.5). This impulse is in contradistinction to "the swindles of desire" Herzog wants to rid himself of. He is in control here as he is not in the final Edvig letter. And this is very far from his distraught reaction in the courtroom scene as it appears in the novel and the later versions. He will go to Chicago, pick up his father's gun, save his child, murder Val and Mady and so be it. But even in early versions this solution is questioned: "So he was flying to his daughter, taking the drug of action. For it was a drug—he knew that. . . . He knew very well, yes, very clearly that June was not being harmed in any direct manner and that . . . he could not really explain why he had come" (B.17.8). Then he reads the Geraldine Portnoy letter (with its description of June in the car), originally placed here, leaving us with an equivocal "whatever he was going to consider, he would consider on the plane." Other early versions indicate Herzog's skepticism in intellectual terms: "I wonder what I was doing rushing here. Impulsiveness, immaturity, morbidity, wastefulness, foolishness that looks like generosity, all that schlemiel nonsense that people take to be the struggle for freedom against bureaucracy-organization, power development. This 'radical innocence' in which I don't believe for one moment and is simply a sign of laziness and limited intellect" (B.17.7). The allusion is to Ihab Hassan's study, which follows perhaps uncritically the alienation line, with its hipster, criminal and ashcan heroes.[8] Bellow, as we have seen, has little use for this typology. He refines his criticism in a later version, this time in the police station scene: "I wonder . . . what the gun did signify today. . . . Perhaps it was the schlemiel in me that chose this symbol—the radical innocence that looks for disasters and then must obviously be relieved of its responsibilities, the pure heart of burlap, the child-man. But this must stop" (B.21.40,340). Radical innocence is another expression of the fag-end Romanticism Herzog attacks in some of the letters. Another version of about this time counters this immoralism with his own more traditional roots. Thinking of Junie in the car, he wants to kill Gersbach: "But being a civilized man, more or less Jewish, he limited his act to fantasy or imagination and took legal measures instead" (B.21.9,249). This brings to mind a remark of Father Herzog's pertaining to his hijackers: "I knew they wouldn't kill me. They were Jews" (B.19.36,192). In his refusal to give the physical blow, Herzog is his father's son. "Can you shoot a man?" asks Pappa's clever sister. "Could you even hit someone on the head?" (H,p.145). Herzog recalls this soon after he foregoes his own murderous impulse (H,p.258). Yet another earlier version is a preface to withdrawal: "People who do evil are coming to think that they are more authentic and truthful. . . . First I want to find out what they are doing with my daughter. Juliana has a right to prefer Valentine to me. There's nothing criminal about it. But June—a little girl brought up by vulgar liars or even psychopaths" (B.17.17). This is a somewhat confused version of his feeling in the novel, though it continues in a very elevated vein: " 'Though with high wrongs, stuck to the quick,' as Prospero says, 'yet with my nobler reason gainst my fury Do I take part. The rarer action is in virtue than in vengeance.' Once committed to the grand project of being, in that special and distinguished sense, human, a man is left with no alternative" (B.17.17). Okay, but better the ironic comedy of the novel than such high seriousness. Low seriousness is what Bellow is after. In the new comedy a sense of humor is the better part of salvation and this involves seeing yourself as well as your enemies in proportion.

The novel itself undercuts the element of suspense. We are given preliminary indications of how things will turn out. Writing to Zelda, who had feared for the life of Mady and Val, Herzog says, *I'm no criminal, don't have it in me*" (H,p.41). This proves to be true. Even in his most despairing moments, Herzog says, "if, even in that embrace of lust and treason, they had life and nature on their side, he would quietly step aside. Yes, he would bow out" (H,p.52). In the end, Mady is associated with murder more definitely than Herzog. Herzog thinks of "the terrifying menstrual ice of her rages, the look of the murderess" (H,p.63). And when she views him in the police station, her look was made to kill. It "expressed a total will that he should die" (H,p.301). But the will is not the act and there will be no murder in this novel. So centered in consciousness, even potentially physical explosions are absorbed by it. Radical innocence could not be much more than an elaborate joke in a novel critical of negative transcendence. Herzog, it turns out, is as good as his convictions. The murder scene itself has little but minor verbal revision (e.g. "kill" becomes "shoot or choke" (H,p.255,B.23.4,58). It was "right" from the start.

That this is the psychological crux of the book is born out by the instantaneous release Herzog feels. *The human soul is an amphibian and I have touched its sides*" (H,p.257f.). As this figure, borrowed, perhaps unconsciously, from Nietzsche ("Nietzsche Contra Wagner," *Viking Portable Nietzsche*, p. 663), indicates, Herzog's resiliency has passed the test: "how good it felt to breathe!" (*H*,p.258), better than chest pains. Now, even the masses have no trouble taking flight. "*Think!*" writes Herzog, having not given up on that activity. "*Demographers estimate that at least half of all the human beings ever born are alive now, in this century. What a moment for the human soul!*" (*H*,p.258) Maybe this flight takes us into an empyrean, but the psychological point is clear enough. The weight of numbers which had oppressed now releases. It is now Herzog's turn to comfort the sick. This he does in the mock-*liebestodt* of Lucas Asphalter and his chimpanzee. Yes, *le coeur a ses raisons*. The scene is a *reductio ad absurdum* of reactive depression.[9] Asphalter, as his name suggests, shows that you don't have to be a Romantic poet to be severely depressed. You can be a Romantic scientist, as interesting macadam. In this scene, Herzog is healthy enough to laugh at heartsickness. "It's one of those painful emotional comedies," says Herzog, perfectly summarizing the meaning in a phrase not present in early versions (B.17.8). He might almost as well be talking about his own love life. The Asphalter scene provides us with a comic analogy to another aspect of the action, this time ideational. It is a parody of existentialism as dread and death philosophy, as modernist orthodoxy. This parody is a late inclusion. In one late version, Luke does "nudity" exercises to overcome his mind-body dualism (B.22.5,318); these become exercises in "facing your own death" (B.23.4). "Face death. That's Heidegger," says Herzog (*H*,p.270,B.23.4,99). Ironically, what Luke sees in this exercise is life in all its bulging sensuousness—his fat-assed old aunt saved from a fire, or big burlesque broads playing softball. The lengthy attack on the existentialists with which the chapter concludes—"God is no more. But Death is. That's their story."—does not appear until late (*H*,p.271–273, mostly not in B.22.6). To this philosophy of anguish, Herzog prefers an older wisdom. He quotes Blake to make his point: "I really believe that brotherhood is what makes a man human. If I owe God a human life, this is where I fall down. 'Man liveth not by self alone but in his brother's face. . . . Each shall behold the Eternal Father and love and joy abound.' "[10] Despite the awareness of his own shortcomings, the line between potato love and this assertion is a fine one. And Herzog's previously expressed skepticism on the subject indicates that the assertion is authentic only as a polarity of exhilaration. More convincing is the social expression of brotherhood with which he concludes: "The real and essential question is one of our employment by other human beings and their employment by us" (*H*,p.272) Herzog's exuberance is one of a number of indications that his depression is over and carries enough authenticity with it so as to establish a psychological balance, if not buoyancy, in the remaining part of the book.

If we look, for example, at the two most important letters of this section—those to Mermelstein and Nietzsche—we see familiar thematic material considered now with little apparent pain. In a recent study, Professor Mermelstein has stolen Herzog's thunder, but Herzog is above any deep professional envy, insulated in part by his newly found self-satisfaction. More than this, he is not personally disturbed where he may well have cause to be. There is a contrast here with the animal contempt he felt early in the novel for Shapiro and to some extent still feels. The substance of the Mermelstein letter, a defense of *"those of us who remain loyal to civilization"*—there is an almost corporate confidence now expressed in the plural—in the face of *"people playing at crisis, aliena-tion, apocalypse and desperation"* (H,p.316f), is not new, except for the refer-ence to Kierkegaard. The latter half of this epistle, its most memorable part, seems to be the last revision in the novel (B.23.5, Galley 16), another case of best, or most quotable (including the fragments above) saved for last. An earlier reference to Mermelstein spoke of Herzog's study as being "about romanticism as the scattered effects of a disintegrated Christian tradition" yielding aliena-tion, where Herzog needed "community, consensus, prayer, responsibilities and all the rest of it" (B.21.29,243f.). This tired formulation is recast and *"What this country needs is a good five-cent synthesis"* finds its proper place (H,p.207). The argument in the actual letter to Mermelstein—it is not only the situation which is funny, but the name, with its suggestions of murmur, worm or weasel, followed by stein yet—is more clearly about contemporary than Christian apocalyptics. So, for example, a reference to Shapiro's book is changed from "The Roots of Vico in Patristic Literature" (B.17.8) to "From Luther to Lenin, A History of Revolutionary Psychology" (B.22.6,369). Herzog correctly explains Kierkegaard's position: *"truth has lost its force with us and horrible pain and evil must teach it to us again"* (H,p.316), but then goes on to reject this idea. *"More commonly,"* he holds, *"suffering breaks people, crushes them, and is simply unilluminating. . . . We love apocalypses too much, and crisis ethics and florid extremism with its thrilling language. Excuse me, no. I've had all the monstrosity I want"* (H,p.317). In an earlier version, Herzog's resistance to Kierkegaard ("a marvelous fellow") is not so clearly articulated. He tells us what Kierkegaard means, adding, *"I do not claim to be an expert in this matter. I don't compare the evils I have known to truly gruesome evils such as we have all heard of. My life is a fairly ordinary one. . . . But what is this truth or seriousness that Kierkegaard thinks Hell must teach us? Is it that eternity must be recovered for the present moment, that the man who fingers all universals must leak away must disintegrate?"* (B.21.41,371). Once again we see how late final intellectual formulation comes. The point of the Kierkegaard letter(s), finely made in the later revision, is to cast Herzog's suf-fering in bold relief. He was the man, he suffered, he was there, but let us not succumb to the temptation to consider suffering honorific. It is frequently, all too frequently, meaningless. The morally real can be perceived in other ways as well.

Coming between the letters to Mermelstein and Nietzsche, as a bit of comic relief perhaps, is a letter about the size of the rats in Panama City. Herzog, sounding like a cross between late Faust and Leopold Bloom, thinks of a constructive way of dealing with them. Why here? If the rat is considered a symbol of nihilism, so often the case in modern literature, we see the point of this letter's placement. Having just exposed the danger of religious nihilism, Herzog, in his letter to Nietzsche, for him the master of those whose view is aesthetic, will expose the danger of aesthetic nihilism.

The letter to Nietzsche has the "gaiety" the philosopher admired and is characteristic of Herzog's found equilibrium. Addressing itself primarily to *Nietzsche Contra Wagner*, Herzog agrees with Nietzsche's negative revaluation of Wagner's music as a bogus Christianized Romanticism for mass consumption for "the sick . . . the idiots . . . (the) Wagnerians,"[11] and would agree with his judgment that Mozart has the "gracious, golden seriousness." Nietzsche saw that living in "a period of reaction *within* reaction" as he did, an "age of national wars," may help "such an art as Wagner's to a sudden glory, without thereby guaranteeing it a future," adding, with some ironic prescience that "the Germans themselves have no future" (*VPN*,p.668f.). Herzog also speaks of *"that sickly Wagnerian idiocy and bombast"* but chides Nietzsche on his own Wagnerian propensities as manifested in a phrase like the "luxury of destruction" (*H*,p.309, *VPN*,p.670). In doing so Herzog questions the clarity of Nietzsche's distinction between the tragic or Nietzschean figure suffering from overfulness, which as a young man the philosopher once saw in Wagner, and the "revenge-against-life" figure, suffering from impoverishment. In Goethe we do clearly see "excess" as creativity, in Wagner, most notably in the Romantic Christianity of *Parsifal*, "hatred" as creativity. So complete is Wagner's selling out of his earlier art that Nietzsche hopes *Parsifal* is really an elaborate irony. "After all," he says in a funny line, "Parsifal is operetta material par excellence" (*VPN*,p.674). This aspect of Nietzsche's argument is related to the sort of connection that Herzog makes between Romanticism and modernism, on the one hand, and Christianity or otherworldliness, on the other. We have described Bellow's resistance to Flaubert in these terms. It is no accident that Nietzsche also cites Flaubert as the apostle of "hatred" as creativity, "a new edition of Pascal, but as an artist, with the instinctive judgment deep down: 'Flaubert est toujours haissable, l'homme n'est rien, l'oeuvre est tout' " (*VPN*,p.671). Nietzsche laments Flaubert's "selflessness", calling it "the will to the end, in art as well as in morals" (*VPN*,p.671). In Wagner's case, Nietzsche can only wonder, "Did the *hatred against life* become dominant in him as in Flaubert?" (*VPN*,p.675). So far so good. But Nietzsche himself favours an aesthetic aristocracy and from a diametrically opposite position shows an equal contempt for "the ordinary life," which usually means, in political terms, the assumptions of democratic liberalism. "*John Stuart Mill:* or insulting clarity" Nietzsche quips in *Twilight of the Idols* (*VPN*,p.513), and, later in that work, "Liberalism: in other words, herd-animalization" (*VPN*,p.541) Herzog wonders about Nietzsche's invocation of the Dionysian spirit and its power "*to endure the sight of the Terrible*," the spirit which allows itself "*the luxury of Destruction*" (*H*,p.319,*VPN*,p.670). When Herzog says that these expressions have a Germanic ring he is turning Nietzsche's contempt in on himself. For "the Dionysian god and man," says Nietzsche, "what is evil, senseless, and ugly seems, as it were, permissable, as it seems permissable in nature" (*VPN*,p.670). How these immoralists argue from "nature!" Sade is perhaps the first in modern times. Herzog will not grant Nietzsche his immoralist assumptions, any more than he will grant that "mildness, peacefulness, and goodness" must imply a "saviour" (*VPN*,p.670). Throughout his career Bellow has been skeptical of the heroic view and even Nietzsche can not win him over. *"Where,"* wonders Herzog, *"are the heroes who have recovered"* (*H*,p.319) from the Dionysian luxury of Destruction? Herzog values Nietzsche's immoralism to the extent that it sees through and articulates the falsity of the age, including liberalism as the property of the educated rabble. But the philosopher's high-minded approach to destruction is too much like murder. Great pain may be an ultimate liberator of the spirit, but one must be around to gain from the experience. *"No survival, no Amor Fati,"* quips Herzog. Love of necessity, even when it is love of one's own sickness, implies a lover. Herzog points to the dubiousness of Nietzsche's arguments and to its peculiar susceptibility to perversion. Implied is the use to which Nietzsche was put by Nazism, the qualities of which Nietzsche himself despised.

This is made explicit in earlier versions of the letter. "The Nazis asserted the most absolute freedom which only the Dionysian power can claim—the power to endure the sight of the terrible, the questionable, this luxury of destruction" (B.18.9). Nietzsche would have disputed the claim that what he said had application to a state, a military idea, or perhaps anything German. Somewhat more accurately Herzog states in another draft, "you are speaking of some idea of an artist rather than any sort of factual historical existence applicable to the majority of us. . . . I do not wish to test my power to endure the sight of the terrible." Herzog prefers "a different view of Nature, the one, namely, which holds that in us the Evolutionary process has achieved a different power, that of self-consciousness and that Nature looks at itself in mankind. It has entered the mental zone. In this, 'Blood' culminates in 'Mind' and they are not such violent opposites after all" (B.17.8). But is Herzog certain enough even of his own self to stay very long with this optimistic, apparently romantic, metaphysics?

Later in the drafts (B.21.40,236) Herzog comes back to Nazism. He writes Nietzsche that *"to me Wagner has always been appropriate program or background music for people who are plotting a pogrom. Thus I imagine the Wahnsee Conference on the Final Solution with that horrible Siegfried on a record, shattering sword after sword."* (The Siegfried theme was, in fact, commonly used in Nazi propaganda.) Herzog again questions "the luxury of destruction" expressing nonetheless a sympathy for Nietzsche: *"Humankind is in fact losing its ancient forms of personality. Whether a new spirit of destruction should be involved is of course a different question . . . all of this about new beasts shambling off to Bethlehem to be born is simply nonsense."* He concludes again with the notion that blood may culminate in mind.[12] In sum, the Nietzsche letter is a final critique of modernism, giving some assent to its authority, done with no bitterness, but with a healthy humor. It is all well suited to Herzog's hard-won emotional balance.

For all its concentration of effect, for all its mental depth and psychological turmoil, for all its argumentation and change of scene, the novel takes place in five days, with recuperation at Ludeyville (another joke-name, town of the lewd) being the sixth. This adds verisimilitude to Herzog's conversion to sanity.

We come out of the pit with him. "But it was only a week—five days? Unbelievable! How different he felt. Confident, even happy in his excitement, stable. The bitter cup would come round again, by and by" (*H*,p.326). In a sense, this level-headed view has been present from the beginning. An early draft has the novel titled, "Alas and Hooray" (B.18.12). It is clear that the break with Mady has actually brought him "joy," these last two letters, among others, being written "in tranquil fullness of heart" (*H*,p.313). Herzog has resisted various temptations to dehumanization, to a Wasteland identity, affirming what remains of a moral view. It is appropriate that this "archaic" type utters an almost secular prayer in conclusion. It is not simply a case of not being able to let go of Poppa. "Thou movest me," Herzog says, explaining his feeling in natural images. "Something produces intensity, a holy feeling, as oranges produce orange, as grass green" (*H*,p.340). If this is an expression of the attribute of holiness it is an expression intimately allied to the attributes of Nature. If this is faith it is a faith of feeling, in its way Romantic, a product of the heart, recalling to Herzog the words of Rousseau—*je sens mon coeur et je connais les hommes*. Subtly he adds, "I couldn't say that for sure." Whether he really knows his heart or not the feeling is there. And whether he knows his heart or not may not be of the utmost significance. Both of the Romantic and beyond it, an apostle of the ego and a critic of it, Herzog turns to God as an act of the natural man recognizing the limits of Nature. His quest has brought him to affirm the primacy of moral authority, or God.

Notes

1. John J. Enck, "Interview with Saul Bellow," *Wisconsin Studies in Contemporary Literature*, 6 (1965), 157.

2. The much revised and copious Herzog mss. are held by special collections of The University of Chicago Library. They are arranged and numbered largely in chronological order beginning with B.16.1 and ending with B.23.5.

3. Concerned with some possible ambiguity in this formulation, I asked Bellow for a clarification to which he responded: "Real ideas transform, electrify. In the intellectual world people trade in ideas for worldly profit. The men advance their careers, the women add them to their attractions, making themselves more exciting. Just more Dior or Helena Rubenstein" (in a letter from "Jerusalem May 24 77"). I have, therefore, left my original description unchanged.

4. The Sono episode, like the Napoleon St. sequence, appears in a fragment which apparently antedates the mss. of the novel. In *Don Juan's Marriage* the names are Kikiku and Bryer. There is a womb-bath and Bryer considers marrying Kikiku.

5. Much comes to light in the revisions by way of minor characters. It is worth looking at the metamorphosis of one of these to get a more precise view of the richness of the whole cloth. Valdepenas, the cabbie, will do as an illustration. In his earliest incarnation, he is an anonymous cabbie who advises Herzog not to lose any sleep over the bums who wipe the windshield (B.17.5). Next we see him as Teddy, speaking more vivid Newyorkese: "I'll tell you a coincident" (B.17.9). He is not yet the aggressive, sexual Teodoro Valdepenas of the later versions. The name itself, like so many in the book, gets at the essence of the character, at once an actual Spanish name and a mock-Latin version of heroic phallus. By B.21.13 we see him combing his thick hair and grooming his little moustache, recognizing Herzog as the older guy who kissed that young-looking chick and interposing some of his own wisdom on the subject. "I broke up with a sixteen year old broad last week. I come in, she's reading a book. I say, 'Baby, listen, with Teddy you don't read books.' I slapped the

book out of her hand," a macho gesture which stands in sharp contrast to Herzog's fumbling with his Tikhon-Zadonsky-reading wife. Not that this is the solution. When the girl says, "Okay so let's get it over with" (B.21.13,280), he assures her that Teddy's gonna take his time. In the novel it is, more realistically, a magazine, and his retort to the girl is spicier: "In my hack, that's where I hurry. You ought to get a punch in the teeth for talkin' like that." He concludes to an astonished Herzog, "A broad eighteen don't even know how to shit" (H,p.223). Valdepenas, a Puerto Rican who knows some Yiddish (the fat guys who pay the window cleaning bums "shiver in their pupick"), some genteel phraseology (it finally comes out just right—"You know, I think I got a coincident to tell you"), and, of course, street talk ("Keep sockin' away, Doc") is an example of that New York candor which Herzog finds so striking. Each of the parenthetical examples appears in the late B.22.5,267ff., showing again how Bellow often saves the best, or most memorably formulated, for last.

6. Fydor Dostoevsky, *Notes From the Underground*, trans. Ralph Matlaw (New York: Dutton, 1960), p. 23.

7. Dostoevsky, p. 31.

8. Ihab Hassan, *Radical Innocence* (Princeton: Princeton Univ. Press, 1961).

9. There is some question as to the accuracy of this label as Herzog applies it to himself. Analysts I have spoken to seem to think that this describes a state more severely alienated than any Herzog inhabits.

10. Blake, "The Four Zoas," *Selected Poetry and Prose of Blake*, ed. Northrop Frye (New York: Modern Library, 1953), p. 236.

11. *Nietzsche Contra Wagner*, in *Viking Portable Nietzsche*, p. 667. All subsequent references to Nietzsche will be from this volume and cited in the essay as *VPN*.

12. Elsewhere, Herzog's references to Nietzsche are not so balanced or "cheerful." In an early draft of the Strawforth letter, he writes that "Whitehead, Ortega and Nietzsche are the modern writers who deal with risk. This is nothing but the Social Darwinism on which many writers, notably Bernard Shaw, blame the disasters of this century "(B. 18.12,376). Again, an uncomplimentary reference: "Curious how the Continental disdain of British genius as lacking in original conceptions betrays ideological disorders—Nietzsche's contempt for Darwin's mind is an example" (B.18.12,141). Finally, and most critical of all: "You never hear me crying out about the decay and degradation of the highest values, as if I represented these values. Like a Nietzsche or a Burckhardt or a Henry Adams, or any of those Christian Fatalists or two-bit prophets of doom who call themselves Royalists, Classicists, Aristocrats (B.21.29). Here he simply links Nietzsche, for whom he has much admiration, to the strain of modernism, for which he has no admiration at all.

Nature and Social Reality in Bellow's *Sammler*

Robert Boyers*

One is apt to hear a great deal in our time about the return to nature and about the apocalyptic renovations likely to attend success in such an enterprise. It is as though, having failed quite miserably as a culture to manage our problems, having failed even properly to define them, we had decided that our only hope lay in pronouncing them less monstrous than they had originally appeared, and surely available to the rhetorical reductions we have collectively trained ourselves to execute. This is nothing new, of course. One has only to be modestly familiar with the vagaries of cultural fashion since the time of the French Revolution to recognize in contemporary cycles of reaction and renewal the rehearsal of a very old drama, and nothing has been so frequently proclaimed as original and promising in all these years as the tired notion of nature and the attributes of sheer being unmodified by cultural directives of any kind. There have been wide divergences among the various spokesmen for nature, to be sure, and one who has read carefully, say, Rousseau's *Confessions* or *Social Contract* cannot easily commit the error of linking him uncritically with German despoilers of the idea of culture in the Nazi period. What has generally characterized the best, the most enduringly useful of these spokesmen, though, is not really difficult to formulate. I speak of their resistance to the notion that reality conforms to rather simple laws, or that ambivalence towards one's society and prospects can be resolutely banished once an appropriate perspective is realized. That such resistance has been exemplary in the work of men like Goethe and Rousseau seems to me indisputable, but the romantic tradition they represent seems today everywhere in ruins, its legitimate heirs confused and hysterical in more instances than one would care to recite.

It has seemed to me for some time that we have in Saul Bellow a more hopeful variant of the romantic disposition than we had any right to expect. Surely, with a very formidable body of work behind him, he has shown us how difficult it is even for the most sensible of men to abandon the idea of nature to which American writers have been so uniformly compelled. He has, moreover, modified that idea and enlarged the context in which it is conventionally treated. Whether in so doing he has succeeded in making the idea more persua-

*Robert Boyers, "Nature and Social Reality in Bellow's *Sammler*," *Critical Quarterly*, 15 (1973), 251–71.

sive, or has stripped it of a singularity we always thought it had, we cannot decide confidently as yet. What is clear is that an element one could discern even in an early novel like *The Victim* has moved steadily to occupy a central position in Bellow's more recent fiction. What I propose to examine here is the idea of nature in Bellow and its relation to two others: the idea of social reality, and the idea of character conceived both in its moral and aesthetic dimensions. To do this, it seems a good idea to focus on Bellow's 1970 National Book Award winning novel, *Mr. Sammler's Planet*, for it is a compact volume with rather few characters and a carefully limited perspective on everything. It has, in addition, a sympathetically drawn protagonist whose intelligence is so fine as to filter a very great range of ideas and events. In *Mr. Sammler's Planet*, the idea of nature must necessarily be evoked as a complex and tantalizing thing, for the mind that entertains it is nimble and endlessly active. While it treats the idea of nature not as a learned treatise might, but as a learned work of fiction infrequently can, Bellow's novel allows us to consider the degree to which the idea can be compelling in a culture like ours.

Probably the most striking and insistent note sounded in *Mr. Sammler's Planet* is the protagonist's cry of alarm against what he calls '. . . the peculiar aim of sexual niggerhood for everyone.' What he means by this is not as simple as one might expect, for Sammler, no less than Bellow, seems rather confused about just what constitutes 'sexual niggerhood'. Clearly the expression depends for its resonance on the stereotype of the black man as somehow more intimately 'tuned in' to the rhythms of his own pulse than other men and as therefore more at ease with the demands of his own sexuality. From this stems the familiar notion of the black man's demand for instant gratification of every sensual whim, and the growing attractiveness of this attitude for many millions of white Americans recently liberated from outworn inhibitions. Crudely considered, the stereotype is not altogether misleading, though the human reality it ostensibly illuminates is largely concealed by so vague an image. Similarly, one would not want to take issue with the notion that demands for instant gratification have been sounded with increasing regularity even in those segments of the culture one would not ordinarily have looked to for such sentiments—I am thinking here especially of the intellectuals in American society, but the phenomenon is as current in European circles as it is in this country. Why Bellow's Sammler should be as exercised by the whole thing as he is we may justly question, however, for he is rather attracted by just those kinds of spontaneity and avowals of potency one is apt to identify with the stereotyped image of the black experience we have come largely to accept. It is not that Sammler is, or has been, an erotic type, if we may use so imprecise a term, or that his is a forcefully expressive personality of the sort we may mistake for erotic command. He is very much concerned, though, with what his intellectual enemies the existentialists call authenticity, and if he is less aggressive than they are about the wearing of masks and socially sanctioned ritualizations of concealment, he is never far from cynicism about the games most of us play, and we are not surprised to hear him say, 'To be nearer to nature was necessary in order to keep in balance the achievements of modern method.' In the long run, one has a good sense of what Sammler thinks on the subjects of war, peace, brotherhood, family, the responsibility of intellect, and the like, but one will be hard put indeed to locate a consistent pattern in these views. Not that we have any right to demand that Bellow provide one, of course, for what he does give us is a rich and believable character whose ambivalence moves us to the degree that it resists easy resolutions of every kind. Where the character Sammler succumbs to such resolutions, to patterns that would explain every particular view and experience, he strikes us as a little pathetic, hardly persuasive.

Mr. Sammler, for example, is not altogether moved in a negative way by the 'niggerhood', sexual and otherwise, he has reason to descry. Readers of the novel will remember his compulsive returns to a west-side New York bus to observe a handsome, elegantly attired black thief at work picking the pockets of passengers. Now it is nothing so fashionable as the fascination of the absurd that Sammler experiences on these daily excursions of his, but a positive admiration for carefully plotted depradations carried out with an assurance, style, and conviction that are almost calculated to embarrass an observer with the comparatively anxious and petty manoeuvres to which he himself is habituated. Sammler reflects on the thief as follows:

> The black man was a megalomaniac. But there was a certain—a certain princeliness. The clothing, the shades, the sumptuous colours, the barbarous-majestical manner. He was probably a mad spirit. But mad with an idea of noblesse.

Sammler suffers for this black man when he is finally cornered and humiliated, suffers for him not because he is a mere mortal who has fallen on bad times, but because the idea of noblesse he somehow incarnates has been wantonly soiled by those who have no real sense of what noblesse might mean for all of us. One is tempted, surely, to share Sammler's attitude, but it is a little hard to do so if one does not understand what it is he admires in the black man. Can one seriously admire a man for his sumptuous clothing and confident demeanour? What can the idea of noblesse amount to when it is embodied in a petty thief who shows absolutely no concern for his victims as people, and who brutally affronts an old man like Sammler as he does? (The thief, in a scene one is not likely to forget, traps Sammler in an apartment-house and exposes his sex-organ to him as an unmistakable sign of his mastery.) So much that Sammler says in the novel seems sensible and clear that one is almost willing to grant that he is right about the black man, that it is we who are blind to certain qualities largely absent in our experience of the modern world. It would be unfortunate to acquiesce in such temptations, though, for, as Bellow would himself say in his most lucid moments, we know better, and what we know Bellow has had a hand in teaching us. Surely the glorification of madness, whether princely or banal, is not a project one would associate with Bellow, nor with Sammler. Who would we expect to understand more clearly how the flight into psychopathology can be at best an abstract gesture, in that it contains no concrete criticism of the reality it would reject? That this is no easy criticism to produce we are aware, for we have lost all secure touch with what older writers might have called the concept of normality, and only such a concept can enable one to account for madness, to gauge its depth and consider reasonably its attraction. In all the talk of 'sexual niggerhood' we overhear in *Mr. Sammler's Planet*, and despite the vivid evocation of a virile black man subversive of established western values, we are given very little sense of those particular social conditions that make possible the phenomena Sammler reacts to so unhappily. We never really understand why the black man, not merely in his person but as an emblem of values and life-styles, should have been permitted to move into the centre of western culture and to emasculate its older traditions.

What we can say, then, is that if the black man is not at the very centre of Bellow's novel, the styles and values associated with him most definitely are, and to the extent that they weigh heavily on Mr. Sammler, they must concern us. These values and styles, only loosely imagined in the course of the novel, are about as close as we can come to what Bellow thinks of when he turns to the idea of nature. Obviously, it is not the nature of trees and blue skies and tip-toes through the tulips, nor the nature of pastoral swains and woodland nymphs, to which Sammler is drawn. Like other protagonists in Bellow's fiction, he is at least partially drawn to the idea and image of nature red in tooth and claw. Strange? Perverse? Not really, for Sammler is a survivor of a tradition forcibly isolated from pastoral pleasures of every kind. A Jew who has but barely escaped death in a Nazi concentration camp a quarter of a century earlier, Sammler is a gentle man, almost passive really, but in his heart he wishes he were a bit less civilized, less passive, that Jews in general had been less prone to play the role of victim to conquerors of every type. Nature for Sammler is purpose combined with the strength and energy to realize its wishes, grasp for its dreams no matter how unpleasant or occasionally indecorous. That this nature is necessarily envisioned as a little mysterious and frightening in Bellow's work is no surprise, for even substantial physical size and strength are insufficient to convince Bellow's protagonists that they are men capable of confronting the real world in all its harshness.

We think of Asa Leventhal, the central figure in Bellow's early novel *The Victim*. Though he is hardly an intellectual, and hardly the throwback to old-world dignity we meet in Sammler, he is nonetheless a prototype of Bellow's latest protagonist. Without rehearsing the details of his story, we may say he is victimized because he does not know how to look at nature, let alone deal with it maturely. One well-known critic complained of Bellow several years ago that his protagonists' sense of sin and excess was boyish, and when one thinks of figures like Leventhal and Augie March, one is hard put to disagree. When we meet Leventhal he is living alone, his wife having gone to visit a parent for a while. We see at once that he is ill-equipped to live by himself, and he is subject to morbid uncertainties, the prey of distressing memories out of a past that should have been settled and buried. He remembers an affair his wife was having with a married man while she was making plans to marry Leventhal, and he thinks of this as of an event so absolutely terrible and incomprehensible as to constitute a reality from which he must forever be excluded. Just so is he awed at the small spectacle of his neighbour's dog panting in pleasure as its belly is rubbed, wholly given over to delight in the moment. Attracted to an emblem of sheer abandon, Leventhal relates to the dog as a mysterious and wonderful creature, again existing at a level of feeling Leventhal cannot acknowledge as potentially his as well. When his friend tells him to get close to himself later in the novel, Leventhal seems to grasp what he means, that he must acknowledge his own propensity towards a variety of feelings and experiences he has sought resolutely to repress or to banish. What Leventhal must learn is that there need be no absolute victims, no total oppressors, only men who do injury to one another and who are capable of forgiving both what they have done and what has been done to them. But like Bellow's other protagonists, Leventhal never really learns this as well as he should, and he is therefore inordinately tempted to view as reality only what is sordid and ruthless. All the rest is suspect as mere sentiment or idea.

So the nature Sammler looks upon in the guise of a handsome black thief is a nature ruthless and sordid, and all the more attractive for being so. In a sense one may say this nature is conceived as a corrective to the humane sentiments and gentle manners in which Sammler feels somewhat enclosed, though at the same time he is very much at home with old-world manners and assumptions. What Sammler suspects is that the other nature, the nature one associates with the divine flow of things passively regarded, is not really the sort of thing one can rely upon in the modern world, much as one would like to, and much as Sammler relies upon it from time to time. The nature to which Whitman and other American writers have delighted in yielding themselves is here rejected as inadequate, for it is unrealistic in its trust and in its failure to discriminate between a sense of the universe and a sense of social fact. That Sammler never successfully formulates or understands the distinction on an intellectual level only attests to the great difficulty western humanistic intellectuals have had in thinking in such terms. Sammler tells us he has abandoned most of the books he has read in and thought about in his life, so that he might dwell almost exclusively with Meister Eckhart, whose mystical works contain injunctions against entertaining notions of multiplicity and difference, of limitation and quality. Would Meister Eckhart have been gripped with admiration for Sammler's black thief? It is, of course, a preposterous suggestion, but it points up rather clearly the intellectual failure of Sammler's formulations, and of Bellow's fictional project conceived as a philosophical enterprise. No doubt it is possible by way of explanation to assert that it is Bellow's intention to dramatize Sammler's failure of insight, but we have no way of discerning just where Bellow's perspective deviates from Sammler's. It is hardly legitimate to claim that a character's revealed failures in insight constitute a necessary triumph for the novelist who has permitted us to see them. Unless the novelistic intelligence is unmistakably distinguished from a single character's perspective, as it is so often in Flaubert and in James, we can have at best a richly ambiguous confusion. We may not have a philosophical triumph, which is precisely what the wise-man accents that permeate *Mr. Sammler's Planet* would lead us to expect.

But we have not determined as yet precisely what is this nature to which Sammler is drawn and whose incarnation is the black thief. Is this nature no more than reality bluntly conceived? I should have to say that it is not, for reality would seem to me at least a complex of events and objects and living things which cannot be evaded or denied. Mr. Sammler's black man is something else altogether, for he *can* be evaded, can be denied. In his actuality he is as strange, as unrevealed to Sammler as though he had never seen him. Nature for Sammler is a fictive realm which can endow human beings with wondrous attributes otherwise undreamed of by cautious old-world Jews committed to esoteric speculations of an altogether otherworldly sort. Which is to say that for Sammler, nature is an idea, and as an idea it is available to manipulations whose basis in subjective need in no way compromises the persuasiveness of the idea. It is a nature practically protean in the number of shapes it can be made to assume. In Sammler's hands it serves at once to assuage a sense of alienation, of otherness, and to enforce it as a badge of distinction. On the one hand he will insist upon the viability of mystical experience, unorthodox though it may be, upon the necessary dissolution of that multiplicity we perceive in the physical world, upon the sensation of oneness with all that exists. This is the perspective of Meister Eckhart, so forcibly impressed upon us in *Mr. Sammler's Planet*. On the other hand we have a nature which is nothing if not multiplicitous, a nature which is movement, passion, struggle, disorder, the singular personality impressive precisely in the degree of its defiant singularity.

To ask which nature Sammler prefers is to compound the confusion. I think it is possible to conclude that he thinks he is on the side of Meister Eckhart and the mystics, but that he actually occupies several positions at once. Would he agree with Wittgenstein in the *Tractatus* when he asserts that 'the solution of the problem of life is seen in the vanishing of the problem'? Surely this is to deny nature, if nature has anything whatever to do with what we ordinarily call reality, and if reality can be said to grip us by the throat from time to time. Problems conceived as difficulties in linguistic operations are surely susceptible to manipulations such as would please a Wittgenstein, but it is doubtful that Bellow would be satisfied with that sort of solution, or with that sort of problem. The problems he posits for his characters are not problems of mere explanation, not a matter of simply getting things straight or establishing manageable linguistic dimensions in which the problem can be more beneficially reconstituted. When Bellow's Augie March tells us, 'That's the struggle of humanity, to recruit others to your version of what's real', he does so with some sort of conviction that this is ultimately an impoverishing struggle, that to become more attached to the version than to the reality it should serve or represent is a great misfortune. What is so baffling in our experience of Bellow's work, though, is that virtually all of his resolutions, certainly in the works of the last fifteen years or so, amount to simply getting things straight or rearranging the terms of a problem so that it at least appears more manageable, or less important. What does the mystic do if not banish problems conceived at a secular level? To seek to move beyond desire, for example, is to avoid having to determine appropriate objects which can satisfy that desire. Whether the character is Henderson the rain king, Moses Herzog, or Artur Sammler, we have in Bellow's more recent fictions the exaltation of a will to banish conflicts whose resolutions imply decision and discrimination. A decision is made at the conclusion of *Henderson The Rain King*, but it does not emerge from the novel itself, nor from anything the main character has learned in the course of his adventures. The decision is willed rather than achieved, and it is asserted largely at the expense of fundamental realities the novel has resolutely impressed upon us. I do not know any serious commentator who has found that novel's conclusion satisfactory. There is nothing like a concluding decision reached in *Herzog*, nor is there one in *Sammler*. Both decide, basically, that there is little point in the endless discriminations and explanations to which their lives have been largely committed. It is fitting that the final words of *Sammler* should be, 'For that is the truth of it—that we all know, God, that we know, that we know, we know, we know.'

What we know, according to Sammler, has a lot to do with the mystic bond men like Meister Eckhart have told us so much about. Secure in our affirmation of this bond, so Sammler's thinking goes, we shall be secure in knowing the terms of responsible behaviour towards our fellows, we shall be decent men and women, grateful children and generous parents. Is it human nature to be thus secure, to seek simply to fulfil the terms of our contract with God which in our heart of hearts we know and understand? This is more difficult to answer, surely, for one can hardly claim that mystical affirmations are natural, that the discounting of physical phenomena is a thing readily accomplished even by the most mundane intelligence and flabby will. Nature mystics, from Wordsworth to Rimbaud and Tennyson, have of course described states of blissful absorption into boundless being achieved almost spontaneously, without the sort of disciplined attentiveness and wilfull self-denial we associate with St. John of the Cross, or with T. S. Eliot, for that matter. What seems clear, though, is that the trust and spontaneity of a Wordsworth, lovely and moving though their expression can be in his poems, are simply not of the sort a sensible man can long maintain. That, in Wordsworth's words, 'Nature never did betray the heart that loved her' is a gorgeous sentiment, but the grotesque developments in the life of Wordsworth's own sister Dorothy ought surely to have altered his faith in such a sentiment. Sammler's gentler nature, the nature he identifies with the mystic affirmations of Eckhart (rather than with the nature represented by the black thief), is not really very different from Wordsworth's, is similarly easy, accepted almost deliberately as against the facts. In an extended discussion between an Indian scholar named Govinda Lal and Sammler, we note especially the following exchange:

> Lal: 'I believe you intimate that there is an implicit morality in the will-to-live and that these mediocrities in office will do their duty by the species. I am not sure. There is no duty in biology. There is no sovereign obligation to one's breed. When biological destiny is fulfilled in reproduction the desire is often to die . . .'

Sammler: 'When you know what pain is, you agree that not to have been born is better. But being born one respects the powers of creation, one obeys the will of god—with whatever inner reservations truth imposes. As for duty—you are wrong. The pain of duty makes the creature upright, and this uprightness is no negligible thing. No, I stand by what I first said.'

Surely Lal's remarks seem the more cogent and sensible in this exchange, but we must remember that Sammler is a hard man to pin down. Only thirty pages earlier in the novel, speaking wistfully of Tolstoy's humanism, he reminds himself and his companion of a scene in *War and Peace* in which the French General Davout spared the life of Pierre Bezhukov: '. . . they looked into each other's eyes. A human look was exchanged, and Pierre was spared. Tolstoy says you don't kill another human being with whom you have exchanged such a look.' Prodded by his companion to explain his sentiments upon recalling such an incident, he remarks: 'I sympathize deeply. I sympathize sadly. When men of genius think about humankind, they are almost forced to believe in this form of psychic unity. I wish it were so.' And further, '. . . though it's not an arbitrary idea, I wouldn't count on it.' Which is to show only that Sammler is of many minds on many issues, that his attraction to Meister Eckhart and the black thief is no more contradictory really than his attraction to abstract ideas of widely varying merit and implication. That nature should be for Sammler at once an exhilarating idea, no matter how disparate his varying conceptions of it, and also a rather sickening notion laced with a kind of emotional excess he finds intolerable, should not surprise us once we have come to terms with Bellow's work. One may find it all a little dismaying, nevertheless, for it is not merely a narrow, a petty consistency that we fail to find in Bellow. What we have, again, and there is no getting around the fact, is confusion presented as complex wisdom, is a series of rejections of specious idea constructs which is itself thoroughly founded on intellectual quirkiness and easy indulgence.

We have claimed for Sammler a considerable intelligence and power of discrimination, yet we accuse him of intellectual quirkiness and vulgar expediency. The contradiction is not in the terms we apply, however, but in those confusions that we have cited. These confusions point to more than a split in the central character, a radical ambivalence the likes of which most of us surely know and share. I am concerned with a failure of imagination that refuses to work through the problems it posits at the level on which they are originally conceived. To fail of resolutions that are gratifying, or even modestly acceptable, is no great failure, for we live at a time when all resolutions are held suspect, especially among the liberal and literate people who will constitute Bellow's immediate readership. To introduce into serious discourse, though, considerations and perspectives that banish to irrelevance the central issues or insistently terminate them, is to opt for confusion, the fragmentary rather than the substantive response. And this is surely what we have in *Mr. Sammler's Planet*. For all that the central character is always on stage, for all his intelligence, his fine capacity to associate fluently among diverse materials and to stamp his personality on everything he touches, we necessarily relate to the novel as to a series of brilliant fragments, insights constituted in the spirit of the contemporary probe beloved of speculators in the stockmarket of ideas. We may love or dislike Sammler himself, and surely that is a constituent of our response to the novel as a whole, but we will want as well a more coherent vision of possibility than the novel affords.

Some years ago, in an essay entitled 'Art and Fortune', Lionel Trilling wrote of some of our best novelists that they '. . . have mixed what they personally desired with what they desired for the world and have mingled their mundane needs with their largest judgments. Then, great as their mental force has been, they have been touched with something like stupidity, resembling the holy stupidity which Pascal recommends: its effects appear in their ability to maintain ambivalence toward their society, which is not an acquired attitude of mind, or a weakness of mind, but rather the translation of a biological datum, an extension of the pleasure-pain with which, in a healthy state, we respond to tension and effort; the novelist expresses this in his co-existent hatred and love of the life he observes. His inconsistency of intellectual judgment is biological wisdom.' The passage has always seemed to me rich and provocative, and surely it has a great deal to say about the idea of nature we have been considering. It speaks, after all, of 'a biological datum', of 'biological wisdom', in fact, and these are clearly notions dear to Sammler. For Sammler thinks he knows 'what is what', speaks often of 'fated biological necessities', and has something more or less definitive to say about everyone he encounters, as though confirmed in his judgments by some exalted authority seated deeply in his very blood. What the authority says corresponds roughly to the attitude of 'holy stupidity' Trilling briefly describes, and might be put as follows: Be a judge, but don't believe overmuch in the necessity or absolute validity of your judgments; believe that man is good, looking at the species archetypally, but understand that in fact we are miserable and cruel to one another and have it as our fundamental project in life to overcome disgust; embrace only what is mystical, aesthetic, spiritualized, but be, at all costs, reasonable. No doubt about it, these are the messages Sammler turns over and over in his head, these are the imperatives to which he responds. Where the biology comes in is in our resignation to these contradictory imperatives as a kind of wisdom, in our feeling that nature enforces such contradictions as necessary, if not always satisfying to the critical intellect. None of this is a matter of cultivating experiences sufficient to convince us that what is, is. Experience has very little to do with it. In the view to which Sammler subscribes, we come to know what is necessary through an operation of mind which is not exercised by specific phenomena, by the accumulation and consideration of sensible experiences. Every mind must know by itself, somehow, what is necessary and true, those things that cannot be other than they are. A mind which cannot discover these things by itself will never understand them at all. We must anticipate lawfulness, form, regularity in nature, which is to say in the created universe, we must respect the rightfulness and necessity of some organizing principle, though we may not make regular contact with it. Duty will consist in our standing unperturbed, unintimidated in the midst of complexity, before the spectacle of inexhaustible contradiction.

This is all very well, it seems to me, but it does not yet refute the charges we have brought to bear in witness of Bellow's novel. 'Inconsistency of intellectual judgment' against a background of secure conviction in the orderliness of nature and the abiding authority of reasonable feelings is but an aspect of the problem, an aspect which gives us less trouble than others, I might add. What we really cannot understand in considering Sammler is what he desires for the world, to use Trilling's idiom, how he explains to himself the idea of society and its relation to nature. To 'maintain an ambivalence' towards one's society is at least to have some sense of what it is, how it operates, what obligations participation in its processes entails for the individual. This sense is difficult to improvise, for it is customarily rooted in a profound conception of necessity that takes into account both the peculiar, temporary needs of the self and the past it is impaled on. Sammler does not appear wholly to avoid the dilemma Bellow once described in an article, as follows:

> American novelists are not ungenerous, far from it, but as their view of society is fairly shallow, their moral indignation is non-specific. What seems to be lacking is a firm sense of a common world, a coherent community, a genuine purpose in life.

I do not think Bellow's view of society is shallow—surely *Mr. Sammler's Planet* communicates the texture, the very feel of contemporary life as vividly as any novel we can name. What we must say, though, is that it is not sufficiently historical. We do not know what are the forces that have brought us to the moment the novel documents. In fact, there is no development of any kind in Bellow's novel, for while presenting to us a central figure who is nothing if not historical, Bellow is definitely more concerned with the revelation of the human condition. This condition we understand all too well in the first twenty-five pages of the book. As we read on, we come more and more to feel the absence of 'a coherent community' as an aspect of the human condition, despite perpetual reminders as to the uniqueness of the present moment. The abstraction of 'the human condition' finally is identified with reality itself, so that it becomes almost impossible to think of 'a common world' or 'coherent community' as concrete potentialities within the domain of contemporary experience. The novel, in other words, denies us the possibility of a social reality that is not a direct reflection of a corrupted nature, conceived here largely in static, immutable terms.

Set in such a context, the projects of selfhood assume a vaguely mystical air, and the attitudes that shape experience seem eccentric and insistently private. The strange thing about this, though, is that Sammler should stand out so clearly from all the others in the novel. While they do not collectively form anything like a 'coherent community', surely they have a good deal more in common with one another than any of them have with Sammler, who often reminds himself of his distinction: 'Mr. Sammler did feel somewhat separated from the rest of his species, if not in some fashion severed—severed not so much by age as by preoccupations too different and remote, disproportionate on the side of the spiritual, Platonic, Augustinian, 13th century.' Is it simply that Sammler cultivates more assiduously than others certain aspects of personality which are relatively exotic in our time, or is it that he is really different as the result of some peculiar endowment more biological than cultural? The novel definitely stresses the cultural domain as the source of Sammler's distinction— continually he is referred to as a survivor of a very special kind, an old-world Jew with expectations and manners derived from an earlier world originally more orderly and decorous, later more unequivocally cruel and murderous, than the contemporary scene. Yet Sammler's mysticism does not seem at all a necessary outgrowth of his derivation from an old-world European tradition, the essential flavour of which was anything but occult and mysterious even in its darkest ravages. It seems to have emerged full-blown from nowhere, a wondrous flowering in old age. It is described in the novel not as an evasion of reality but as a commitment to a deeper, more abiding reality than mundanity impresses. That is to say, while Bellow wishes us to relate to Sammler as the product of a special cultural and social environment no longer available to us except by way of historical imagination, he evokes the character, in all his attitudinal dimensions, as a force of nature, something marvellous and unaccountable. No doubt, Sammler would not seem so marvellous and exotic were he presented to us with fewer explicit reminders of his difference, and did he not himself insist upon this so strenuously. In a universe of human beings struggling to keep afloat, to nurture some sense of individual, if not of communal, purpose, a man whose habitual mode is 'aesthetic consumption of the environment' is bound to seem extraordinary.

What remains problematical is the degree to which social reality in this novel reflects nature, or perhaps we should say, what is prior to culture. If Sammler's mysticism and his separateness cannot be strictly accounted for in terms of social realities either suggested or explicitly described, can we account any better for the other characters in the novel? Surely they do not seem to be forces of nature. In fact, each is the product of a situation Sammler himself would have us believe he grasps, a situation that is unmistakably cultural and social as far as he is concerned. What has happened, Sammler tells us, is that we have become so civilized, technology has had its way with us for so long, that it is no longer possible for most of us to think 'nature' as we could in an earlier time. Even to say the word is to realize how little it resonates with the strangeness it once had. Where once nature called to mind primal energies and the necessary risks entailed in openness, it now has more to do with what Philip Rieff, in another context, calls 'calculated spontaneity'. Here is a description taken from the novel, a description of New York as the setting in which these various lives must make their way:

> You opened a jewelled door into degradation, from hypercivilized Byzantine luxury straight into the state of nature, the barbarous world of colour erupting from beneath. It might well be barbarous on either side of the jewelled door. Sexually, for example,

the thing evidently, as Mr. Sammler was beginning to grasp, consisted in obtaining the privileges, and the free ways of barbarism, under the protection of civilized order, property rights, refined technological organization, and so on.

What Bellow is giving us, in other words, and what Sammler sees, is a universe in which the very idea of nature has been altered, confused, deliberately turned around in such a way that it does not mean what it used to. And as the idea of nature has been wilfully perverted, so is it difficult any longer to think of social reality in the customary ways. Obviously, to think of the one idea is in some sense to compare it to the other, and this has become more and more difficult to do. The self has no secure home either in nature or in society, for neither constitutes a firm reality to which it can relate with confidence. Where once it was possible to speak of one's nature and authenticity in terms of understanding one's position in society—a fact brought home to us in Erich Auerbach's discussion of the 17th century French idiom *se connaître* as signifying both recognition of oneself and of one's position in the social world—we have now reached a time in which it seems futile even to speak of the one in the context of the other. That this is not an entirely familiar situation we may be certain. Even Rousseau, whose exaltations of nature we hear so much about these days, had a very specific sense of the coherent community, and understood that there could be no natural man in the modern world, at least no natural man in the old sense. Whoever urged men to drop out, to cultivate their own impulses and pleasures in an exclusive sense, denied them access to reality, and that reality for Rousseau was clearly social. Though it was not desirable for men to require others to tell them what to want, it was necessary that modern men keep in mind the sense of themselves as contingent beings, as social and historical figures confronted with particular inexorable demands. In *Emile*, we read that 'Good social institutions are those best fitted to make men unnatural, to take away man's absolute existence and give him a relative one, to absorb the self into the common whole, so that each individual no longer regards himself as one, but as part of a larger totality, and is aware only of the whole.'

The passage does overstate Rousseau's fundamental position, as a matter of fact, but it is clear that social reality was to him no spectre to be casually dismissed or wilfully transcended. It was there and one had to deal with it. Individual impulse could be nurtured only under conditions that might threaten to limit its gratification, and this the individual himself would have to acknowledge and approve. So disaffected is Mr. Sammler from his own social reality, so disgraceful is it, in fact, as it is presented in Bellow's novel, that the responsibilities Rousseau outlines seem more and more impossible to recommend or to fulfil. The dilemma is easy enough to explain. For Rousseau and for Bellow, particular social conditions have encouraged a whole variety of unfortunate behaviours which hinder the development of trust, affection, and confident selfhood. For Rousseau, however, these social conditions must be met head-on by a generation of people who have been properly trained to decide for themselves what are their real needs and what are the peculiar contours of their independent selfhood. This selfhood is understood in advance to be fragmentary and insufficient, since to be whole it must acknowledge contingency and control itself in the interests of communal purpose. For Bellow, insofar as his position is clear at all, there is an authentic selfhood that is individual and perpetually resistant to the claims of social conscience, indeed even of the social-reality principle. This resistance is an aspect of Sammler and constitutes perhaps the most favourable aspect of his character structure, in Bellow's view. That such resistance can take several forms, Bellow knows very well, it must be said, and there can be no doubt that he feels strong aversion to some of them. Of madness and the attraction to coolly spontaneous violence he has Sammler reflect as follows: 'The middle class had formed no independent standards of honour. Thus it had no resistance to the glamour of killers . . . Madness is the attempted liberty of people who feel themselves overwhelmed by giant forces of organized control. Seeking the magic of extremes. Madness is a base form of the religious life.' Despite these aversions, however, and no matter how deeply felt and persuasive we feel Bellow's expression of them to be, his notion of genuine and positive resistance is largely insupportable, whether in terms of social reality or of individual human nature. It involves a syndrome of gestures and assertions which the psychoanalyst Leslie H. Farber has described as a distension of will, a willing of what cannot be willed, given what the individual agent happens to be. Bellow wants his protagonist to be a reasonable man, a humble though learned *mensch* even as he wants him to be something a little more exquisite, a mystic in touch with occult realms. For a man who in *Herzog* so eschews potato love, that awful inclination to get rid of one's peculiar burden of selfhood by merging with the mass and proclaiming the supremacy of the universal, he seems strangely at ease with a passage like the following in *Sammler*:

> No force of nature, nothing paradoxical or demonic, he had no drive for smashing through the masks of appearances . . . that one should be satisfied with such truth as one could get by approximation. Trying to live with a civil heart. With disinterested charity. With a sense of the mystic potency of humankind. With an inclination to believe in archetypes of goodness.

In other words, while we must not feel ourselves absolutely 'overwhelmed by giant forces of organized control', and while any sense of coherent community is surely out of the question for the foreseeable future, 'the mystic potency of humankind' is a plausible idea to which we should cling for dear life, though surely it cannot provide those 'independent standards of honour' for want of which the middle classes are literally destroying themselves. Altogether a difficult set of propositions to recommend. We know, of course, that it is not the business of any novel to recommend particular behaviours, and we would be gravely mistaken were we to translate Bellow's propositions into actual suggestions offered us in the spirit of persuasion. Yet there is no doubt that we must take these propositions seriously, and to do so we must look at them concretely, with a specific sense of what they portend. If the novel is, in some sense, as

Lawrence argued, The Book Of Life, we have an obligation to read it as real men and women occupying a more or less real and still habitable universe, not as hypothetical readers bent on mere aesthetic consumption of the sort Sammler imagines himself committed to. Sammler tells us that 'he had no drive for smashing through the masks of appearances', but we know that he is drawn to 'archetypes of goodness' and to mystical affirmations. Perhaps he insists upon both because he is confident of neither. Yet he is presented to us as very confident indeed, despite the modesty he wears so well to ensure that he will not give offence. Again, the question we must ask is, why this fundamental confusion in a novel that takes as its central intelligence so astute a mind as Sammler's?

Rousseau proclaimed the indissoluble relation between the nature of civilized man and the socialization process to which he would inevitably succumb. Bellow understands all too well this relation, but prefers to deny rather than to confirm its necessity. Authentic selfhood, radical integrity, consist for Bellow in the capacity to think of the mundane behaviours conditioned by social reality as fundamentally inane and finally insignificant. The specific and the finite are to him in the long run hideous and intransigeant, especially in the degree of their relativity, the fact that they do not have an absolute value to which all of us can readily attest. When he looks about him at the range of human possibility, at the varieties of actual human behaviour and values clashing as fanatical ideologies, he feels sick at heart, and yields to the desire to step, perpetually, back. He wants to think of nature as of something antecedent to civilization, something the social process cannot really touch, though it can obscure it a little. What is so terrible, though, is that Bellow cannot really imagine this nature. It comes to us always besmirched, corrupted, deliberately exotic as though conscious of its own implausibility. In The Victim, it is communicated in the guise of the panting dog owned by a Puerto Rican janitor, but it finally calls to the mind of Bellow's protagonist sexual adventurism and depredations of various kinds that Bellow finds not only exotic but disgusting. In Henderson the attempt to make contact with nature, one's own and the broader nature conceived generically, is involved in disciplined identification with the spirit of the lion, an identification Henderson himself never really achieves. In Sammler the most potent image of nature is the black thief riding the New York City bus lines, dressed in impeccable western splendour but described as '. . . this African prince or great black beast'. What these various images of nature have in common is the element of primary animal vitality, but none of them is generated in a context that espouses the return to nature in an authoritative way. The emotional context in each case is clouded by guilt and by a self-consciousness all the more poignant in Sammler for being so complexly developed.

That guilt and self-consciousness colour Bellow's fictions should come as no surprise, for what neither he nor his protagonist-spokesmen can freely abide is the decision to pursue selfhood apart from the more general responsibilities social reality customarily enjoins upon us. In The Victim, Leventhal feels painfully out of touch with the sordid realities Allbee resolutely thrusts before him, and suffers over his incapacity to respond sympathetically, with an emotion less tainted by horror and revulsion. In *Henderson* we have the resurrection of the service ideal, of the notion that we have no right to live for ourselves alone, that we must consecrate our lives to something greater than the enhancement of sensual pleasures. If the novel does not quite encourage a specific communal ethic, the spirit of the novel certainly instructs us in the special beauties of a life hallowed by purposes ratified and enforced by a community. For Sammler, though guilt may not be precisely the word to describe his characteristic reflections, there is a distinct discomfort associated with his sense of distance from the life of his fellows. Though he can denounce others for their failures of filial devotion, he relates to his own daughter Shula with a lofty amusement and distress which never amounts to genuine intimacy. He accuses the young of having 'no view to the nobility of being intellectuals and judges of the social order', but he recognizes somewhere in his depths the impoverishment of being a judge without at the same time allowing oneself to participate in the conventional foibles of social creatures.

What Sammler is strongly impressed by is culture, but lacking a firm grasp of social reality, he is unable meaningfully to impress it upon others. How can they relate to Sammler if not as to a magical figure to whom one periodically pays homage without doing him the honour of adopting him as a model? His notion of culture is so special a thing, so rarefied, and though he speaks of judging the social order, he has virtually no sense of how men and women may be expected to live under particular conditions, what demands it is legitimate to make of them. Of experience, mostly brutal and alienating, he has had a belly-ful, but he has become too much the adept at converting it to moral lessons and exempla to make use of it in establishing intimacies with others. He is a touch-ing figure, but the odour of death does cling to him, as he himself suspects. It is not just that he is old, that his life has largely run its course, but that he thinks of himself as old in a special sense, as inhabiting another order, of being in touch with arcane truths not permitted people who consider themselves contempo-rary. Convinced that nature is corrupted at its very source by imposing social organizations that have been taken in by individuals and elaborated as commu-nal structures of consciousness, he has decided that it is better to transcend nature than to work to improve it. He does not want to deal with a reality that is continuously uncivil and unlovely, though the novel makes it clear he will go on dealing with it, evasively to be sure, but persistently nonetheless. He will accept that perversions of nature are the most exotic and exciting things around, that he is almost as susceptible to their fascination as are most of his contemporaries, but he will insist all the while that there are mystic archetypes, human bonds we know and ratify in the blood, unutterable realities beside which social reality and perversions of nature are as insubstantial shadows. Of course, the tension is a necessary one for the would-be mystic, who cannot completely transcend the things of this world. Were he to be successful in such an enterprise, he'd have nothing left to transcend, nothing to sustain his ardour. The mind would go entirely dead, challenged by nothing, all phenomena having been reduced to absolute inconsequence. Sammler's mysticism is selective, asserted when he feels just weak enough to require an 'out', when the specific density of objects and the clamourings of other pathetic selves for solidity and permanence become more oppressive than he can bear. For the encroaching and devouring event, perpetually subverting our tenuous equilibrium, Sammler would substitute absence, only he projects this absence, this steady negation of the phenomenal, not obsessionally but modestly. In the face of the unanticipated and irregular, the accidental and individual, Sammler retreats to the universal and archetypal. His devotion is more to truth than to reality, a preference not without dire consequences for the novelistic project, at least. For though we find a comparable commitment in the work of 19th century melodramatists like Balzac, the social structure set as a backdrop for individual development in their works so convincingly revealed character and established the necessity within which relationships could take root and unfold that there was no danger of projecting eccentric behaviour as if it were a force of nature pure and simple.

Can it be that the failure of the modern world to furnish models of strength wedded to integrity and civility has forced upon Bellow the stratagems he employs? Is it fair to say that the moral impoverishment everywhere illustrated in the daily routines of the social order has literally driven writers like Bellow into fragmentary and confused elaborations of an idea of nature that cannot possibly deal with our shared experience in a satisfactory way? Surely our time is no worse than many others, a fact one hears oneself repeating with a regularity that is apt to become deadening, but there are differences in the ideas we have of ourselves and of our possibilities as social beings when we compare this period to others. Sammler himself suspects as much when he says that 'Unanimously all tasted, and each in his own way, the flavour of the end of things-as-known.' Western cultural history has long been taken with the idea of apocalypse, no doubt, but never before has apocalyptic thinking so dominated a secular age. When Sammler wonders, at another point, 'To a lunatic, how would you define a lunatic?' he follows the thought with, 'And was he himself a perfect example of sanity? He was certainly not. They were his people—he was their Sammler. They shared the same fundamentals.' Sammler does not characteristically identify himself with others so explicitly—we have already stressed his sense of personal distinction, his notion of himself as a judge—but it is telling that at least at one lucid moment he should recognize the fundamental disorientation of the entire period, a disorientation so pervasive that it is not possible even for Sammler wholly to elude it. Under such conditions, how are we to be objective, how are we to discriminate between values, between human affections, how are we to make sense of the social reality we must reclaim for our better purposes? How are we to distinguish between nature as inherent, as something given and fundamental, and nature as spurious or corrupt, though no less immutable for all that.

Mr. Sammler is no misanthrope. He feels there is something in each of us that deserves to be preserved and extended, some essence that can be nurtured by our learning to imitate what is good, by adopting proper models. 'Make it the object of imitation to reach and release the high qualities´, he tells us, 'But choose higher representations'. What he encourages is not idolatry but imitation, and this is all to the good. What is problematical, of course, is the very existence of appropriate models. Higher representations are simply not available to most of us, who will demand something more immediate. Lacking these, we shall decide, most of us at any rate, that we had best learn to get along without models, and shall cease the pursuit of ethical heights. It is this that so discourages Sammler, and why we find him so often 'considering the earth itself not as a stone cast but as something to cast oneself from—to be divested of.' Unable actually to manage this, Sammler posits a nature that is, if not edifying, at least essential. Though reality is more than he can tolerate, though human beings are in general too silly and clinging to be borne, he will have for himself a deeper dimension of reality, a dimension he can invest with whatever qualities he finds lacking as he looks about him. Princeliness, unself-conscious brutality, subversion as primal need rather than defensive gesturing: these are the fancies he frequently entertains. To be sure, Sammler likes from time to time to lose himself in the music of the spheres, to listen for that finer harmony mystics say they are able to hear. But there is a perspective in which the mystic's nature and the nature of the black thief coalesce. Both are called into being by an aesthetic attitude, a demand that there be achieved an adaptation of phenomenal reality to human faculties and human wishes. That we are denied such an achievement in our mundane lives does not mean that we may not continue to nurture a hope of its coming to pass. We speak here not of simple delusion, but of faith in the impulse to transcend, not of the drive to reshape actuality but to imagine the possibility of another dimension. The moral component is lacking here, not because it is in any way inimical to Sammler, but because in the social world he inhabits it more and more assumes the barrenness of a gratuitous emotion. It has nothing to feed on, no models of consistent behaviour to imitate. Where it appears at all it takes the form of empty rhetorical gesture without impact or meaningful extension. The nature to which Sammler turns, no matter how disparate the modes in which he conceives it, bespeaks the still potent combination of imagination and nostalgia. For Sammler, what he dreams and aspires to in his abstract, ruminative way may never have been, but may still be invested with an aura of preternatural pastness, as though it had been, and might still be. Sammler is not interested in reclaiming nature for the present generation, or for some cloudy future available to utopians and visionaries. To the degree that it exists at all, he wants it for himself alone. He is generally disturbed only when his customary aesthetic consumption of the environment is riddled with stimuli it cannot accommodate, images that refuse to be imaginatively transformed by the mystic's determined internal decrees.

We continue to care for Sammler, though, and it must be because his mysticism is inhibited by more than a vestige of conventional sanity. He remains always a figure to whom we can relate, whose distinction has not, for all his occasional pretensions to the contrary, wholly removed him from the turmoils with which we associate genuine reality. He leaves us with the impression of a man we might have a great deal to do with, who is as little content as most of us have been with the edifice of reason as it has come to us in our time. If his mystical impulses lead him to ignore what many of us know of necessity, his memory is still vivid, and he knows in his better moments how foolish it is to demand what 'the sum of human facts', as he puts it, cannot yield. Where he disappoints us is in his continuing incapacity to get beyond the realm of senti-mental affirmation to a more acute apprehension of social reality. We are not inclined to demand of him that he abandon his ideas of nature but that he somehow manage to place them in the perspective in which they belong.

To make this point more clearly, and it is surely a crucial point in these considerations, it is instructive to examine a key passage occurring near the end of Bellow's novel. Riding along in the automobile owned by his favourite nephew, Sammler notices a crowd gathered in the street to watch a fight of some sort. Getting out of the car and coming closer, he sees that the fight is between the black pick-pocket and Feffer, a young man of Sammler's acquaint-ance to whom he has confided his experiences of the black man. As the fight proceeds, Sammler feels himself growing physically ill and profoundly aware of his weakness: 'He was old. He lacked physical force. He knew what to do, but had no power to execute it.' There, if you will, is the dilemma that Sammler can do nothing to resolve or to overcome. He knows what to do, not what can actually be done, but what ought to be done. We must be careful to see that it is not moral knowledge as such that Sammler would invoke here, but a knowledge of propriety that is a function of a resolutely aesthetic attitude. From a strictly moral point of view, and to the degree that moral laws are at least in some sense communally sanctioned, it is proper that the black thief be brought to justice, that he be prevented from further depredations. This is not a consideration that carries much weight with Sammler, though he had himself earlier informed the police, to no avail, of the black man's conduct. For Sammler, what matters is that two men are fighting with one another on the streets of New York, provid-ing a spectacle that is singularly unedifying and unsavoury.

After a while, Sammler's estranged son-in-law Eisen comes along, carrying a sack of metal pieces which he will use in his work as a sculptor. Sammler pleads with Eisen to break up the fight, insisting that it must be done at once. The younger man complies, stepping in to do what he can, but finds that the black man is a difficult fellow to put down. They struggle, and Eisen begins hitting his opponent with the weighted sack, to Sammler's horror and amaze-ment. Stung by Sammler's angry reproaches, Eisen responds: ' "You can't hit a man like this just once. When you hit him you must really hit him. Otherwise he'll kill you. You know. We both fought in the war. You were a Partisan. You had a gun. So don't you know ... If in—in. No? If out—out. Yes? No? So answer." ' Against which we read, 'It was the reasoning that sank Sammler's heart completely.'

Now I do not see anything especially heartless or inhuman in Eisen's reasoning. What he says makes good sense, though obviously it reflects his intellectual limitations. Were the occasion less pressing and perilous, perhaps even he might have explained his behaviour more elaborately, but without the sort of flourishes a Sammler might applaud. We may not like to think of contemporary life in New York as similar to a state of war, but it is clear that for many of its inhabitants that is what it has become. That such people, subjected as they are to acts of effrontery and violence almost every day, are not apt to be enthusiastic about turning the other cheek or 'taking it easy' should come as no shock. Nor is Eisen mistaken when he says, 'If in—in'. For that is precisely what too many people of humane and liberal persuasion refuse to acknowledge. One does not need to line up with the pigs, to be thought of as a repressive brute, because one has done what is necessary to restore order and protect one's narrow life-space in the immediate terms available to individuals in the social realm. Sammler is almost right when, recognizing the dilemma we earlier cited, he says that 'To be so powerless was death'. To attempt to hold together a social order and restore to sanity an entire culture on the basis of modest gestures and whining sentiments is a form of deadly foolishness—and that is something we must not only see but renounce as well. This seems clear to me, at least.

That Sammler will continue to see, but never come to renounce the foolishness, is similarly clear. We persist in our affection for him because he is a decent and interesting man, no matter how confused, because he has suffered a great deal, and because he is actually old, not just belligerently old-fashioned. Powerless as he feels himself, and as his sentimental idealism ensures that he must be, it is no wonder that he should conceive nature as he does, or that he should proclaim the merits of undifferentiated being. Such a resolution is, after all, entirely credible and acceptable for a man who cannot act effectually to stem the tide of events, even those that affect him most closely and visibly. To demand an aesthetic response to human experience, a response that includes recognition of enduring, *natural* human obligations is to ask of most of us, alas, more than we can manage, or want to. Sammler is not an acceptable model for most of us, nor are his ideas of nature, social reality and authenticity such that we ought to acquiesce in them indiscriminately. He is, however, a portrait of a very special and moving individual who raises a great many questions about our lives. Saul Bellow may not know any more certainly than Mr. Sammler the precise shape and direction of his own sentiments, nor the social implications that may follow from them. But there is no doubt that he knows the terror and confusion that beset those of us who try to take in and respond responsibly to the contemporary experience.

Mr. Bellow's *Sammler*:
The Evolution of a
Contemporary Text

Keith Cushman*

When Saul Bellow is asked about his working method as a novelist, he sometimes tells a story about an American tenor making his debut at La Scala. The tenor sings his first aria, and the audience goes wild with applause, thundering out cascades of bravos and insisting that he sing the aria again. The tenor repeats the aria and receives even more uproarious approval. Once more the audience demands that he repeat the aria. After the exhilarated tenor performs his aria a third time, the audience is more demonstrative than ever and demands a fourth performance. The tenor, deeply moved, steps forward to the footlights to thank his listeners. He tells them of all the long years that have led to this night: the encouragement from his mother, the family scrimping and saving that made music school possible, the small parts he sang in provincial houses at the beginning of his career, and his slow progress as he worked his way up to La Scala and this greatest evening of his life. He thanks the audience from the bottom of his heart—but isn't it time to get on with the opera? How many times do they want him to sing the aria? A voice from the audience answers: "You must sing until you get it right." And that, says Saul Bellow, is his working method.[1]

Bellow is an inveterate reviser. A new work by Saul Bellow emerges only as the end product of a long and complicated process of rewriting and reformulating, persistently dedicated to "getting it right." He has said that when he begins a new novel he has to "thresh and sift and winnow until I have a clear notion of what I'm up to."[2] Even after he has "discovered" the general shape and outline of the novel, the job of threshing, sifting, and winnowing continues. Characteristically this process of alteration and refinement is not finished until the time that the new book goes to press.

E. M. Forster's remark about writing, quoted with approval by Bellow, bears on his own compositional habits: "How do I know what I think until I see what I say?"[3] To Bellow, the work-in-progress is an artistic and intellectual experience that the writer engages himself in. Potentially it is an experience without end, for each new immersion in the process of revision is certain to

*Reprinted from *Studies in the Novel*, 7 (1975), 425–44.

change the work of art. Bellow himself acknowledges that he cannot bear to read some of his novels because of the "mistakes" on every page.[4]

One striking example of Bellow's devotion to "getting it right" is the interview with Gordon Lloyd Harper published in the third series of *Writers at Work*. The substance of the interview came out of two recording sessions which totaled no more than ninety minutes. The actual tapes, however, were just the beginning:

> Following each taping session, a typescript of his remarks was prepared. Bellow worked over these typed sheets extensively with pen and ink, taking as many as three separate meetings to do a complete revision. Then another typescript was made, and the process started over. This work was done when the interviewer could be present, and again the changes were frequently tested on him.[5]

The published interview emerged only after five weeks of meeting and revising two or three times a week.

With such care lavished on a seventeen-page interview, it is not surprising that the labors that go into a novel, from conception to completion, are prodigious. In this essay I propose to concentrate on the making of *Mr. Sammler's Planet*, the novel which won Bellow his third National Book Award. *Mr. Sammler's Planet* is especially endearing to textual scholars because it was published in two different versions. It was serialized in the November and December 1969 issues of the *Atlantic*, and then the Viking Press brought it out in book form early the next year. The differences between *Atlantic* and Viking versions are considerable. As we shall see, the *Atlantic* text is but one important stage of Bellow's efforts to get his novel right.

Bellow is scrupulous about preserving the various holographs, typescripts, and galleys that go into the composition and production of his works. He has an obvious interest in and respect for the process that produces his novels. The rich and abundant materials that went into the creation of *Mr. Sammler's Planet* are on deposit in the Department of Special Collections in the University of Chicago Library. This essay could not have been written without Saul Bellow's generous permission to explore and make use of these materials. I wish to thank him and the Special Collections staff for their kindness and cooperation.

The scholar with access to all the extant *Sammler* materials has an excellent ringside seat from which to observe the creation of a masterwork of recent American fiction. The textual critic's ideal is to be able to account for and verify every word that found its way into the Viking text; inevitably that is an unattainable ideal. Nevertheless, the materials for *Mr. Sammler's Planet* are so replete that the scholar is granted the illusion of coming close to his ideal—or at least of seeing it, miragelike, in the middle distance.

My primary aim in this essay is to provide a sense of how *Mr. Sammler's Planet* evolved. Rather than attempting a definitive textual study, I want to offer an idea of the kinds of materials that exist for such a recent novel and to indicate the nature of the textual problems that arise. I will have an imaginary editor of the future in mind, and this essay will be something of a prologomena to the textual study of *Mr. Sammler's Planet*. I will also be using the *Sammler* materials to illustrate the working method of our most distinguished living novelist. It also seems especially worthwhile to comment on the two very different published versions of the book.

Let me begin by roughly outlining the *Mr. Sammler's Planet* deposit. The earliest materials are holograph fragments in which the protagonist is not Artur Sammler but Meyer Pawlyk and his daughter is not Shula but Rosa. A few pages of these fragments were deposited in the University of Chicago Library as early as 1967. The first complete version of the novel is a holograph written out in four notebooks and entitled *The Future of the Moon* (the working title right up to *Atlantic* publication). In this version the protagonist begins as Artur Mendelsohn, but by page 8 he has become Artur Sammler.

A typescript was prepared from these four notebooks; this typescript is extensively revised in Bellow's hand. In turn a second typescript was prepared incorporating the revisions in the first typescript. It is this second typescript which is the basis for the copy-text used by the *Atlantic*. Bellow slightly revised a carbon copy of this second typescript and sent it to the magazine. The carbon of the first four chapters was xeroxed by the *Atlantic*. The xerox displays printer's proofmarkings, including the inevitable house styling; each chapter is marked "Nov. Atlantic." No xerox was made of chapters five and six. These chapters were printed directly from the carbons Bellow had sent. The carbons for both chapters display printer's proofmarkings and much house styling. Both are marked "November Atlantic" even though these two chapters comprise the second installment that was not printed until December.

Meanwhile Bellow had sent a xerox of the uncorrected second typescript to Edward Shils at Cambridge University. Shils, the eminent sociologist and Bellow's colleague on the Committee of Social Thought at the University of Chicago, annotated this xerox copy of the second typescript. The Shils annotations that Bellow chose to incorporate show up for the first time in the Viking Press galleys.

The Viking galleys were set from the *Atlantic* text, and they are extensively revised. The key revisions are found in a set of galleys marked "Duplicates." Even at what would seem to be the final stage of composition, new pages of typescript are found at several key junctures in the text. In these instances Bellow did so much revising that he wrote out portions of the final text in new typescript. In other words, some of *Mr. Sammler's Planet* was never set in galleys because Bellow revised these portions so extensively *after* the book had been set in galleys.

The Viking Press edition completes the story. To recapitulate, the earliest materials are the Pawlyk holograph fragments; then comes the *Future of the Moon* holograph written out in four notebooks; then the heavily revised first typescript from which a second typescript was produced to be sent to the *Atlantic*; *Atlantic* galleys and *Atlantic* text; Viking Press galleys including some revisions by Bellow based on annotations made by Edward Shils in a xerox copy of the second typescript; and finally *Mr. Sammler's Planet* as published by Viking early in 1970. Here and there additional typescript pages, somewhat difficult to place in the compositional sequence, turn up. But essentially the preserved order is close to complete and fairly easy to piece together.

Perhaps the most interesting materials of all are the earliest—the various Pawlyk holograph and typescript fragments. It seems unlikely that all the Pawlyk materials are extant. The nature of the holograph and typescript indicates that more than one stage of composition was involved; perhaps several were. It is also hard to determine how far Bellow went with this preliminary version of his novel. There are sixty-four pages of Pawlyk materials on deposit. One holograph fragment runs continuously for twenty-nine pages, but the Pawlyk fragments consist mostly of bits and pieces one or two pages in length. The bits and pieces also tend to be versions of the same pages over and over again. For example, the sixty-four leaves of Pawlyk materials include five different versions of the opening of the novel, each just one or two pages long. All sixty-four leaves belong to the early portions of the novel as we know it, and most are from the very beginning.

It also seems highly probable that Bellow made use of these Pawlyk drafts—and perhaps additional Pawlyk drafts no longer extant when he wrote out the four holograph *Future of the Moon* notebooks. Unmistakable traces of many passages in these fragments can be found even in the Viking text of the novel. Many phrases, sentences, and even whole passages survive nearly intact all the way from the earliest formulations through the completion of the novel.

This point is worth illustrating. The twenty-nine page fragment that is by far the longest of the Pawlyk fragments comprises a nearly clean typescript that was obviously a fair copy from earlier versions. It includes a visit to Sammler by Angela, his rich and promiscuous great-niece. One passage in this visit contains the following sentences:

> She crossed her legs on a chair too fragile to accommodate such thighs, such curves. She opened her purse for a cigarette, and Pawlyk gave her a light. She loved his manners. The smoke came from her nostrils and she looked at him with cheerful slyness, she the beautiful maiden, he the old hermit in his cell (I, 7, 24).[6]

Notice how similar this is to a passage in the second chapter of the Viking text of the novel:

> She crossed her legs on a chair too fragile to accommodate such thighs, too straight for her hips. She opened her purse for a cigarette, and Sammler offered a light. She loved his manners. The smoke came from her nose, and she looked at him, when she was in good form, cheerfully with a touch of slyness. The beautiful maiden. He was the old hermit (V 70).[7]

Keep in mind that I am comparing this bit from an early Pawlyk typescript with a parallel passage from the final text, dating from at least two or three years later. Even though it is hard to find many instances in which parallel passages are so similar, still, one must conclude that the Pawlyk materials figured directly in the evolution of the novel. They cannot be considered fragments from an abandoned draft.

It seems certain that the various Pawlyk fragments help explain the remarkable fluency of the holograph *Future of the Moon* written out in those four notebooks. The four notebooks can hardly be considered a first draft. Instead Bellow was to some extent—and sometimes to considerable extent—making use of earlier drafts. The one great mystery is how much Pawlyk material there originally was.

Inevitably, the Pawlyk materials are most interesting for the way they differ from the completed novel. The revelations that follow are not intended to be earthshaking. The Pawlyk fragments show Bellow at work at his regular job of threshing, sifting, and winnowing, figuring out what he is up to. One should not make too much of conceptualizations and formulations that are probably quite tentative. At the same time it is fascinating to find so many unfamiliar details mixed in with elements of the novel easily recognizable to readers of the first edition.

To give you an idea of what the Pawlyk materials are like, I will quote in full a fragment that is surely the earliest extant. This version of the opening of the novel runs to a little more than a page of holograph. Bellow made many changes and corrections in the passage as he wrote it, crossing out words, phrases, and large parts of sentences. The less than perfect punctuation also suggests the rush of composition:

> At an El station in the Black Belt, in the street at the foot of the gray, horrible stairs ancient in wear if not in years, two young Negroes, mere boys, jumped Pawlyk. They hurt him badly and took his wallet. There were other Negroes, waiting for the bus, but no one helped. It was one of those icy Chicago days when Sixty-third St., thanks to the wind, is not too fetid. Elderly, foreign (anyone could tell that) heavy, Pawlyk with a bleeding eye was picking himself up when the squad car came, a blue cyclops, and the police took charge. Brief inquiries were made. No one knew a thing. Pawlyk was unable to say "purple windbreaker" or "brimless fedora" in English. His vocabulary was academic. On the whole the police were very decent. Pawlyk was not looking for sympathy. Over the years his objectivity had become very deep, and even at such a moment, with the blood forming thick drops in his eye, he refolded his handkerchief, undemonstrative.[8]

The most striking feature of this passage is its setting in Chicago rather than New York City. (As it turned out, readers had to wait until *Humboldt's Gift* for Bellow to return them to Chicago.) The four other versions of this scene found among the Pawlyk fragments are all set in Queens. Of course the mugging of the uncharacteristically "heavy" protagonist is a trial run for the important episode involving the princely and elegant black pickpocket whom Sammler sees at work on the bus, who notices Sammler watching him, and who follows Sammler to his apartment building lobby and exposes his genitals to him as an idiosyncratic but unmistakable warning. It goes without saying that the pickpocket offered Bellow richer thematic implications, not to mention a particularly arresting opening to the novel.

The Shula who appears in the Pawlyk fragments is very much the Shula of *Mr. Sammler's Planet*—except that her name is Rosa. Shula's violent husband Eisen is present in much the same language that is found in the Viking text, and so is Sammler's nephew Gruner, the important character whose death moves

Sammler to the beautiful farewell testament that concludes the novel. However, Gruner had not become a gynecologist in the Pawlyk materials; instead he is a meat wholesaler doing business with restaurants. Again it is obvious that the change in Gruner's profession heightens thematic implications in a novel so expressly concerned with life and death and the future of our planet. In one fragment Gruner's children are two respectable married daughters rather than the promiscuous Angela and the wildly eccentric Wallace.

To complete the cast of characters, Pawlyk's wife is Celia rather than Antonina. She perished in the Warsaw Ghetto rather than the mass grave from which Sammler, Lazarus-like, escaped. One passage in the longest of the Pawlyk typescripts offers a reminiscence of the nature of the marriage between the protagonist and his wife, something we learn nothing about in the *Atlantic* and Viking texts. Several of the Pawlyk fragments refer to Mary Pawlyk, the aged widow of one of the protagonist's cousins but a character not found in the novel as the world knows it. Finally, Dr. Govinda Lal, the Indian scientist whose manuscript on the possible settlement of the moon has been stolen by Shula, thus triggering much of the novel's action, appears in only one fragment and as an anonymous South African. Rosa/Shula reminds her father that she borrowed the manuscript for him two weeks ago and that the author has to return shortly to South Africa. This one brief exchange does not make it clear whether or not Rosa/Shula has stolen the manuscript, although it seems probable. Even in the Viking text Shula first describes the manuscript as being on "short loan" (V 50). Lal surfaces for the first time in his Indian incarnation in the *Future of the Moon* holograph notebooks.

The sixty-four leaves of Pawlyk holograph and typescript are all that is left of the *Ur*-form of the novel. Some ideas were immediately discarded, but others survived through the final text. And even in passages that were quickly dropped from the work-in-progress, Bellow often retained phrases and insights that seemed right. There is a sort of creative economy here. Once Bellow has gotten a phrase right, he is apt to keep it—even though everything surrounding that phrase may be discarded.

The four *Future of the Moon* notebooks comprise the next stage of composition. These notebooks add up to a complete and completely recognizable version of the novel from beginning to end. The first paragraph of the first notebook is almost word-for-word identical with the Viking Press first paragraph. The concluding paragraph of the fourth holograph notebook, after one trial run, differs only in minor detail from the concluding paragraph of the Viking Press edition. There is manifest evidence of revision throughout these notebooks, some of it so extensive that it should be considered fresh composition. At the same time, as I have suggested, it also seems clear that these notebooks build on earlier versions.

In the four holograph notebooks Bellow seems to be trying to get down on paper a solid complete version of the novel, a working text from which he could proceed. When the notebooks were completed, Bellow had essentially found *Mr. Sammler's Planet*. A good deal of trial-and-error went into the Pawlyk drafts, but with the completion of the *Moon* notebooks the basic outline, characters, and incidents of his novel—and indeed the sequence of actions, ruminations, and interspersed memories—were all in place. The Pawlyk fragments show Bellow looking for Mr. Sammler and his story; the *Moon* notebooks constitute the first draft of *Mr. Sammler's Planet*. All the subsequent typescripts and galleys and texts should be understood as revisions of the book he first got together in the *Moon* notebooks.

The *Paris Review* interview includes an intriguing description of the style Bellow developed in *Henderson the Rain King* and *Herzog*. These remarks also seem to me to reflect on the composition of *Mr. Sammler's Planet:*

> I wouldn't really know how to describe it. I don't care to trouble my mind to find an exact description for it, but it has something to do with a kind of readiness to record impressions arising from a source of which we know little. I suppose that all of us have a primitive prompter or commentator within, who from earliest years has been advising us, telling us what the real world is. There is such a commentator in me. I have to prepare the ground for him. From this source come words, phrases, syllables; sometimes only sounds, which I try to interpret, sometimes whole paragraphs, fully punctuated.[9]

Not I, not I, but the wind that blows through me! Bellow's account of the voice within sounds like a recollection of D. H. Lawrence listening to the promptings of his demon.[10] Artistic creation is viewed as an experience that the writer participates in and indeed submits to. The writer must listen carefully if he is to seize the best words out of the flow.

This passage is also an accurate description of the ruminative style of *Herzog, Mr. Sammler's Planet,* and *Humboldt's Gift.* In *Sammler* Bellow makes us believe that we are directly in contact with the "primitive prompter or commentator" within his elderly protagonist. Artur Sammler goes through his days, responding to the world around him, trying to make some sort of sense of it. The substance of the narrative is Sammler's consciousness. The novel's rich stream of association with its interplay of intellect, imagination, and memory obviously owes a good deal to Joyce.

This quality of Bellow's art achieves a natural culmination in *Humboldt's Gift,* which was in part dictated to a typist. In contrast—and not surprisingly— none of *Mr. Sammler's Planet* was dictated. The spoken word seems everywhere discernible in the exuberant, richly comic *Humboldt,* whereas the "voice" in *Sammler* is much more inward and meditative.[11]

One could argue that the evolution of *Mr. Sammler's Planet* from the earliest holograph fragments to the final printed form consists of Bellow's continuing effort to hear the "commentator within" as truly and accurately as possible. Some "whole paragraphs, fully punctuated" did emerge right at the start and remained, virtually intact, throughout the composition. Other passages were rewritten over and over again: this is especially true of the lengthy conversation between Sammler and Govinda Lal at the Gruner house in New Rochelle and of great chunks of the concluding pages of the book. Bellow's efforts to get his novel right proceeded at an uneven pace. The passages most difficult for the inner commentator to get right are the passages most frequently and extremely revised.

I can best illustrate the nature of the revisions by tracing a passage from its formulation in the *Moon* notebooks to its final form in the Viking text. The passage I will use was selected almost at random. The patterns of revision it displays are characteristic of the process of revision as a whole.

Bellow made use of his own experience covering the Six Days' War in the Middle East as a correspondent for *Newsday* to provide Sammler with his memories of that war. The passage I have selected is found near the end of the fifth chapter on page 251 of the Viking text. It is part of the largest flashback to the war.

Father Jewel, soon to become Newell, is a Jesuit priest working as a war correspondent. Sammler is obviously struck by this man of God with his full fund of military expertise, as is demonstrated by the following passage in the fourth of the holograph *Moon* notebooks:

> Father Jewel, a war expert, was only too keen to show and explain the war to Mr. Sammler. He named the guns, identified the tanks, the calibre of the shells. He could not read the Russian letters stencilled in white on green metal. Mr. Sammler read for him *Gorkiskii Autozavod*. In the clumsy ballooning, battle dress, meant for jungles, the Jesuit walked in the desert. Look out for mines, he said. See how easily the Jewish shells had pierced the Russian armor And see the reddish, the mauve the unnatural colors of napalm. It made a characteristic clinker, said Father Jewel of green tinged salmon pink. A whole little war, miniature but as real as any other—savage because the Arabs had threatened massacres in Tel Aviv, and this Army Jews had lost their fear of death. "You can see that, can't you?" (I, 4, unnumbered).

Many words are cancelled like the "Army" that became "Jews" as indicated. The casual punctuation also suggests that Bellow was mainly trying to get the words down on paper. Cleaning up and polishing would come later.

This passage has two forms in the first typescript draft that was prepared from the *Future of the Moon* holograph notebooks. After this first typescript text had been completed, Bellow rewrote the Six Days' War flashback so thoroughly that eight pages needed to be retyped. The original rejected version of the passage contains much the same contents found in the holograph notebook, but the passage has been slightly rearranged and made more concise:

> Mr Sammler and Father Jewel took a walk up the road. "Just look out for the mines," said the priest. he could not read the Russian letters stencilled in white on the tanks. Mr Sammler read them for him. "*Gorkiskii Autozavod*." Father Jewel knew the names of the guns, knew the calibres, the ranges, the thicknesses of armor. In clumsy ballooning battle dress meant for the jungle, conspicuous in the desert. "And see that color—that's napalm, sure as anything." It made a characteristic clinker of green tinged salmon pink. See all that reddish, all that mauve out there. Those Jews were tough. It was a real little war, you know. He meant that after all they still could kill. They kept the respect of mankind (I, 12, 205).

When Bellow rewrote the original version of the big Six Days' War flashback in the first typescript, he made the passage we have been scrutinizing even more concise. The description of the priest's inappropriate uniform is deleted, and his revelation about Israeli napalm is more neatly formulated. In addition Jewel for the first time becomes Newell (a name which quietly alludes to the changed order of established things):

> As Mr Sammler and Father Newell walked together, they were warned not to step from the road because of mines. Sammler read out for the priest the Russian letters stencilled white on the green tanks and trucks: *Gorkiskii Autozavod*, most of them said. Father Newell seemed to know a lot about gun calibres, armor thickness, ranges. In a lowered voice, out of respect for the Israelis who denied its use, he positively identified the napalm. See all that reddish, all that mauve out there? Salmon pink with a green tinge in the clinkers was the sure sign. It was a real little war. These Jews were tough (I, 12, x–4).

This version in the first typescript of the novel is essentially the text that made its way into the *Atlantic*, and the Viking text is not very different from it.

I should also point out that what seems to be a minor textual error enters at this juncture. Although it is only an error in punctuation, it throws off the meaning slightly. If Father Newell indicates the napalm and lowers his voice "out of respect for the Israelis who denied its use," that means that there are also Israelis who *do not* deny the use of napalm to journalists. It seems doubtful that Bellow means to suggest that, and consequently there should be a comma after "Israelis." That is one for the Bellow editor of the future to think about.

The above passage was reproduced exactly in the second typescript that was prepared; it is this version that was submitted to the *Atlantic* for magazine publication. There are only three variations from this passage in the revised *Atlantic* galleys. A holograph emendation by Bellow changes "from the road" to "off the road." The two other variations are changes in spelling only: "stencilled" becomes "stenciled," "calibres" becomes "calibers." Both spelling changes can be found in the printed galleys, and they bring us up against the long-standing problem of bibliographic treatment of accidentals. It seems pretty clear that the changes were made by an editor in the interest of standard house spelling. Bellow's spellings—"calibre" and "stencilled"—are accepted spellings, though "caliber" and "stenciled" are preferred. The future editor of Saul Bellow will have to decide between the author's spelling or the preferred American spelling used by the editors at the *Atlantic* and Viking Press. This will not be a decision of major proportions, but in its own modest way the question is a thorny one.

The passage in the revised *Atlantic* galleys appears word-for-word in the *Atlantic* text of December 1969. There are, however, a few changes in the passage as it is found in the corrected Viking galleys. The passage we have been examining immediately follows a rather grisly description of corpses decaying in the desert sun. In the Viking galleys Bellow interpolates: "A strange flavor of human grease. Of wet paper pulp. Mr. Sammler fought his nausea." As a result, Bellow changes the beginning of the next sentence from "As Mr. Sammler and Father Newell walked" to "As he and Father Newell walked." There is one other change. In the *Atlantic* Newell "positively identified the napalm." In the corrected Viking galleys Newell simply "identified the napalm." After the description of its characteristic color and effects, a new sentence is interpolated to pick up further the priest's characteristic speech and special interests: "Positively napalm" (III, 1, galley 74). Interestingly, there is no hard evidence that Bellow himself was responsible for the changes that appear for the first time in the Viking galleys, though it seems certain that he was. No extant galleys show these changes in his hand; instead one finds the changes already printed in a set of galleys marked "Revised proof" and "for author." The issue is further confused because these galleys do contain a good deal of holograph revision in Bellow's hand. The commonsensical conclusion is that an earlier state of galleys existed and that Bellow made the changes there. Once again however, editorial judgment must be called on if the text is to be established.

The Viking Press text of the passage is identical with the corrected Viking galleys. The evolution of the passage displays a certain amount of verbal accretion, but essentially the process is one of refinement. The only important exception to this generalization is the interesting pattern of expansion involved in the revision of the *Atlantic* text of the novel, a pattern I will be describing later. The *Moon* notebooks present the novel in rough form, but it is unmistakably the novel we know. The various revisions in typescript and in the *Atlantic* galleys put the novel into sharper focus and make the details cleaner and clearer.

So far in talking about the *Sammler* revisions, I have concentrated on the gradual, painstaking, and somewhat laborious process in which the writer engages himself with his text over and over again, each time altering it in the direction of its ultimate form. I have borrowed Bellow's own metaphor and spoken of him as listening to the voice within, trying to hear and heed its dictations as accurately as possible. But of course the voice within is not the only voice a novelist listens to while he is writing a novel. Bellow is not uncharacteristic in seeking the comments of an outside reader whose judgment he respects. Bellow made use of the comments Edward Shils recorded in his xerox copy of the second typescript. In a curious way one could say that *Mr. Sammler's Planet* is something of a collaborative effort. At any rate the book would be slightly different if Bellow had not sought out Shils's comments and taken them seriously.

The Shils annotations are not extensive, but they do have a distinctive local interest. They show up as revisions in the Viking galleys, which means that Shils's comments are incorporated in the Viking text but not in the *Atlantic* text. Some of Shils's annotations merely point out verbal and syntactical awkwardness. For example, he points out the following sentence from early in the novel: "He had reconsidered the whole question of Anglophilia with numerous cases of Salvador de Madariagas, Mario Prazes, André Maurois, and Colonel Bramble" (NAt 97).[12] With Shils's prompting this sentence became: "He had reconsidered the whole question of Anglophilia, thinking skeptically about Salvador de Madariaga, Mario Praz, André Maurois, and Colonel Bramble" (V 6).

More interesting, however, are suggestions by Shils which alter the substance of the novel as well as its syntax. It is Shils who relocates Sammler's

Bloomsbury address, suggesting that Great Russell Street would have been a little seedy even in the twenties and thirties and providing a list of alternatives from which Bellow selected Woburn Square. At one point in the *Atlantic* text "the Sammlers lived in Bloomsbury" (NAt 104a); at the same point in the Viking text they lived "in Woburn Square, Bloomsbury" (V 28). The same change shows up in the fifth chapter when Lal is asking Sammler about his London years. In the *Atlantic* text Sammler says he lived "on Great Russell Street near the British Museum" (DAt 110b); in the Viking first edition this appears as "in Woburn Square near the British Museum" (V 210). On his way home from the Six Days' War Sammler stops off in London and visits "his old flat in Great Russell Street" (DAt 124a) in the *Atlantic*, "his old flat in Woburn Square" (V 253) in the Viking first edition. However, Mr. Sammler's change of address is responsible for one obvious mistake in the Viking text, for at one point the address simply did not get changed. Early in the novel Sammler, thinking about the same period in his life, remembers his days "when he lived in Great Russell Street"—and he does so in both the *Atlantic* (NAt 101b) and Viking (V 19) versions.[13] It is especially easy for human error to creep in when changes like this are being incorporated. Think of the notoriously corrupt first English edition of *Women in Love* in which the name of Halliday's mistress has generally been changed to Minette but sometimes remains Pussum—and in one paragraph Minette and Pussum coexist almost side by side, causing desperate readers to assume that they are two separate characters.[14] The future editor of Bellow is sure to want to domicile Mr. Sammler in only one place at a time in Bloomsbury during the twenties and thirties.

Shils's English expertise is also called into service in the case of Maynard Keynes, a Bloomsbury acquaintance of Mr. Sammler. Shils points out that Keynes did not become a baron until the forties, a time when Sammler was trapped in Poland. As a result "Lord Keynes" (NAt 101b) in the *Atlantic* is reduced to "Maynard Keynes" (V 19) in the Viking text because Sammler knew him before the war. Shils is also responsible for another interesting minor variation. In the *Atlantic* version we learn that Sammler's niece Margotte Arkin always speaks of her late husband Ussher "as her Man" (NAt 102a). Shils points out the possible confusion between this phrase and its German origin—*Mann* means both "man" and "husband" in German—and the somewhat different connotations of the phrase when its associations are with the blues. As a result, in the Viking text Margotte speaks of her late husband, "Germanically, as her Man" (V 20). I will mention only one change suggested by Shils and incorporated by Bellow. In the *Atlantic* text Sammler, on his way back to New York from the Six Days' War, notices "that the British advertising industry had discovered the female nude, and that most posters in the Underground were of women in undergarments" (DAt 124a). Shils remembers the same phenomenon with greater accuracy, and in the Viking first edition Sammler observes that "most posters along the escalators of the Underground were of women in undergarments" (V 253).

There is no difficulty in establishing the authority for the changes suggested by Shils, for they show up in Bellow's hand as revisions in the Viking galleys. Bellow did not make use of all the suggestions. I personally agree with Shils that the book would profit if some of the lengthy intellectualizing in the Sammler-Lal scene in New Rochelle were trimmed, but this is a suggestion Bellow ignored. The use of the Shils commentary is one of the most fascinating aspects of the making of *Mr. Sammler's Planet*. The case of Mr. Sammler's Bloomsbury address also demonstrates the textual problems that can result from such outside assistance, no matter how sound and helpful that assistance is.

The copyright page of the Viking Press first edition includes the laconic information that "this book originally appeared in *Atlantic Monthly* in a different form." Even if the texts of the *Atlantic* and Viking editions were identical—which is anything but the case—the forms of the two versions would be worth commenting on. For example, the *Atlantic* reader had to wait an entire month between November and December of 1969 if he wanted to finish the novel. The book is divided after the fourth chapter, and there is even a nice curtain as Sammler leaves Gruner at the hospital, promises to return the next day, and prepares to ride to New Rochelle. Readers of Dickens's big part novels were able to proceed from month to month without benefit of any recapitulation of the earlier action, but the December 1969 installment of *Mr. Sammler's Planet* in the *Atlantic* begins with a 461-word summary of the November installment. This summary twice mentions that Sammler lived in Bloomsbury during the thirties though the novel makes it clear that he lived there in the twenties as well. The summary does not mention Sammler's humiliation by the students during his lecture at Columbia, one of the most vivid episodes in the novel, nor does it mention his encounter with Walter Bruch, a character who does not reappear in the December installment. This synopsis was written by Bellow himself, but this is impossible to know unless you see the corrected typescript for it among the *Sammler* materials on deposit at Chicago.

In addition the *Atlantic* text includes fifteen illustrations inserted at various points on the printed page, eight in the November installment and seven in December. These illustrations appear to be pen-and-ink drawings photographically reproduced. The artist, whose name is Cossi, is nowhere credited. The rather stylized and quite effective drawings mostly depict cityscapes, though a few represent portions of urban interiors. They are uniformly bleak and somber. The *Atlantic* reader is apt to have a somewhat grayer impression of *Mr. Sammler's Planet* than the Viking reader because of these illustrations.

One other nonverbal difference between the *Atlantic* and Viking texts has minor but interesting bearing. Each version is of course divided into six chapters, but in addition there are breaks in the text at five points in the *Atlantic*: one in 1, one in 2, two in 5, and one in 6. Only the last of these two internal breaks shows up in the Viking text, and it cannot be discerned whether the decision to eliminate the other three was made by Bellow or a Viking editor. Without a break the reader experiences continuous flow, but a break in the text signals the reader to expect that he is embarking on something at least slightly different. Consider the point in the fifth chapter at which the weighty dialogue between

Sammler and Lal is rather mercifully interrupted by the water flooding out from the burst pipes. In the *Atlantic* there is a break after Sammler's last enormous seven-paragraph monologue and before Shula's question about the water—a break that signals the novel is shifting gears. There is no such break in the Viking edition: Bellow wants the intellectualizing more obviously undercut (dampened?), and he also wants to keep the continuity going. Both of the internal breaks that remain in the Viking text are there to signal definite lapses of time. However, one of the two—Mr. Sammler meditating in bed after the day that ended with the burst pipes—is not noticeable because the break comes between the bottom of page 246 and the top of page 247 and only one line has been subtracted from the top of 247. We can be sure that Bellow did intend these last two internal breaks, for they were part of the novel from the beginning. Nevertheless, one of the two is not observable unless you happen to be looking for it. I do not aim to revolutionize textual criticism with this observation, yet it is a matter that does make a difference.

Of course the main difference between the *Atlantic* and Viking texts is the words. A collation of the two texts reveals that there are substantive differences on nearly every page. Most of these revisions can be traced to the extensively revised galleys for the Viking edition. These galleys were set from the *Atlantic* edition, and Bellow could not resist one final opportunity to make the novel as strong as possible.

I am not suggesting that he wrote a new book at the last minute. The Viking edition differs from the magazine text in detail more than in substance. Bellow already had a clear sense of the book he was writing when he wrote out the version of the novel found in the four holograph *Future of the Moon* notebooks. The *Atlantic* and Viking texts display only one rather secondary difference in plot. Yet the Viking edition seems to me quite obviously the richer and more refined version of the text.

The one plot difference is easily described. In all completed versions of the book Dr. Govinda Lal is perceived as new blood by both the widowed Margotte and the eccentric spinster Shula. In the *Atlantic* text love has already begun to bloom for Margotte and Lal. Near the end of the novel Mr. Sammler stops off at his apartment en route from New Rochelle to the hospital to pick up some family papers that Gruner wants him to bring. In the *Atlantic* version he meets Margotte and Lal, and they chat briefly. It is obvious that romance is budding between Margotte and the Indian scientist: "Before the much taller Mr. Sammler these two people, delighted with each other, seemed to announce how lucky they were. Lovers like to parade their good fortune. Let the world see that Love is still Love" (DAt 133b). The brief scene somewhat incongruously asserts the power of love in the face of death, for when Sammler reaches the hospital he discovers that Gruner is already dead. In the Viking text Margotte has invited Lal home to lunch, but that is as far as she has gotten.

As with all the other stages of revision, Bellow's revisions of the *Atlantic* text show him changing individual words, improving phrases, making pronouns clearer, altering and tinkering here, there, and everywhere. He catches a number of minor errors in the magazine text, and as historical time marches on, the New York Central becomes the Penn Central. The reader will also discover that the lengthy and highly intellectual exchanges between Sammler and Lal have been freely revised, reformulated, and rearranged, possibly in an effort to make the speeches work better in terms of character and the central thematic concerns of the novel. Most of the last twenty pages or so of the novel were also subjected to this sort of sweeping revision.

The large-scale rewriting found in these two portions of the book deserves closer scrutiny than I have space for here. Significant as it is, however, it still does not constitute the most important revision of the magazine version. I believe that that distinction belongs to a pattern of local expansion found throughout the Viking text. As I have noted, the habit Bellow has acquired of listening to the commentator within is related to something like free association. Each time Bellow goes back to his novel-in-progress the commentator has more to comment on. The voice within plays off not only the characters and experience Mr. Sammler encounters but also the words and the train of thought that are already down on paper.

Mr. Sammler's Planet communicates itself to the reader as a book of mature "wisdom." Of course it is anything but a tract, for Sammler himself has a difficult time being sure of his beliefs—or even being sure what his beliefs are—in the chaotic world in which he finds himself in his old age. Nevertheless, the success of the novel depends in part on the credibility of the ideas, insights, reflections, and ruminations that nearly always comprise most of the substance of Sammler's thoughts and Sammler's spoken words. Furthermore, the thought process must itself be persuasive, for part of Bellow's strategy is to involve the reader in exactly the same questioning and inner agonizing. If the reader truly participates in the ruminative experience of the novel, he is more likely to accept the guarded affirmations the novel offers.

All this is by way of accounting for the pattern of expansion so clearly discernible in the last version of the novel. Bellow makes the thoughts and speeches of Mr. Sammler richer, stronger, and more complex by the simple device of judiciously adding to them. These expansions add significantly to the novel's intellectual density at the same time they make the book a fuller and more rewarding aesthetic experience.

One could select passages for illustration almost at random, for they are found throughout the final revision. The galleys for the Viking edition are studded with such passages in holograph. For example, the following sentences are added to a passage early in the novel in which Sammler is talking about the Nazis with Margotte and criticizing Hannah Arendt's notion of the banality of evil: " 'Is such a project trivial? Only if human life is trivial. This woman professor's enemy is modern civilization itself. She is only using the Germans to attack the twentieth century—to denounce it in terms invented by Germans. Making use of a tragic history to promote the foolish ideas of Weimar intellectuals' " (V 18–19). A learned historical gleaning enriches a lengthy meditation on contemporary sexuality: "Oh yes, the Templars. They had adored the Muslims. One hair from the head of Saracen was more precious than the whole body of a Christian. Such crazy fervor! And now all the racism, all the strange erotic persuasions," (V 33). An entire paragraph is added near the beginning of the third chapter:

> Drop a perpendicular from the moon. Let it intersect a grave. Inside, a man till now tended, kept warm, manicured. Those heavy rainbow colors came. Decay. Mr. Sammler had once been on far more easy terms with death. He had lost ground, regressed. He was very full of his nephew, a man quite different from himself. He admired him, loved him. He could not cope with the full sum of facts about him. Remote considerations seemed to help—the moon, its lifelessness, its deathlessness. A white corroded pearl. By a sole eye, seen as a sole eye (V 105).

The most important feature of this interpolation is its statement of admiration and love for Elya Gruner. Gruner's moral and human worth are at the center of the novel; it is Sammler's beautiful eulogy of his dead nephew that closes the book so brilliantly. This passage shows that Bellow was aware that he needed to prepare the reader more fully for the importance of Gruner. Consequently we have this elegant paragraph, a miniature fantasia played on important themes in the novel: death, resurrection, the mystery of life, the moon. It is this sort of addition, part of a consistent pattern of expansion and enrichment, that makes the Viking *Mr. Sammler's Planet* a better book than its *Atlantic* counterpart. These examples are but a minimal sample of the differences that exist between the two published versions of the novel. A detailed comparison of the two texts would be well worth the effort of a textual critic.

All the revising Bellow does, especially his habit of revising right on into the early stages of production, increases the chance that there will be errors in the final text. If you want to publish a novel that will be free of textual error, it is better to save time and not even write the book. I do not pretend to have located every error in the text. I mean only to illustrate the sort of error that can creep into a book published by a major American press in 1970 despite all the techniques and advantages of modern book production.

I have already pointed out the instance in which Mr. Sammler is located in the wrong Bloomsbury address and the missing comma in the passage about Israeli napalm. A more glaring error is found in an exchange between Sammler and the chauffeur Emil before they drive from Sammler's apartment to the hospital at the end of the novel:

> He stopped Emil from getting out of the car for him.
> "I can work the door myself."
> "We're off, then. Open the bar, pour yourself a drink."
> "I hope the traffic will not be too thick."
> "We'll go straight down Broadway."
> "Turn on the TV."
> "Thanks. No TV" (V 282).

Did you catch the mistake? According to the way these speeches are set up, Emil invites Sammler to have a drink, Sammler wonders about the traffic, Emil tries to reassure him about the traffic, and then *Sammler asks the chauffeur to turn on the television set and the chauffeur declines!* The last two speeches are of course just backwards: Bellow means for Emil to be asking Sammler to turn on television just as he has asked him to have a drink, and it is Mr. Sammler who declines. The mistake is all the more curious because the exchange is printed correctly in the *Atlantic:* "We'll go straight down Broadway. Turn on the TV." "Thanks. No TV." This mistake must have been a printer's error, for the speeches are printed in the incorrect manner in the Viking galleys. Neither Bellow nor an editor caught the error, and it stands in the first edition.

Thinking of friendship and human attachment in the *Atlantic* text, Sammler reflects: "That was for your young person, still dreaming of love, of meeting someone of the opposite sex who would cure you of all your troubles, heart and soul, and whom you would cure and fulfill the same" (DAt 115a). As printed in the Viking galleys and in the Viking first edition, an extraneous preposition mysteriously insinuates its way into the conclusion of this sentence: "meeting someone of the opposite sex who would cure you of all your troubles, heart and soul and *for* whom you would cure and fulfill the same" (V 224). The extra "for" garbles the meaning and takes the sentence beyond the boundaries of English syntax. I believe that the author or an editor erroneously introduced the preposition; no one subsequently caught the mistake.

Bellow's habits of revision may be responsible for another minor oddity of the Viking text. Near the end of the novel in the midst of the final big quarrel between Sammler and Angela we learn: " 'Yes,' said Angela. She was furious. With Dr. Cosbie, with Wallace, with Widick, Horricker. And she was bitter with Sammler, too" (V 297). Four pages later we read something that sounds familiar: " 'That's right,' said Sammler. She was angry with Wallace, with Cosbie, Horricker. He did not want to add himself to the list" (V 301). These pages from near the end of the novel were heavily revised, and the passages cannot be matched up with the *Atlantic* text. The revision in this part of the novel involved much rewriting, much rearrangement, and much rephrasing of passages already written. It is possible that Bellow included both these passages in order to emphasize Angela's wrath and the imminent danger of a serious falling-out with her great-uncle. It also seems highly possible that the two passages are really two versions of the same passage and that one should have been cut out.

Bellow has said that he has no "ascertainable working method. I get up in the morning and I write." I hope I have illustrated something of the lengthy, intricate, and fascinating process through which the job gets done. The evidence clearly demonstrates that he is the "very dogged" and "very persistent fellow"[15] he says he is.

I have also intended in my discussion of the evolution of *Mr. Sammler's Planet* to offer a sense of the opportunities—and problems—available to the textual critic working in the area of contemporary fiction. If this essay has seemed something of a grab bag, it is because I have wanted to present a wide variety of textual issues. The copious materials for *Mr. Sammler's Planet* comprise a rich and bountiful gathering of holographs, typescripts, galleys, and separate published texts. In this plenty there is much for the textual scholar to ponder, much for him to learn, more than a little for him to puzzle over. If he pursues his labors diligently he will find that he has traveled a long way toward understanding a first-rate work of contemporary fiction and how it came to be the novel it is.

Notes

1. Question-and-answer session at Woodward Court, Univ. of Chicago, 15 April 1975.

2. Ibid.

3. *Writers at Work: The PARIS REVIEW Interviews*, 3rd ser. New York, 1967, p. 184.

4. Question-and-answer session, Woodward Court.

5. *Writers at Work*, p. 179.

6. I will use this form to cite unpublished materials included among the 1969 Bellow deposit in the Univ. of Chicago Library. This particular citation indicates Box I, Folder 7, p. 24 in the 1969 Bellow deposit.

7. I will incorporate references to the Viking Press first edition of the novel (New York, 1970) using this abbreviation. The reader must be careful not to confuse this first edition with the Literary Guild edition also issued early in 1970. There are many physical differences between the two books, including different typefaces. For my purposes the books are easily differentiated: the first edition has 313 pages, the Literary Guild edition 316 pages.

8. This is my only quotation from the 1967 Bellow deposit at Chicago. This passage is found on two unnumbered holograph leaves in Box VI, Folder 11 of the 1967 deposit.

9. *Writers at Work*, pp. 183–84.

10. Lawrence speaks about the dictates of the "demon" within in the introductory essay he wrote for the *Collected Poems* of 1928. This essay can be found in *Phoenix: The Posthumous Papers of D. H. Lawrence*, Edward D. McDonald, ed. (New York: Viking, 1968), pp. 251–54.

11. An article by Karyl Roosevelt in the Sept. 8, 1975, issue of *People* (pp. 60–63) describes Bellow at work dictating *Humboldt's Gift*. A week later I verified that Bellow did not use dictation in writing *Mr. Sammler's Planet* by asking him as he strolled by my apartment. Such a source of evidence is not available to the textual critic working on *The Scarlet Letter*.

12. This abbreviation refers to p. 97 of the Nov. 1969 issue of the *Atlantic*. The abbreviation for the Dec. 1969 issue is DAt. In most cases the page number is followed by an "a" or "b." Most of the novel is printed in long double-columns: "a" citations will be found in the left-hand column, "b" in the right.

13. This error is surprising since Shils made his suggestions about changing Sammler's address on the back of the typescript page where this passage appears.

14. The best discussion of this textual problem in *Women in Love* is found in Robert L. Chamberlain, "Pussum, Minette, and the Africo-Nordic Symbol in Lawrence's *Women in Love*," *PMLA*, 78 (Sept. 1963), 407–16.

15. Question-and-answer session, Woodward Court.

Artists and Opportunists in Saul Bellow's *Humboldt's Gift*

Ben Siegel[*]

Easily the novelist most successful in capturing contemporary life's realistic and grotesque aspects has been Saul Bellow. Now past sixty, he has for more than three decades proved himself this country's most profoundly serious and exuberantly comic observer. If many writers today resort to "impressionistic journalism and innovative fantasy," he retains a "Tolstoyan appetite"[1] for serious ideas. Indeed, ideas are Bellow's primary material, and usually they entangle themselves in his characters' perceptions and emotions. Despite his intellectual concerns, however, Bellow is basically a storyteller, and one who remains in the major tradition of conscious realism, with its intense characterizations and detailed, textured descriptions of its heroes' every physical and mental action.

He has been described as having emerged from an "ancient Jewish tradition of alarm wedded to responsibility."[2] His social concepts and interpretations bear this out. His fiction derives much of its strength from his grasp of the cultural implications of his characters' behavior and emotions. His central Jewish loners and lamenters are perceptive, critical, overextended urban beings; they tend to separate themselves from families and friends while they strain to bring order and coherence to their private lives. For these bedeviled seekers, the pressures and constraints come as often from without as from within. Most suffer not only from minds tormented by personal fears but also from an unfeeling society's frequent indignities. As a result, their lives often become desperate battles against not merely their own capricious, self-serving appetites but also against the wants and wishes of family members and intimates, friends and strangers.

Yet despite their antic involvements, his characters reassert Bellow's unflagging humanism. Every individual, he insists, should adhere to a human measure or mean. Even his least cerebral heroes seek to convert America's social chaos into coherent traditional notions about character, morality, and fate. Some critics have accused Bellow—especially with *Mr. Sammler's Planet*—of souring in his humanism, liberalism, and social expectations. "There can be little doubt," notes Malcolm Bradbury, that the "high ironies" of recent Bellow

[*]Reprinted from *Contemporary Literature*, (Spring 1978), 143–64.

fiction "betoken a sceptical withdrawal from . . . contemporary consciousness . . . and a cold eye . . . [toward] the contemporary circus."[3] Bradbury is only half-right. For if Bellow does view present social and moral disorders with a skeptical or "cold eye," he has hardly withdrawn from current happenings or ceased to care about those affected by them. Moses Herzog and Artur Sammler, for example, express concern not only for the cultural drift evident at every turn but for their own urges toward detachment or withdrawal as well.

Bellow is even more deeply involved with contemporary life in *Humboldt's Gift*.[4] Here narrator Charlie Citrine is nagged by guilt at having immersed himself in personal pursuits. He has closed his eyes, he laments, and "slept" through momentous historical events. Citrine's troubled ruminations enable Bellow to explore again, directly and unequivocally, American morals and expediencies—this time as they operate in the 1970s. He does not fit, admittedly, current definitions of the "experimental" novelist. He retains instead specific and basic literary commitments to realism; in short, his plot structures derive from story and character, and his people exist in a tumultuous but recognizable world. Yet Bellow is hardly a static thinker or writer. In each novel he not only records meticulously his evolving responses to setting and culture, but he also ventures beyond his previous imaginative perimeters to make playful use of shifting narrative styles and forms. His realism often shades into romanticism and the absurd, into social comedy and black humor, into psychology and the picaresque, into philosophy and satire. These elements enrich *The Adventures of Augie March, Henderson the Rain King, Herzog, Mr. Sammler's Planet,* and now *Humboldt's Gift*. In these novels Bellow reaffirms that the comic view offers the most valid means of grasping an American scene by turns tragic or absurd, or both. But laughter alone, he makes clear, is never enough. In *Humboldt's Gift*, therefore, as in his earlier novels, he mixes historical speculation and "metaphysics" with his vivid pathos and "mental farce."[5]

Here his turbulent world overflows as usual with things and noises and human needs. If he evokes again his fierce love of Chicago, he leavens his nostalgia with recollections of life among such New York literati as Philip Rahv, Sidney Hook, and Lionel Abel—and especially of his troubled friendship with the poet Delmore Schwartz. Moving along the periphery of that life are such political or social figures as Adlai Stevenson, the brothers Kennedy, Jacob Javits, and Harry Houdini. Others, like Dwight Macdonald, Richard Blackmur, and Carlos Baker, are thinly disguised, but play more central roles. These people, appearing in real and imagined events and places, present two familiar interlocking Bellovian themes. The first theme details the dangers posed to the artist in America by worldly success, with its inevitable attachments of money and fame, sex and excitement, and, often now, crime. Bellow has emphasized repeatedly in his fiction the gap between America's professed ideals and practiced compromises, between its high aspirations and low opportunism. The artist or writer's function, as he sees it, is not merely to expose but to help mend the rift between these divided value areas.

Centering on a live writer and a dead poet, Bellow tries to define the artist's role in a society lured away by its massive material substance from its cravings for mind and beauty. In a culture so fragmented the artist too often meets professional failure, if not personal disaster. For despite his early dreams and plans, he—no less than businessmen and lawyers—generally ensnares himself in a typical American compromise, as Charlie Citrine puts it, of "crookedness with self-respect or duplicity with honor" (p. 221). This moral confusion, Bellow suggests, is caused primarily by the artist's refusal to confront "the main question . . . the death question" (p. 332). In other words, the artist, like his fellow Americans, frequently fails to consider the moral or ethical—much less the spiritual—aspects of his goals and behavior. As so often in the past, Bellow is following (albeit more cynically) Walt Whitman, here the Whitman of *Democratic Vistas* and of "Out of the Cradle Endlessly Rocking."[6]

Saul Bellow embraces moral, ethical, and spiritual problems. His second theme is vintage Bellow: the comic pathos of a vain intellectual's efforts to age with style and dignity. Bellow writes of the deeply felt loss of dead kin and friends, focusing primarily on that sharpest of human anxieties, the fear of death. Probing this and related areas, he fashions a long, loose, funny/sad narrative of a crucial five months, in 1973–74, in the life of an embattled writer. During that December-to-April span, Charlie Citrine seeks higher significance in his life and possible ways for his soul to transcend or defeat death. Bellow shapes his hero's untiring monologue not into chapters but into unnumbered segments brimming with social details and philosophic speculations, narrative flashbacks and quick transitions. Charlie Citrine is the picture of the successful American man of letters. He is a cultural historian and biographer who has won Pulitzer Prizes for books on Woodrow Wilson and Harry Hopkins. He has rejected academic rewards to garner fame and money for a hit Broadway play. Top magazines have commissioned him to write articles on the Kennedys and other national leaders, and the French government has made him a Chevalier of the French Legion of Honor. Clearly, his is a life to admire in a success-loving age. Yet if he is so successful, why is he so blocked. Charlie wonders, in his joy and work? Why is he so accomplished in several worlds and at ease in none?

A major reason is his character. History may intrigue Charlie and literature and art fascinate him, but daily life baffles him. Indeed, unhappy events have in recent years been shattering his lengthy "slumber" of money, fame, and middle-class comforts. At fifty-six, he is losing his looks, his hair, and his paddle ball game. He owes his publishers $70,000 for advances on books he will never write. His ex-wife and a battery of lawyers, judges, and tax experts are stripping him of funds. So is his old friend Pierre Thaxter, a flamboyant literary con artist with a scheme for launching an intellectual quarterly. In short, despite his subtle, perceptive intelligence, Charlie is an easy mark for crooks and cranks and greedy friends.

Material problems are not his only worry. Of late, Charlie has been experiencing pangs of guilt and responsibility. He feels he should help alleviate the modern day's spiritual and cultural shortcomings—as if they were his personal obligation. He is also haunted by recollections of his close friend and mentor, the poet Von Humboldt Fleisher.[7] Now seven years dead, Humboldt had been the big, blond, new bard whose thin volume of early lyrics, *Harlequin Ballads*, had helped shape the literary landscape of the 1930s and 40s. But his book's title suggests the clownish aspects of Humboldt's character and fate. Charlie had read Humboldt's first poems while still a University of Wisconsin graduate student. Charlie is a native of Appleton, Wisconsin, the home of Harry Houdini, "the great Jewish escape artist" (p. 435). The magician's feats are repeatedly evoked and prove to be a paradigm of Charlie's dreams of escaping middle-class life and pressures. For Moses Herzog, the wily bankrobber Willie Sutton had served a similar emblematic role. Houdini and Sutton appeal to Bellow and his heroes as sly illusionists who evade nature and society's laws.

Yet Von Humboldt Fleisher had been the direct agent of Charlie's escape efforts. Eager to enter New York's heady world of high intellect, Charlie had fled the Midwest. He had found his idol in Greenwich Village enjoying, he later recalls, "the days of his youth, covered in rainbows, uttering inspired words, affectionate, intelligent" (p. 341). A generous if disoriented patron and guide, Humboldt had launched Charlie's academic and literary career and filled him with manic, improbable dreams. Exhilarated by life, art, thought, Humboldt was an irrepressible creative force, "a hectic nonstop monologuist and improvisator" (p. 4) and an unending source of wit and wisdom and paradox. If he warned Charlie, for example, to view the dangerous and beautiful rich only as they are mirrored in the "shield of art" (p. 14), he hungered also for wealth and fame. He lusted to be artist and oracle, culture czar and celebrity, and a living link between art and science.

His desires filled Humboldt with "high-minded low cunning" (p. 126) and turned him into a scheming mix of sage, publicist, and tavern prophet. A masterful wheeler-dealer in literary politics, he garnered fellowships and faculty appointments, consultancies and grants. Combining talent and drive, he fashioned himself into one of the exemplary literary successes of the 1930s and 40s and won acceptance as a major American poet. What he wanted for himself, he wanted—or thought he wanted—for others. Convinced that culture was on the rise in America, and that the imminent presidency of Adlai Stevenson would make all things possible, he dreamed of transforming the nation, through its art and wealth, into a new Athens. In such a state, American social forces would be reconciled with Platonic concepts of truth and beauty.

Humboldt could not sustain his "youthful dazzle," and subsequent disappointments and the opposing tensions of poetry and politics exacted a cruel toll. Expending his creative juices on the grant-and-fellowship game, writing little and orating long into the night fueled by gin and barbiturates, Humboldt began to crack. Slipping steadily into paranoia, detecting acts of betrayal everywhere, he lashed out repeatedly at his wife and friends. His special target was Charlie. As the latter's career rose and his own sank, Humboldt turned on his old chum in envy and depression. While Charlie, his writing in demand (and propelled by an ambitious wife), visited at the White House and shared helicopters with the Kennedys, Humboldt was in and out of institutions, feeding his rancor and resentment at his pal for not impeding his fall. Once, from Bellevue, Humboldt phoned Charlie at the Belasco Theater. "Charlie, you know where I am, don't you?" he yelled. "All right, Charlie, this isn't literature. This is life" (p. 156). He even filled in and cashed for over $6700 a blank check Charlie had signed years before at his urging as a friendship bond. The greatest shock for Charlie, however, came years later when he spotted Humboldt—broken, dirty, forlorn—on a New York street corner, a shambling, mumbling derelict. Confused and embarrassed, Charlie hid and then rushed back to his own bustling world. Two months later, he read that Humboldt had dropped dead in a Times Square flophouse.

Now Humboldt is much on Charlie's mind. Haunted by his bad conscience, Charlie mourns his friend's accomplishments and follies and lonely death. He dwells obsessively on his last glimpse of the poet, appraising him less as an individual than as a "cause" or "mistreated talent" meriting "posthumous justice."[8] Humboldt had tried "to drape the world in radiance," Charlie decides, "but he didn't have enough material" (p. 107); and he died essentially of "unwritten poems" (p. 25). Even worse, Humboldt had lain unidentified and unclaimed for three days. The morgue, Charlie muses sardonically, harbored "no readers of modern poetry" (p. 16). Yet Humboldt had died, Charlie observes, as a poet in America is expected to die. He had gratified the public's conviction of the superiority of the practical over the ideal, the material over the aesthetic. Charlie tries, however, to see his friend's death in more positive terms; he wonders, therefore, if Humboldt had not made a "Houdini escape" from the world's madness and distractions. Had he also not embodied, in his personal and professional turmoils, the confusing talents, visions, and drives of a nation committed historically to opportunity and success?

For these and other reasons, Charlie regrets not having been more tolerant and understanding of Humboldt. He wishes now to redeem his friend's reputation and even in some way to carry out his ideas.[9] He would also like to discover why so charged and talented a figure produced so little. By unraveling that riddle he hopes to find answers to his own creative and social dilemmas. For Charlie is as much a victim of his emotional needs and success drives as Humboldt. He is another of Bellow's versatile but aging Jewish intellectual innocents, marked by their "talent for absurdity" (p. 48). Caught up in this era of urban violence and public assassinations, uneasy family life and moral cynicism, he finds his vast knowledge of dusty volumes and esoteric authors of little practical value. "I knew everything I was supposed to know," he complains at one point, "and nothing I really needed to know" (p. 50). His lack of devious, pragmatic strategies leaves him desperately protecting his dignity and principles from a familiar Bellow array of greedy, dissatisfied women, voracious lawyers, and societal demands, diversions, and clutter. These pressures move Charlie to take cynical measure of his country and countrymen. The American had overcome his land's "emptiness," he observes, but "the emptiness had given him a few good licks in return" (p. 93).

Chicago offers ample evidence. The city is Charlie's testing ground. He had grown up there and been drawn back to it. He is, he admits sardonically, "a lover of beauty who insists on living in Chicago." Why? Well, New York may have better talk, he reasons, but in "raw Chicago" one can best "examine the human spirit under industrialism" (p. 108). He is also intrigued by the phenomenon of boredom, and this element pervades his city in a pure, near-mystical state. New York, on the other hand, dilutes its boredom with culture. So anything significantly revealing of the boring human condition, Charlie is convinced, will more likely befall him in his hometown. Ironically, Bellow presents a vibrant, pulsating Chicago that offers quite a stimulating microcosm of the USA. He fashions the city into a living metaphor for the violent, mad, real world that differs so sharply from Humboldt's ideal, aesthetic one. Here Charlie confronts his turbulent muddle of lawyers and alimony hearings, past and present girlfriends and vengeful ex-wife, petty gangsters and greedy friends.

Here also, as so often in Bellow, criminality takes comic forms.[10] Amid his confusions Charlie entangles himself with Rinaldo Cantabile, a small-time Mafia operator, and the plot acquires overtones of black humor. If New York's intellectual ferment had spawned a Von Humboldt Fleisher, Chicago's material turmoils have thrown off the opportunistic Cantabile. "One of the new mental rabble of the wised-up world" (p. 107), as Charlie describes him, this petty racketeer lives totally in the here and now; he is always "one thousand percent" (p. 460) with the action. Meeting and cheating Charlie in a poker game, Cantabile is furious when his victim stops payment on a check written to cover game losses. In revenge, he clubs Charlie's Mercedes Benz into a shapeless wreck. When Charlie does offer the money, he is ritualistically humiliated and insulted. To make matters worse, Cantabile not only tries to replace Humboldt as Charlie's mentor and guide, but he has a Ph.D.-candidate wife who is writing her dissertation on the poet and wants Charlie's help.

Cantabile, like Humboldt and Charlie Citrine himself, proves one of Bellow's great comic figures. He is literally Charlie's "nemesis"—a satanic spirit fated to shatter Charlie's slumber of success and smugness and to compel him to move away from "dead center" and confront his true self. He also personifies the tightening bonds between an upwardly mobile middle class and a shady world of confidence men and mobsters. Charlie's friends view this new social comradeship with indifference. They nourish, like most Americans, a steadily higher gratification threshold and an intense need to escape boredom. One major result of such attitudes is a morally and intellectually uncertain age in which "culture and corruption" are symbiotically entwined. The effects of this turbulent partnership are strongly visible. "What a tremendous force," Charlie observes, "the desire to be interesting has in the democratic USA" (p. 170).

Charlie is fighting hard to shake off both his own boredom and the incessant demands of others. Like Tommy Wilhelm and Moses Herzog before him, however, he is enmeshed in a web of domestic court battles. Denise, his ex-wife, bitter at his having rejected her, has separated him from their two young daughters; now she, her lawyers, and a cooperative judge are determined to teach Charlie some hard, practical lessons by draining him of money, energy, and time. His own lawyers, accountants, and friends prove equally insatiable "reality instructors." Yet, as his name suggests, Charlie Citrine,[11] with ironic, slightly soured, self-deprecatory humor, is wryly amused at his repeated victimizing by these frenetic business toughs, literary con men, and divorce court hustlers who envy his fame and covet his money. For the money, he decides, is the world's money. A capitalist society, for its own darkly comic motives, has granted him temporary loan of huge sums and now is taking its own back. He views his mounting losses, therefore, with bemused detachment, even seeing virtue in the process.

Time and disappointment, however, are having their effect. At fifty-six, Charlie is nearing exhaustion. Yet, exhausted or not, he remains a dedicated womanizer who fights aging by frantic devotion to yoga postures, paddle ball, and body exercises. His current mistress, the young and voluptuous Renata Koffritz, demands marriage, money, respectability. But if she pressures Charlie to marry her, Renata fears his unreliability and imminent loss of wealth. She takes the precaution, therefore, of sleeping periodically with the wealthy undertaker Harold Flonzaley. So blocked and confused are Charlie's relationships here and elsewhere that he is repeatedly tempted to lie down and go to sleep.

Yet he fears already having slept through the high moments of his era and his life. The novel's latter half is suffused with "sleep" images that suggest both Charlie's "bemused worldliness" and his hunger for a higher awareness or consciousness. For if Humboldt had succumbed to high-voltage graspings for fame and success, Charlie has been given to lethargy and self-absorption. While those about him, especially the relentless Cantabile, scheme to destroy his peaceful slumber, Charlie himself now resolves to concentrate his "whole attention" on his time's "great and terrible matters" (p. 194)—those same matters that for decades he had filtered out by turning inward. But he must ponder first Humboldt's blunted career and life. Charlie is not certain how much sympathy either Humboldt or he merits. They both had enjoyed, after all, the best America had to offer: fame, money, audiences, women. If they had gone sour, where lay the fault? Had they misdirected or misapplied their intellectual and creative gifts? Or does fault lie with this country, so rich in diversity and distraction that it ignores or downgrades its creative talents and rewards mediocrity? Whatever the root cause of its dulled aesthetic sensibilities, American society has to answer for its blatant adoration of material success.

Bellow's central figures are never mere passive, blameless victims. The novelist makes clear that the artist in America bears at least partial blame for his failures. Many problems derive from every artist's acute sense of self or of being special. "Remember," observes Humboldt in a letter he bequeaths Charlie, "we are not natural beings but supernatural beings" (p. 347). But for most sensitized, creative individuals to view themselves as "supernatural beings" in a tough-grained technological world is not easy. For many artists it proves even crushing. If they feel at one with the heavens, they draw their materials from life. If given to Platonic speculations about truth and beauty, they hunger for acclaim, luxuries, acceptance. If they strive desperately for purity, achievement, art, they become speculators in mind and profit, sinking almost inevitably to performance, caricature, compromise. Delineating these cultural paradoxes, Bellow resists (more in his fiction than in essays or lectures) easy formulations or explanations. Assigning blame is, to him, not only facile but beside the point.

He expresses serious reservations, however, about the aims or motives of the modern artist—at least as exemplified by Von Humboldt Fleisher and Charlie Citrine. Bellow's doubts are hardly new. He has stated them in his recent Nobel Prize address[12] and on many previous occasions. He had criticized in a 1963 Library of Congress lecture those American writers who smugly mix affluence and radical chic. Such middle-class writers "are taught," he charged, "that they can have it both ways. In fact they are taught to expect to enjoy everything that life can offer. They can live dangerously while managing somehow to remain safe. They can be both bureaucrats and bohemians . . . [or] conservative and radical. They are not taught to care genuinely for any man or any cause."[13] For this reason Bellow expects the reader to take Charlie Citrine seriously. Charlie does come to care about those close to him and about the artist's place and function in American life.

Despite his faults, the artist hardly bears sole responsibility for his marginal status. Who—if not his American history, culture, and countrymen—has taught him to want the wrong things? Contemporary America for Bellow is a politically expedient, science-and-technology-oriented community uncertain about how to employ—much less celebrate—its artists.[14] Filling them with false values, this society then stirs their anxieties and insecurities. "I don't think we know where we are or where we're going," Bellow has told interviewers. "I see politics—ultimately—as a buzzing preoccupation that swallows up art and the life of the spirit."[15] Charlie Citrine shares these uncertainties. Can a poem, Charlie asks himself, transport you from New York to Chicago? Can a novel plot a condominium or an epic "compute a space shot" (p. 155)? In Bellow's America, therefore, writers generally are frustrated and ineffectual, and often they entrap themselves in social roles and institutions whose managers treat them as irresponsible, ungrateful children.

Writers who seek acceptance compound their problems: they appeal to readers or audiences who value all artists' public images over their creative acts, their personal lives over their paintings or novels, their scandals over their music or poems. Is it even possible, then, Bellow and Citrine seem to ask, for the artist or writer in this country to express his true philosophical, religious, or even aesthetic convictions? Yet what worries Bellow and Citrine has fascinated Von Humboldt Fleisher. The collective disappointments of other artists were of little account to Humboldt. For him, as for Walt Whitman, America was promises, opportunities, excitement. America had been his world, and "the world," Humboldt insisted, "had money, science, war, politics, anxiety, sickness, perplexity. It had all the voltage. Once you had picked up the high-voltage wire and were *someone,* a known name, you couldn't release yourself from the electrical current. You were transfixed" (p. 312).

Where a Walt Whitman or Von Humboldt Fleisher saw opportunities, Saul Bellow and Charlie Citrine see pitfalls, indifference, neglect. "The history of literature in America," Bellow has stated, "is the history of certain demonic solitaries who somehow brought it off in a society that felt no need for them."[16] Charlie Citrine voices similar sentiments. "Poets have to dream," he points out, "and dreaming in America is no cinch" (p. 312). Humboldt, having grown desperate, "behaved like an eccentric and a comic subject" (p. 6). Many poets, declares Charlie (picking up the theme of Bellow's 1971 essay "Culture Now"),[17] have become publicists or promoters, campus politicians or public clowns. Thus, for Charlie, Humboldt's fate raises many questions. Was the poet's deepening disenchantment, his sense of being nothing more than his society's superfluous, comic victim, what drove him to destruction? Were his strivings for power and money less mercenary yearnings than symptoms of his growing fears and frustrations? Or was he little more than a "pathetic wool-gatherer" whose "comeuppance" was not only "inevitable" but "somehow correct"?[18] Does Humboldt's fate prove emblematic, in other words, of the artist's dark destiny in American life?

Whatever its prime cause, his friend's pitiful end saddens and frightens Charlie. He is pained especially by Humboldt's strong contribution to his own failure. He is keenly aware that the poet's self-indulgence and lack of discipline rendered him a "farcical" rather than a tragic martyr. Humboldt fed in his life and in his death the popular conceptions that poets are kindred spirits to those "drunkards and misfits and psychopaths" (p. 155) who cannot confront the American reality and for whom "the USA is too tough, too big, too much, too rugged" (p. 118). Humboldt, by chasing "ruin and death," performed in the manner expected of him. Americans derive pleasure from such sad happenings, Charlie sighs, because the poet's failure validates their cynicism.

To make matters worse, Humboldt's pitiful finish, alone and muttering in abject poverty, suggests to Charlie the social and moral confusion not merely of "demonic solitaries" but also of prudent, decorous intellectuals like himself. Has not he acted even less commendably than his erratic, disorderly comrade? Did he not reject Humboldt's physical presence on a public street? Is not his own carefully calibrated success a denial of his friend's failed but somehow valiant life, with its heedless, dramatic mistakes and misfortunes? Not even Humboldt's pathetic hunger for success and fame mitigates Charlie's guilt. Haunted by the dead poet's voice, communing with his own "significant dead," trying to withstand his living debtors, and unable to write, Charlie abandons an ambitious essay on boredom for "interior monologues" on life and death, re-birth and immortality.

Ironically, Charlie Citrine (like Saul Bellow) has been a tough-minded realist committed firmly to a cause-and-effect balance between man's past and present and between his inner and outer worlds. Now, painfully aware of an aging body and diminishing lifespan, he refuses to believe that the extraordinary human soul "can be wiped out forever." Charlie disagrees, therefore, with those thinkers and theorists who, having lost their own "imaginative souls," dismiss any possibility that man's consciousness can survive death's oblivion. "If there is one historical assignment for us," he argues, "it is to break with false categories" (p. 404) and to accept an "inner being" separate from physical nature's finalities.

Such metaphysical faith or acceptance, however, requires the individual to confront "the big blank of death" (p. 357). Charlie turns for help to the writings of Rudolf Steiner (1861–1925). One of this century's "Scientists of the Invisible," Steiner had moved from German philosophy to an occultist doctrine he called anthroposophy. Rejecting conventional scientific or even theosophical views, he developed a theory of "spiritual science" that involved the study of the human spirit by "scientific" inquiry. Steiner argued for the transmigration of souls, and he advocated self-discipline of mind and body to achieve cognition of the spiritual world.[19] For guidance through the Steinerian maze, Charlie consults a Chicago anthroposophist, Dr. Scheldt. Their conversations dwell on the soul's connections to "a greater, an all-embracing life outside" the physical one—as well as on the plight of the dead, who surround the living but are "shut out" by modern man's "metaphysical denial" (p. 141) of them.

His spiritualistic musings do not prevent Charlie from enjoying the pleasures of the flesh. Several reviewers have dismissed Charlie's interest in anthroposophy, therefore, as a "highly egoistic" one centering on Steiner's ideas of "transcendence and immortality of the self."[20] Yet Charlie makes clear—as had Walt Whitman—that what is true of him is true of all men. Some readers also have seen in Scheldt a counterpart to Artur Sammler's friend Dr. Govinda Lal. That Indian scientist, too, advocated "extraterrestrial reality." The rationalistic Sammler, however, rejected such fanciful views for life on a troubled earth. Charlie Citrine, on the other hand, driven by "frenzied longings" for existential possibilities beyond this sphere, embraces Steiner's occultist concepts (with their strong Wordsworthian overtones) of the soul's cycle of sleep and wakefulness.

These cogitations are interrupted by more mundane problems. A domestic relations judge rules that Charlie must give his ex-wife most of his money and orders him to post a $200,000 bond. Despite this heavy penalty, Charlie takes off on a European trip, with Renata scheduled to join him in Spain. He makes two stops. He goes first to New York to pick up Humboldt's legacy to him, which consists of a long conciliatory letter, a movie scenario they had collaborated on, and a Humboldt original film treatment. Charlie then heads for Texas, to Corpus Christi (an ironic reference, perhaps, to his physical-spiritual meanderings). He wants to see his older brother Julius through a serious operation. Julius Citrine merits a novel of his own. A heavy-eating, fast-moving real-estate tycoon, he has the dash and drive of a Eugene Henderson or Von Humboldt Fleisher. A maker and loser of fortunes, he wheels and deals on the very eve of open-heart surgery. Charlie, despite his interest in occultist metaphysics, retains the traditional Jew's respect for family, the past, and conventional burial rites. Julius does not. His views on death and burial reflect both his restlessness and his ease with the American here and now. "I'm having myself cremated," he tells Charlie. "I need action. I'd rather go into the atmosphere. Look for me in the weather reports" (p. 387).

Julius proves a born survivor, however, and Charlie heads for Madrid. There he learns that Renata, having saddled him with her mother and son, has eloped to Italy with her undertaker. Though crushed, Charlie realizes that losing Renata was inevitable. Does not Death (here mortician Flonzaley) always ensnare Beauty? Still he mourns his loss of sexual pleasure and especially those gifts of youth—excitement, stimulation, pride—that Renata had provided to soften the advancing years. Finally alone in Madrid, and nearly broke, Charlie resumes his meditations. He hopes to reorganize his life and to reconcile his mystical readings with his rationalistic "head culture." His growing sense of the tight interplay between man's inner and outer worlds, of the soul's power to escape into the supersensible, convinces him that the respected Western thinkers of the last three centuries offer little guidance. Most bothersome is the seeming exhaustion of modernist ideas of art and the poetic imagination so cherished by Humboldt and himself. These ideas, centering on art's ultimate value, have emphasized metaphor, language, and style as the basic purveyors of truth, beauty, and immortality. Such concepts, Charlie now feels, have lost validity in this America of horrendous distractions and temptations. As a result, the sensitive individual finds it difficult to sustain an ethical imaginative life amid the materialistic erosions of science and art.

Charlie also finds it difficult to age and die—much less fail—with dignity in a society cherishing youth, money, and sex. His attempts to establish rapport with the accepted representatives of modern intellect and high culture have left him few solid, conventional beliefs, and his future efforts to reconcile mind and spirit will not be easy. He can expect little help, he realizes, from a "learned world" that disdains anthroposophy. Undaunted, he rejects all rationalist denials of communication between physical and spiritual worlds, as well as all arguments against the continuing life of the soul. Charlie is convinced that it is modern man's failure to interpret the cosmos, to read its subtle, suggestive signs, that has turned the world turbulent. "Real life," he insists, derives from the singular "relationship between *here* and *there*." But how, he wonders, is he to get *there* from his tangled *here*?

Despite his doubts and uncertainties, Charlie determines to leap beyond tangible human facts and passions. "I meant to make a strange jump," he declares, "and plunge into the truth. I had had it with most contemporary ways of philosophizing. Once and for all I was going to find out whether there was anything behind the incessant hints of immortality that kept dropping on me. . . . I had the strange hunch that nature itself was not *out there* . . . but that everything external corresponded vividly with something internal, . . . and that nature was my own unconscious being" (p. 356). Charlie is attracted, therefore, to Steiner's "explanations" of the interplay of each person's outer setting and inner self—to those ideas, in other words, expanding man's awareness of self and cosmos. His readings convince Charlie that the individual's "external world" often blends with the internal to become indiscernible to him. He and it are one. "The outer world is now the inner," he states. "Clairvoyant, you are in the space you formerly beheld. From this new circumference you look back to the center, and at the center is your own self. That self, your self, is now the external world" (pp. 393–94).

Reviewers have expressed surprise at Saul Bellow's visionary turn. This "worldly Chicagoan," they point out, hitherto has been immersed in social realities. How seriously, some ask, does Bellow expect his readers to take Charlie Citrine's "dubious quasi-mysticism"?[21] The more incredulous reviewers have looked for quibbles or qualifications, ironic jokes or subtle satire.[22] But his public comments emphasize that Bellow is strongly taken with Steiner's ideas on the immortal spirit and on the possibilities of the living communicating with the dead; Charlie Citrine, he makes clear, speaks for him as well as for himself. "Rudolf Steiner had a great vision," Bellow states flatly, and he "was a powerful poet as well as philosopher and scientist."[23] He discovered Steiner's anthroposophy, he adds, through the work of British writer Owen Barfield.[24] Both Steiner and Barfield not only exemplify "the importance of the poetic imagination," but they also have convinced him "that there were forms of understanding, discredited now, which had long been the agreed basis of human knowledge." We believe "we can know the world scientifically," Bellow declares, "but actually our ignorance is terrifying."[25]

Bellow's confidence in the occult is reminiscent of Yiddish novelist Isaac Bashevis Singer and his stated acceptance of demons and spirits.[26] Like Singer (and, for that matter, Harry Houdini), Bellow does disparage most occultist practitioners, as well as the "many cantankerous erroneous silly and delusive objects actions and phenomena [that] are in the [physical] foreground" (p. 177). Both novelists are, however, intrigued by the great unknown—by death, rather than by miracles, tricks, or wonder workers. Bellow, despite his basic realism, has often displayed a mystical turn of mind. A careful review of his fiction reveals not only a persistent determination "to break with false categories" but also repeated references to the "illusory" nature of a "successful" life in America. From the dangling Joseph to Artur Sammler, his protagonists are "seeker[s] after cosmic understanding,"[27] spiritual pilgrims convinced life can offer them more than meets the eye. Both Moses Herzog and Artur Sammler, for instance, though tough-minded rationalists committed to confronting "the phony with the real thing," are readers of such mystics as William Blake, Meister Eckhart, John Tauler, and Jacob Boehme; they, too, attempt to satisfy yearnings toward a higher, intuitive awareness. Augie March's earthly friend William Einhorn, it will be recalled, subscribed in the 1930s to the Rudolf Steiner Foundation publications. Charlie Citrine speaks for all Bellovian heroes, therefore, when he reasons that "*this* could not be *it*." One earthly turn is not enough. "We had all been here before," he insists, "and would presently be here again" (p. 89). Though obstructed repeatedly by greedy and unscrupulous "reality instructors," Bellow's stubborn questers are merely slowed, not deterred, in their search for higher knowledge or illumination.

Yet how does Saul Bellow treat the occult here? What precisely does Charlie Citrine's anthroposophy do for him? Clearly, he does enjoy some positive results. If nothing else, Charlie's theosophical readings and reflections calm him; they lift his mind and attention from immediate tribulations to more permanent questions of matter and spirit. Equally clear, however, is Bellow's flexible, even ambiguous, attitude toward "the great beyond." For if Von Humboldt Fleisher indeed "speaks" to Charlie from beyond the grave, he does so in a surprisingly clearheaded, practical fashion. It is the dead poet who rescues the live but floundering historian from his financial problems. He has bequeathed Charlie a film treatment that is a fable of the latter's own life—the tale of an artist destroyed by the pursuit of success. Humboldt has also left him a legally protected but seemingly worthless movie scenario on cannibalism and survival in the Arctic the two of them had concocted years earlier as a joke. Charlie puts it aside, but Rinaldo Cantabile, ever the hyperactive operator, arrives with news that this plot outline has been plagiarized and developed into a currently popular film. The ensuing settlement eases Charlie's financial pressures and provides him a modest security. If no longer wealthy, Charlie is in a position— thanks to Humboldt's gift—to contemplate serenely both past errors and future possibilities; he can look to a life without ambitious struggles or self-loathing, or even boredom.

Through their scenario, therefore, and his own film idea (which also proves lucrative), Humboldt has repaid Charlie money taken in life. More significantly, by "communicating" with Charlie, he has, like Harry Houdini, "defied all forms of restraint and confinement, including the grave" (p. 435), and given substance to Charlie's speculations about an existence beyond this sphere. In this limited sense at least, Rudolf Steiner's claims of a possible dimension transcending the here-and-now exhibit some merit. Yet Charlie's occult speculations are merely that; they are provisional meditations or possibilities to challenge his mind and imagination. They do not carry the novel's thematic burden, and their validity or nonvalidity alters neither Charlie Citrine's nor Von Humboldt Fleisher's character, or the relationship of the two men to each other or to their society. At most, Charlie views anthroposophy as a possible aid in perceiving internal or external truths. If he reveals a mystical bent, Charlie Citrine is otherwise a familiar Bellovian figure whose successes and failures, betrayals and humiliations are clearly "separable from his spiritual pilgrimage."[28]

In fact, he resembles strongly a number of recent literary figures. Solvent again, and seeing himself at a late station in life, Charlie decides to lie fallow for a time and to concentrate on his search for a higher selfhood. Thus he proves to be another "underground man" awaiting the proper moment for a return to an active life. Further, if Charlie is more mystically inclined than either Herzog or Sammler, he shares their conclusions on man's moral contract; like them, he believes the individual, when confronted by death, should respond with dignity and style. Indeed, he has himself long been "dying to do something good" (p. 3), and so he now returns temporarily to America to square accounts with the living and dead. Despite his spiritualism (or perhaps because of it), he views the traditional ritual of Jewish burial as a symbolic act giving order and meaning to the most disorderly life. With his share of the film profits, therefore, he has Humboldt's body exhumed from a large public cemetery for a family reburial. He retrieves also from an old-age home Humboldt's uncle, Waldemar Wald, and a longtime mutual friend, Menasha Klinger, and he helps the two old men set up their own apartment.

The novel's first scene finds Charlie, accompanied by the old men, witnessing the transfer of the coffins of Humboldt and his mother from the public cemetery (Deathsville, New Jersey) to the Fleisher family plot. Here, as in scenes closing his other novels, Bellow brings his narrative concerns into sharp focus. For as Charlie Citrine watches the bulldozing crane tearing the soil and whirring noisily among the dead, his thoughts epitomize Bellow's views on the continuing confrontation of death and life, society and individual, collective technology and solitary artist. "The machine in every square inch of metal," thinks Charlie, had resulted from the "collaboration of engineers and other artificers." Any system derived from the discoveries of numerous great minds has to overwhelm and dominate anything produced by the workings of any single mind, "which of itself can do little" (pp. 485–86). The crane raises, then lowers Humboldt's coffin, and Charlie adds: "Thus, the condensation of collective intelligences and combined ingenuities, its cables silently spinning, dealt with the individual poet" (p. 487).

Bellow's narrative endings have come in for much debate. He closed *Seize the Day* also with a "burial scene"—a strongly promising or optimistic one. He is given to taking leave of his heroes amid nature's invigorating currents: Augie March philosophizing his way through Normandy's frozen terrain, Moses Herzog meditating in his old Massachusetts country house among freshly picked summer flowers, Eugene Henderson running in circles through the Newfoundland snow bearing a young orphan. Each scene suggests a future better than the past. Is there reason, therefore, to doubt a positive intent in his present conclusion?

Certainly here, as elsewhere, Bellow does not rule out redemption. Yet if many readers are confident that better days lie ahead for Charlie Citrine, both Bellow and Charlie now seem less certain and more ambiguous about his future, in this life or the next. Charlie looks into Humboldt's grave, for instance, to see the poet's coffin placed within a concrete casing. "So the coffin was enclosed," he muses, "and the soil did not come directly upon it. But then how did one get out? One didn't, didn't, didn't! You stayed, you stayed!" (p. 487). Bellow may be paying homage to James Joyce, whom he admires, for Charlie here echoes the Irish novelist's meditative Jewish hero, Leopold Bloom. "Once you are dead," sighs Bloom, gazing at the gravestones surrounding Paddy Dignam's burial plot, "you are dead."[29] Charlie finishes his narrative with a wry joke and a graveyard pun that underscores his doubts—and most likely would have pleased Joyce. Menasha Klinger points out a sight unexpected in a New Jersey cemetery even in April: spring flowers. "What do you suppose they're called, Charlie?" Menasha asks. "Search me," Charlie replies. "I'm a city boy myself. They must be crocuses" (p. 487).

Most reviewers have accepted Charlie's response, along with others of the scene's implications, as purposeful signs of rebirth. Admittedly, these blooming flowers—the new season's first pastoral signs of renewal—seem indeed a gift from the dead; they seem to provide more evidence that Von Humboldt Fleisher's true gift is his ability to touch and affect the living even after death. Yet a close attention to Charlie's mocking urban tone and ironic play on words suggests he is certain not that the flowers are *crocuses* but only that all of *us croak*. The need to listen for Bellow's mood and meaning has resulted in reviewers and critics differing more sharply in their interpretations and evaluations of *Humboldt's Gift* than of any previous Bellow novel. They can not agree, for example, whether Saul Bellow here extends his familiar themes and ideas or departs sharply from them.[30]

Most critics and readers should agree, however, that no modern novelist moves as effectively or authoritatively as does Bellow between "allusive metaphysical speculation and racy low-mimetic narrative." Nor do many writers fictionalize with as cutting a comic wit the "competing urges" of flesh and spirit, "money-making and truth-seeking."[31] For that matter, few writers today will risk the critical mockery stirred by hints of man's redemptive possibilities—or by challenges to intellectual fashions of cynicism and predictions of crisis and doom. More to the point, Saul Bellow and Charlie Citrine present the reader with comic yet moving insights into those crucial issues confronting every sensitive individual between his cradle and grave. If their impressions and conclusions fail to convince totally, they can hardly be faulted for failing where no one has succeeded. Certainly they render the human journey more open and challenging than before.

Notes

1. R. Z. Sheppard, "Scribbler on the Roof," *Time*, 25 Aug. 1975, p. 62.

2. Richard Gilman, "Saul Bellow's New Open, Spacious Novel About Art, Society and a Bizarre Poet," *New York Times Book Review*, 17 Aug. 1975, p. 1.

3. Malcolm Bradbury, "The It & the We: Saul Bellow's New Novel," *Encounter*, 45, No. 5 (Nov. 1975), 61.

4. Saul Bellow, *Humboldt's Gift* (New York: Viking Press, 1975). Parenthetical page references in the text refer to this edition.

5. Bradbury, p. 62.

6. Charlie Citrine evokes repeatedly the Brooklyn Bard. In asserting "that Democracy would fail unless its poets gave it great poems of death" (p. 376), he echoes Whitman's declaration from *Democratic Vistas* that "In the future of these States must arise poets immenser far, and make great poems of death" (*Leaves of Grass and Selected Prose*, ed. Sculley Bradley [New York: Rinehart, 1960], p. 541.) Whitman reiterated this conviction in the final two stanzas of "Out of the Cradle Endlessly Rocking" (*Leaves of Grass and Selected Prose*, p. 213).

7. Bellow derives his poet's name from the noted German naturalist, explorer, and diplomat

Friedrich Heinrich Alexander von Humboldt (1769–1859). A prolific writer, Humboldt sought in his works, especially in his five-volume *Kosmos* (1845–62), to formulate a concept of physical unity from nature's complexities and to determine man's place in the universal scheme.

8. Roger Shattuck, "A Higher Selfishness?" *New York Review of Books*, 18 Sept. 1975, p. 24.

9. Here Bellow may be following Henry James. In his short novel *The Aspern Papers* (1888), James traced an admiring critic's desperate efforts to exhume from personal letters the life of the dead American poet Jeffrey Aspern. James asked whether the personality of the artist is distinct from the personality of the man, and therefore the public's legitimate possession. Bellow posed the question more briefly and obliquely in his 1954 story "The Gonzaga Manuscripts," published in *Mosby's Memoirs and Other Stories* (New York: Viking Press, 1968), pp. 111–42.

10. Criminals or would-be criminals and con artists intrigue Bellow. Moses Herzog is concerned with Willie Sutton, and Augie March counts among his friends Joe Gorman and the posturing, gangster-admiring Dingbat Einhorn. Tommy Wilhelm is fleeced by the fast-talking Dr. Tamkin. Artur Sammler not only contends with a menacing thief and pickpocket, but also has to rationalize his nephew Elya Gruner's Mafia connections. These figures all exhibit "style"—even the pathetic Joe Gorman, who, despite a police beating, refuses to squeal on Augie. Here, the irrepressible Cantabile exhibits his own comic style when he tricks Citrine into posing as a mob "hit man" to frighten a debt defaulter.

11. Bellow is on record as having derived "Charlie Citrine" from the name of an old friend, Louis Sidrin: see Richard Stern, "Bellow's Gift," *New York Times Magazine*, 21 Nov. 1976, p. 48. More significantly, however, "Charlie," in Hebrew, is *Chaim*, or "life." Citrine (Hebrew *citron*) is referred to in Jewish ritual as the *etrog;* it is one of the Four Species carried and shaken in the synagogue service on the Feast of the Tabernacles. A large acidic fruit from a small evergreen tree, it has a rough, furrowed surface and a thin outer rind of yellowish-green color. In the "classical period," the *citron* or *etrog* was a popular Jewish symbol on coins, synagogues, and graves. Bellow probably had most of these elements in mind in naming his hero Charlie Citrine. But as if to emphasize the ties between his heroes, Bellow has Charlie apply his own "name" to Von Humboldt Fleisher. "Oh, Humboldt! He was no potato," Charlie observes. "He was a papaya a citron a passion fruit" (p. 161).

12. The most complete text of Bellow's Nobel Prize address that I have found to this date is "The Challenge: A Nobel Prize Winner's Searching Questions on the Value of Literature," *Los Angeles Times*, 30 Jan. 1977, Pt. IV, p. 3.

13. Saul Bellow, "Some Notes on Recent American Fiction," *Encounter*, 21, No. 5 (Nov. 1963), 26.

14. For detailed discussions of Bellow's views on the artist's changing and shrinking role in a modern technological society, see (in addition to his Nobel Prize address) "Machines and Story-books: Literature in the Age of Technology," *Harper's*, Aug. 1974, pp. 48–54, 59 and his "A World Too Much with Us," *Critical Inquiry*, 2, No. 1 (Sept. 1975), 1–9.

15. Walter Clemons and Jack Kroll, "America's Master Novelist," *Newsweek*, 1 Sept. 1975, p. 39.

16. Clemons and Kroll, p. 33.

17. Saul Bellow, "Culture Now: Some Animadversions, Some Laughs," *Modern Occasions*, 1, No. 2 (Winter 1971), 162–78.

18. Jack Richardson, "A Burnt-Out Case," *Commentary*, 60, No. 5 (November 1975), 76. Richardson refers to Charlie, but his questions also apply to Humboldt.

19. An Austrian social philosopher and Goethe scholar, Rudolf Steiner was a founder of theosophy and, in 1902, of the German Theosophic Association. Theosophy, a philosophic system with mystic affinities, explains life in terms of man's inner nature and his faculty for spiritual perception and pure thinking independent of his physical senses. But Steiner later left theosophy to develop a distinctive "spiritual science" that he called anthroposophy. As Steiner and his adherents formulated its doctrines, anthroposophy argues for the existence of a spiritual world comprehensible to pure thought and fully accessible only to the higher faculties of knowledge latent in every

individual. Steiner and his followers organized schools, theaters, and study centers, some of which still exist.

20. Shattuck, p. 24.

21. Gilman, p. 2.

22. Roger Shattuck, for instance, sees Charlie Citrine as speculating "with only half-committed conviction about Steiner's anthroposophy" (p. 24). Pearl Bell is even more adamant. "Nothing in Bellow's earlier work," she declares flatly, or "in brilliant parts of *Humboldt's Gift*" persuades her "that his skeptical intelligence can be in agreement with Steiner's pompous elaborations of the invisible" ("Bellow's Best and Worst," *New Leader*, 1 Sept. 1975, p. 20).

23. See Joseph Epstein, "A Talk with Saul Bellow," *New York Times Book Review*, 5 Dec. 1976, p. 93.

24. Lawyer, literary scholar, anthroposophist, and Fellow of the Royal Society of Literature, Owen Barfield (b. 1898) has published such wide-ranging studies as *History in English Words* (1926), *Poetic Diction, A Study in Meaning* (1928), *Romanticism Comes of Age* (1944), *Saving the Appearances: A Study in Idolatry* (1957), *Worlds Apart: A Dialogue of the 1960's* (1963), and *Evolution of Consciousness* (1976).

25. Clemons and Kroll, p. 39.

26. See, for example, Joel Blocker and Richard Elman, "An Interview with Isaac Bashevis Singer," *Commentary*, 36, No. 5 (Nov. 1963), 364–72.

27. John W. Aldridge, "Saul Bellow at 60: A Turn to the Mystical," *Saturday Review*, 6 Sept. 1975, p. 24.

28. Aldridge, p. 24.

29. James Joyce, *Ulysses* (1922; rpt. New York: Random House, 1946), p. 104.

30. Roger Shattuck expresses the critics' dilemma when he cautions that one should read *Humboldt's Gift* "with great care—with caution even" (p. 21).

31. David Lodge, "Dead Reckoning," *Times Literary Supplement*, 10 Oct. 1975, p. 1173.

Sex: Saul Bellow's Hedonistic Joke

Sarah Blacher Cohen*

The humor in the relationship between men and women in Saul Bellow's novels rests not so much on the pandemonious clashes between male and female, but on Bellow's portrayal of the laughable nature of sex itself. The young Bellow protagonist regards copulation as a rollicking animal game in which he eagerly participates. Although he experiences some difficulty in learning the rules and familiarizing himself with the other players' techniques, he plunges headlong into the game. He enjoys taking an amoral holiday from his quest for a distinctive fate; he welcomes the refuge it affords from those "imposers-upon, absolutists"[1] who want to conscript him to their versions of reality. He also views sex as an expression of love, a way of breaking out of his solitude and merging with another human being. But after the dissolution of one love affair after another, he realizes that he is not the selfless devotee of Eros. He only turned to love to avoid the grimness of the impersonal world. He had permitted sex to fool him into thinking that he had fused with another person and was not alone.

The middle-aged Bellow protagonist regards the human being in the act of mating as a funny creature, what with the devious stratagems and the awkward positions he must adopt to attain so ephemeral a bliss. Viewing copulation as a clumsy, undignified activity, he mocks his own and especially his female partner's tendency to invest it with romantic feelings and elevate it to the status of a universal panacea. Despite his ridicule of the sex act, after weighty internal debate and labyrinthine rationalizations, he indulges in it. It is not so much the physical pleasure that he seeks; rather he deludes himself into believing that he can escape from the anxiety and ambiguity of man's middle position between beast and god by losing himself in the animal. When his brief metamorphosis ends, he is all the more oppressed by his human state. More shame-ridden and constrained than ever, he now sees sex as a joke which his own nature and civilization, notably women, play on him. His distress is short-lived, however, for he soon allows himself to be the butt of another sexual joke. And so the delusion-disappointment pattern continues.

The older Bellow protagonist views sex not as a joke, but as the most vile

*Reprinted from *Studies in American Fiction*, 2 (1974) 223–29.

175

plague on earth, with women and blacks as the chief contaminators. Trying desperately to dissociate himself from the debased mortal state by denouncing the bestial and choosing the divine, he is not able to quarantine himself from the noxious presence of sex. Although he is not a participant of the hedonistic revels of the time, he is still the voyeuristic spectator of them and experiences the lurid thrill of the carnal. Much as he tries to be a god, his reaction to the sexual— either his shrill condemnation of it or his furtive titillation by it—does not allow him to transcend his human nature. Against his will, he, too, is the butt of the sexual joke.

Augie March, Bellow's larky young hero, is primarily concerned with discovering a worthwhile destiny for himself. Most of his time is spent, however, not in self-scrutiny, but in fleeing from the Machiavellis in his life, those "heavy-water brains" (p. 524) who want him to play a supporting role in their fantasies. Often tiring of charting his life's voyage while having to dodge his relentless drafters, he engages in sex as a diversion. Though he is the "by-blow of a traveling man" and "well-stocked, probably by inheritance, in all the materials of love" (p. 47), he does not always have an easy time of it. His sexual initiation is obstacle-ridden and far from idyllic. Unlike a Tom Jones who chances upon ready sexual gratification, Augie must first hoist his invalid employer Einhorn on his back, walk up a tortuous flight of icy stairs in the dark, deposit Einhorn before an astonished whore, choose a nameless woman himself, and then seek his own pleasure. And this pleasure Augie claims *"didn't* have the luster it should have had, and there *wasn't* any epithalamium of gentle lovers" (p. 124). Yet this first carnal adventure does not deter Augie from getting into one erotic entanglement after another. Almost overnight he is transformed from the swain suffering from the pangs of unrequited love for rich girl Esther Fenchel to the Don Juan whose love is very much requited by chambermaid Sophie Geratis. Right after he is trounced by anti-union men for his association with Sophie Geratis, he is restored to his vigorous self by the higher love of the unchaste hunting goddess, Thea Fenchel. Soon after he is critically injured in Thea's iguana-hunting expedition, he recovers to become the very healthy lover of movie star Stella Chesney.

Although Augie initially considers each of these sexual relations as a pleasurable release from the more painful task of self-discovery, he soon views them more as affairs of the heart than of the groin. Believing himself to be the "sincere follower of love" (p. 401), he regards each woman with whom he is intimate as a potential life-long companion to share his lonely "pilgrimage." But after he abandons one companion after another, he realizes he is a more fickle than faithful servant of Venus. Rather than desiring any permanent unions, he sought only "temporary embraces" from any woman who would give him cover from the world's "mighty free-running terror and wild cold of chaos" (p. 403). The magic of sex had charmed him into believing he could be free of this "bondage of strangeness" (p. 523). Though he eventually marries Stella and claims to love her, at the novel's end he is still the solitary "Columbus" exploring the external and internal *"terra incognita"* (p. 536). But since he is Bellow's *"animal ridens,* the laughing creature, forever rising up" (p. 536), he has his comic sense to keep him company.

Moses Herzog is not a "young and glossy stud"[2] like Augie, but a middle-aged cuckolded intellectual who is suffering from the break-up of his marriage and the collapse of his stability. Unable to perform his scholarly duties, let alone govern himself, he heeds the promptings of his lawless id. Unable to cope with the more complicated issues of life, he copes with women. Having writhed in pain under the "sharp, elegant heel" of his former wife Madeleine, he now writhes in pleasure having sex with Ramona Donselle, "true sack artist" (p. 17). Yet Herzog is not consumed with achieving what Mailer in "The White Negro" describes as the "orgasm more apocalyptic than the one which preceded it."[3] His need for order is stronger than his need for orgy. Although he doesn't share the extreme view of Moses Maimonides, the twelfth-century Jewish philosopher who claimed that the Hebrew language was holy because it contained no words for sexual activity or the sexual organs, Herzog does agree with Maimonides that man should control his sexual desires and not be controlled by them. Herzog states that lust is the "most wretched form of human struggle, the very essense of slavery" (p. 219). Yet he cannot free himself from this slavery. It is not that he is driven only by the craving for sensual delight. As a "prisoner of perception" (p. 72) who is "sick with abstractions" (p. 123), Herzog looks to sex as a release from the cerebral. Plagued with so many human difficulties, he hopes through sex to become the insouciant animal. He therefore ingeniously convinces himself that sexual gratification is essential to his health and well-being. He further rationalizes his personal need by generalizing it to a societal need. "The erotic," he authoritatively claims, "must be admitted to its rightful place, at last in an emancipated society which understands the relation of sexual repression to sickness, war, property, money, totalitarianism" (p. 166). Bellow undoubtedly had such a remark in mind when he jocosely informed a French reviewer: "En Amérique, la sexualité est moins plaisir érotique qu'hygiéne indispensable."[4]

Herzog's comic sense, however, does not allow him to remain satisfied with his impressive-sounding rationalization. He soon punctures his high-flown justification for sex by suggesting the *reductio ad absurdum* conclusion that can be drawn from it. "Why, to get laid," he states with tongue in cheek, "is actually socially constructive and useful, an act of citizenship" (p. 166). Although Herzog in his more rational moments mocks the value of sex, in his less rational moments he is persuaded otherwise by Ramona, theoretician of sex and sensibility. Trusting in the power of positive love-making, she urges Herzog to give full expression to his instincts and revel in her style of hedonism. She firmly believes that sexual release cannot only eliminate man's "constitutional tension of whatever origin" (p. 201), but it can also cure the world of most of its ills. One's failure to satisfy the needs of the body, she insists, amounts to a "surrender to malignancy . . . [and] capitulating to the death instinct" (p. 185). To lend support to her claim, Ramona quotes both "Catullus and the great love poets of all times" (p. 202), and cites the unimpeachable arguments of such neo-

Freudians as Herbert Marcuse and N.O. Brown. Along with lecturing about sex, Ramona gives practical demonstrations as well. Appearing as a "tough Spanish broad," a "girlie magazine" tart, or a priestess of the "Mystical body," she presents a vast repertoire of "erotic monkeyshines" (p. 17). Herzog, in turn, is captivated by these "monkeyshines" and responds with "a lustful quacking in his depths" (p. 337). Thus, despite his mockery of the worth of sexual therapy, he is "powerless to reject the hedonistic joke of a mammoth industrial civilization" (p. 166) and eagerly puts himself in the hands of Ramona, therapist *par excellence*. But after a night-long treatment, he is still the same idiosyncratic Herzog with "his problems unsolved as ever," in addition to "a lip made sore by biting and kissing" (p. 207). He had only been a "petit-bourgeois Dionysian" (p. 17) who carried a "heavy-buttocked woman to . . . bed" (p. 154) and awkwardly experienced his spasm of rapture. Herzog therefore blames Ramona for having misrepresented sex, for convincing him that the "body is a spiritual fact, the sinstrument of the soul" (pp. 208–09). Sharing Freud's belief that woman is incapable of denying her instinctual demands for the sake of civilization, Herzog claims that Ramona's sexual theorizing and practices represents a "dangerous temptation which can only lead to more high-minded mistakes" (p. 209). Apparently Herzog will keep on making these mistakes, for after he has served his sentence of hard mental labor and returned to his Berkshire garden of Eden, he has arranged for Ramona-Eve to join him. When he sees her, he hears within himself "the deep, the cosmic, the idiotic masculine response—quack" (p. 337). The fact that he describes this "*quack*" as "idiotic" lets us know that as much as he would like to revert to the animal, he cannot. His comic self-awareness prevents him from possessing the spontaneous enjoyment of sex so natural to the animal and forces him to admit what a calculating, yet bungling mortal he is. His recognition of the humorous nature of sex thus transforms the sex act into something more than just the purely animal. It establishes his imperfect human state. For man, according to Bellow, affirms his middle position between beast and god by attempting through sex to deny this position.

Mr. Sammler, Bellow's seventy-plus "post-coital" man, cannot, like Herzog, look with humor upon the sex act. Suffering from a hardening of his jocular arteries, Artur Sammler has the same contemptuous regard for sex which his namesake, Artur Schopenhauer, expressed: "[Copulation] is an action of which in cold reflection one generally thinks with dislike and in a lofty mood with loathing."[5] Indeed through the novel Sammler is in "a lofty mood" and abhors "creatureliness." A sworn upholder of Apollonian values, he assails what to him are the Dionysian excesses of the times: "the right to be uninhibited, spontaneous, urinating, defecating, belching, coupling in all positions, tripling, quadrupling, polymorphous."[6]

The culprit whom Sammler chiefly blames for these excesses is woman. Like the fifteenth-century inquisitor, Jacob Sprenger, who claimed that all "witchcraft comes from carnal lust, which is in women insatiable,"[7] Sammler believes that women are infernal sex machines, whipping up this libidinal frenzy. The female in the novel who bears the principal brunt of Sammler's misogyny is Angela Gruner, his spoiled and dissipated grand-niece. Although she is Bellow's caricature of the emancipated woman who is more enslaved than liberated by the free expression of her sexuality, Sammler in his unvocalized monologues upbraids her for being a vile temptress of the flesh. Like the prophet Isaiah, castigating the "daughters of Zion" for their "stretched-forth necks . . . wanton eyes" and provocative adornments,[8] Sammler censures Angela for her stretched forth bust, whorish eyes, and "microskirts." Disgusted by her "experiments" in "sexology" (p. 278), he regards her lewdness as the worst form of the Roman paganism sweeping the country.

Herzog had good cause for his character assassinations of Madeleine, who for such a long time ground her heel into his groin. But Sammler has never been personally wronged by Angela and thus his criticism of her seems unduly harsh. Obviously he needs to vilify Angela to dissuade himself from being attracted to her. Whenever he meets her, he is particularly responsive to her "powerful message of gender" (p. 70). He notes the brand of tights she wears, the kind of Arabian musk she uses, and the type of swagger she employs to "enhance the natural power of the bust" (p. 31). In addition to being taken with her undisguised sensuality, he derives a vicarious thrill from listening to her disjointed tales of unbridled eroticism. If for some reason she neglects to describe all the graphic particulars of her affairs, he imagines the lurid details.

It is Angela and women like her, Sammler believes, who have elevated black men to the position of erotic leadership in the sexual revolution they have started. For Angela's notion of what constitutes the perfect man for women— "a Jew brain, a black cock and a Nordic beauty" (p. 66)—has become the sexual ideal for society at large. And the black man, once he realizes he is so prized for his virility, becomes arrogant and flaunts his sexual prowess.

Sammler does not have to rely on secondhand reports of black genital supermen. A black pickpocket, discovering that Sammler has witnessed his operations, corners him in a vacant hotel lobby, makes public his privates, and threatens him with his formidable penis. The symbolic intent of the confrontation is obvious: in this day and age reason and decency are subject to intimidation by brute, lawless forces.[9] What is not so obvious is the fascination the supposedly righteous feel for those of sexual and criminal abandon. On the one hand, Sammler, sharing Schopenhauer's view that the organs of sex are the instrument of the powerful, unprincipled will, shrinks in dread and horror before the thief exhibiting his weapon of malevolent potency. But, on the other hand, Sammler purposely takes the same bus, secretly desiring a reenactment of the thief's masterful exploitation of the "slackness, the cowardice of the world" (p. 47). Similarly, Sammler has mixed reactions about the thief's capture. When he sees him throttling Lionel Feffer, the sensation-and-money-hungry college student who tried to photograph him in action, Sammler regards the black thief as a lethal beast whose glaring sexuality makes him even more repugnant. But when Eisen, his ex-son-in-law almost destroys the thief, Sammler finds "a certain princeliness" in the black man and admires his "barbarous-majestical manner" (p. 294).

Sammler does not want to acknowledge the "ludicrous inconsistency" (p. 291) of his attitude toward the black thief or Angela. At the time it is less disturbing to dismiss them as warped entertainers "in the great fun fair" who "do this droll mortality with one another" (p. 294). When, however, his nephew Elya Gruner dies, a man whom Sammler considers a fallible, yet saintly being, he is compelled to recognize that he himself is not a flawless divine collector of deviants. By claiming to prefer "lunar chastity" (p. 67), while furtively relishing earthly prurience, he has acted less than human and certainly has not adhered to his original intention of acting more than human. Looking to Gruner as his model, he hopes now to act exactly human, which means he will not deny having "galloping impulses" and will not remove himself from "crazy streets, filthy nightmares, monstrosities come to life" (p. 74). As long as he inhabits this planet, Sammler vows he will be openly involved in its "confusion and degraded clowning" (p. 313).

In *The Adventures of Augie March, Herzog* and *Mr. Sammler's Planet,* Saul Bellow depicts sex as the comic leveler, preventing individuals from viewing themselves as brutes of the flesh or aristocrats of the spirit. Initially fooled by the alleged powers of sex, the youthful and middle-aged Bellow heroes look to it as a source of perpetual ecstasy, an end to loneliness, a reprieve from thinking and a release from all fears. The older Bellow hero recoils in disgust from it and considers himself infinitely superior for his celibacy. But when indulgence in sex or abstinence from it does not improve their lives, they chastise themselves for their gullibility. If, however, they have a sense of humor, they soon laugh at themselves for being taken in by the joke of sex. Made aware that they cannot become at one with the beast or the angels, they struggle to come to terms with their more taxing, yet more fulfilling, mortal state.

Notes

1. Saul Bellow, *The Adventures of Augie March* (New York: Viking Press, 1953), p. 524. Subsequent references to this edition will be made in the text.

2. Saul Bellow, *Herzog* (New York: Viking Press, 1964), p. 154. Subsequent references to this edition will be made in the text.

3. Norman Mailer, "The White Negro," *Advertisements for Myself* (New York: Berkeley Publishing Corporation, 1966), p. 321.

4. Pierre Dommergues, "Recontre avec Saul Bellow," *Preuves,* 17 (January, 1967), 41.

5. Artur Schopenhauer, *The World as Will and Idea,* Vol. 3, "On the Assertion of the Will to Live," quoted in Eva Figes, *Patriarchal Attitudes* (New York: Stein and Day Publishers, 1970), p. 122.

6. Saul Bellow, *Mr. Sammler's Planet* (New York: Viking Press, 1970), p. 33. Subsequent references to this edition will be made in the text.

7. Jacob Sprenger, *Malleus Maleficarum* ("Hammer of Witches"), quoted in Eva Figes, *Patriarchal Attitudes,* p. 64.

8. Isaiah 3:17, King James Version.

9. For further discussion of what the black thief represents see my book, *Saul Bellow's Enigmatic Laughter* (Urbana: University of Illinois Press, 1974), pp. 181, 189–91.

Saul Bellow: The Hero in the Middle

M.A. Klug*

Saul Bellow has been something of a resident alien among recent American novelists. While his work is soaked in American experience, it does not appear to develop out of the tradition of any of his immediate predecessors in American fiction. He has said some kind words about Dreiser, but he is not a direct descendant of Dreiser or of any of the other naturalists. His work does not emerge out of the generation of Fitzgerald and Hemingway, nor does it spring from the social realism that Bellow grew up with in the thirties. Critics, trying to locate Bellow in a literary context, usually link him with French or Russian novelists or with a Jewish tradition that is not specifically American. While Bellow has certainly been more cosmopolitan than most American novelists, he has not simply turned away from the American tradition. From the beginning of his career, he has consciously tried to avoid what he sees as the extremes of the modern American tradition and at the same time to contain those extremes as the central conflict within his own work.

Bellow has described American literature as a "succession of encounters between rival claimants".[1] As Bellow sees it, the "unfortunate result of this progress by contrasts in American literature is that it always produces exaggeration".[2] From his point of view, this impulse toward exaggeration was built into origins of modern American fiction. It was in part generated by a reaction against the "orthodox optimism" of post-Civil-War American life and its expression in literature. As Bellow puts it, the early "realists and naturalists in their anger and moral zeal turned Horatio Alger inside out".[3] While the conventional novel of the late nineteenth century specialized in contrived triumph, the novelists of the naturalist and realist tradition moved to the opposite pole of inevitable defeat. They looked straight through that cliché of the "smiling aspects of American life" and discovered what has become in its turn another cliché, "the destructive element". Reality came to mean bad news and a little later worse news. The best novelists of this emerging modern American tradition found their authority in death. We see the proof of their commitment to reality in the way they drive or follow their heroes into its arms. McTeague,

*Reprinted from *Dalhousie Review*, 56 (1976), 462-78.

Clyde Griffiths, Frederick Henry, Gatsby (the list could go on indefinitely) all discover the real to be the image of their own mortality.

With their polarized view of reality, the naturalists and realists were inevitably committed to polarized views of the self. Over and over they return to two conflicting notions of the self, which doubtless correspond to conflicting elements within themselves and in a broader sense within American culture. On the one hand, the "loss of self" which Wylie Sypher describes in modern European literature was also taking place in American fiction from the nineties onward. The naturalists and realists see the ordinary self (the self of mass or collective man unredeemed by any ideal pursuit) as submerged in total paralysis. It simply drifts in a death-like trance at the lowest possible level of consciousness. In contrast to this passive image of the ordinary self, the external environment which surrounds it represents overwhelming force. At times the force is social or natural, at times it is anonymous. There is nothing of the melodramatic glamour of any Second Fall into the quotidian in all of this. In the United States the finite has a plainer face. Hurstwood worries about the price of liver. George Wilson gathers dust beside his eternal gas pump.

But the early naturalists and realists never totally surrender themselves to the image of the doomed ordinary self. While they show this self as being absorbed in its environment, they also retain a deep strain of romantic individualism. The heroic or ideal self of popular nineteenth-century American fiction was not simply killed off. The early naturalists and realists transform it into a sort of necessary illusion. They glorify the pursuit of the ideal or heroic self even though they see it as doomed. Their central characters are usually romantic artists of the self. They try to create their being in the image of their own idea of perfection. In order to undertake this self-creation they must turn from reality to illusion. In the work of Norris, Dreiser, and later Fitzgerald, this pursuit of the perfect self is only undertaken by central characters who have immense vital energy and are protected by their own ambition or naivete from seeing the futility of their quest. The Hemingway hero senses the futility from the start and can only pursue his ideal self by willfully restraining his imagination and intellect. While the quest for the perfect self is no final defense against destructive reality, it does allow a sad residue of nobility. The heroic self can at least put up a fight against the forces that simply swallow up the Hurstwoods and Wilsons. Ironically this fight comes to mean power over and against nature and the ordinary self. The hero is drawn into a primal conflict with reality and pits the force of his individual will against the destructive force of the environment. The early naturalists such as Norris, Dreiser, and especially London were as fascinated by the ruthless pursuit of power and by maniacal striving as they were with the processes of dissolution and human impotence. In the next generation the brutal ferocity is gone, but Gatsby in his struggle for a Platonic self and the Hemingway hero in his struggle for mastery in the face of destruction are the legitimate heirs of Wolf Larsen, Frank Cowperwood, and S. Behrman.

On the surface this cosmic gloom and the simultaneous obsessions with self-perfection and power may seem paradoxical. If it is, it is an old paradox that can be traced back to the earliest beginnings of the American tradition and beyond. Probably Augustine and Pelagius came over on the same boat. At any rate the extreme pessimism on the dark side of Calvinism has always co-existed with an American version of the romantic quest for self-perfection. It is just these polar extremes which have held Bellow's attention throughout his career. He not only sees them as the shaping forces of American literature but of American history and culture as well. Most importantly he sees them as the continuing terms of conflict within the American psyche. While Bellow rejects both orthodox optimism and orthodox pessimism, both the idea of human impotence and romantic striving after self-perfection, the tension between these contrary forces supplies much of the drama of his work. His minor characters are for the most part grotesque incarnations of one or the other of these extremes. His central characters contain these extremes as the terms of their psychological conflicts. It is here that Bellow's efforts to create an image of the human self can best be seen in relation to the naturalists and realists. Bellow's heroes contain both the heroic self and the ordinary self. The roles which the naturalists and realists tend to assign respectively to their central characters and their minor characters, Bellow locates within his central characters as the basis of their conflict. His heroes are driven in pursuit of self-perfection and at the same time paralyzed by immersion in a hostile environment of death. Life appears to them as a choice of nightmares, just as it does in the work of the naturalists and realists: on the one side a life of frenzied striving after an impossible self-perfection, on the other total surrender to death by immersion. Unlike the characters of the naturalists and realists, Bellow's heroes refuse this choice of nightmares. His characters move towards a comic resolution, and in order to achieve it they must discover both a new sense of reality and of self. In following them through their conflicts towards this comic resolution, we can see the extent to which Bellow incorporated some of the central assumptions of naturalists and realists into his work while at the same time moving beyond them.

The most consistent aspect of Saul Bellow's fiction is the psychology of his heroes. From Joseph, the dangling man, to Artur Sammler,[4] Bellow's central characters all have pretty much the same psychological conflict. Each of his heroes hungers for what he instinctively knows is a decent life, for love, for human brotherhood, for communion with God. At the same time each is betrayed by the demands of his own ego, which insists upon absolute freedom, absolute power, absolute understanding. The traitor ego seeks to create an ideal self and flies beyond all limits. It will settle for nothing short of self-perfection. Joseph, Bellow's first hero, speaks of a "bottomless avidity" which drives him to prize himself "crazily" and to reject any life that falls one thousandth of an inch "short of its ultimate possibility".[5] In varying degrees all of Bellow's later heroes have this same raging ego, endlessly barking "I want, I want". It drives them in pursuit of special distinction, personal destinies, separate and unique fates. In its most extreme form, it perverts the instinctive need to be at one with other men and with God into a desire to control all other men and to become God.

But while Bellow's heroes are ego driven towards a perfect freedom, they live the negation of their desire. They cannot create their own natures and for the simplest of reasons. They have *inherent* natures, finite and imperfectible. That is the message that external reality brings. The world keeps saying "death", and for all of their evasions, Bellow's heroes, on one level of their being, believe it. Joseph knows that "we are sought and expect to be found" (*DM* 122). Like it or not, Henderson finally acknowledges what all the corpses keep telling him, "Here, man, is your being, which you think is so terrific" (*HRK* 137). For Herzog, too, "Death waits . . . as a cement floor waits for a dropping light bulb" (*H* 290). All of Bellow's heroes believe in death, and they also believe that they owe it to themselves to be immortal. This conflict determines the way that they characteristically see the world. In their frustration they condemn all reality. The conviction that death is real comes to mean that all reality is death. Reality exists to annihilate them. Any hope, any consolation is an illusion, just as the desire for immortality is an illusion. As Sammler sees, the earth becomes a terror because it is the grave (*SP* 182).

For Bellow's heroes the recurrent image of this reality of death is the modern city. They see the buildings, the institutions, the multitude of unknown bodies as the substance of death itself. The city exists as a machine for mass-production and mass-murder. To be a part of it is to be swallowed into nothingness, to lose not only the hope of immortality but also the hope of a unique or individual life. Even Augie, who tries the hardest to familiarize his world, believes, in his worst moments, that Chicago means his non-existence:

> Around was Chicago. In its repetition it exhausted your imagination of details and units, more units than the cells of the brain and bricks of Babel. The Ezeckial caldron of wrath, stoked with bones. In time the caldron would melt . . . as before the work of Egypt and Assyria, as before a sea. You're nothing here. Nothing. (*AM* 458).

And just as the ego is inevitably in conflict with external reality, it is inevitably in conflict with another part of the self. The flipside of "bottomless avidity" is bottomless contempt. All of Bellow's heroes despise themselves for falling short of perfection. Joseph is sure that he conceals some inner rottenness. Asa Leventhal is always ready to believe the worst of himself. Tommy Wilhelm continually addresses himself as the "jerk", the "hippo", the "clunk". And so on through to Sammler with his mellowed repertoire of self-insults. What lies behind this is a perverse urge for pure states. If the self cannot be perfect then let it be worthless. The essential dynamic of Bellow's heroes arises from the pull of these two extremes. On the most active level of their being, they are romantic egoists drawn to some pure and absolute freedom. Denied this pure state, they turn in disgust from their environment and from their own natures. While they yearn to romp with God, death and mass society which surrounds them whisper that they will be nothing in this world and the next. Here they come very close to Otto Rank's description of the neurotic as *artiste manqué*. They all have the artist's impulse; they want to create themselves in the image of perfection, make themselves immortal. They fail to complete this act of self-creation because a part of them which corresponds to the ordinary self sees in destructive reality and in death the futility of all quests for perfection and for individual immortality.

As a primary defense, all of Bellow's heroes turn from what they think of as reality and attempt to live in a private world of protective illusion. They strike a coward's bargain and submit to the suffering of an interior life in order to escape greater suffering and death outside. For example, just after Henderson arrives in Africa, he stumbles into an understanding of his own flight from reality; he sees that he arranged to have himself abducted into illusion in order to make "death more remote" (*HRK* 74). Later, as the lion of death charges down on him, the same understanding returns with much greater clarity: "But oh, unreality! Unreality, unreality! That was my scheme for a troubled but eternal life" (*HRK* 307). In almost every Bellow novel there is a moment when the hero literally turns his face from death and looks out the window. The best example shows up in *Herzog*. In a powerful passage, Moses drifts back across the years to remember the death of his mother. He realizes that in dying she tried to convey the simplest message, *"My son, this is death"*. Moses chose "not to read this text":

> He came into her room when she was dying, holding his school books, and began to say something to her. But she lifted up her hands and showed him her fingernails. They were blue. As he stared, she slowly began to nod her head up and down as if to say, "That's right, Moses, I am dying now." He sat by the bed. Presently she began to stroke his hand. She did this as well as she could; her fingers had lost their flexibility. Under the nails they seemed to him to be turning already into the blue loam of graves. She had begun to change into earth! He did not dare to look but listened to the runners of the children's sleds in the street, and the grating of peddlers' wheels on the knotted ice, the hoarse call of the apple peddler and the rattle of his steel scale. The steam whispered in the vent. The curtain was drawn (*H* 234–35).

On one level this passage is literal description; on another, it has the symbolic force of a dream. As his mother is transformed into the common earth, Moses turns away to the subjective realm of random impressions, separated by his fear, like a drawn curtain, from death and the external world. This flight from death and finite reality into subjectivity, which is so important a part of Moses' psychology, shows up in all of Bellow's heroes. All of them instinctively hope to keep themselves safe within their own thinking. By the time we get to *Mr. Sammler's Planet*, flight becomes a characteristic of the whole American culture. Over and over in that novel, the first moon shot represents society's mass rejection of this earth which is our grave.

As a fortification against death and a hostile environment Bellow's heroes literally hole-up. They are habitual lodgers, residents of a succession of narrow, locked rooms. When they are driven into the streets, they move instinctively towards the safety of blind corridor or subway. Joseph bleeds out his time in a "six-sided box" (*DM* 92). Asa Leventhal keeps himself secluded under lock and key. Henderson fiddles away in his basement cell. And so on through to Sammler in his West Side bedroom. They all discover that holing up is a lot like digging their own grave. They run from death in the streets to a metaphoric death within the walls of their own being. Of all Bellow's heroes, Sammler is most harried. His reality has little time for metaphor. It pushes him into a mass-grave in Poland, into a private tomb of the Mezvinski family, where he was "so to speak a boarder" (*SP* 90), and finally into the New York subway to re-encounter "death, entombment, the Mezvinski vault" (*SP* 120).

Bellow's heroes seek out a temporal hideout, just as they do a spatial. The past becomes another safe box, another fortification against death. Tommy Wilhelm, Henderson, Herzog, Sammler all retreat into the past partially in an attempt to resurrect their own dead within the memory. But here again the flight from death leads only to death. Instead of bringing the dead back to life, Bellow's heroes take up residence with them. Henderson sums it up: "the dead are my boarders, eating me out of house and home" (*HRK* 287). Bellow's heroes also seek a kind of personal immortality in the past. Over and over again they return to the scenes and memories of their childhoods as a permanent retreat against time. As a result there is a childishness about them which a number of critics have pointed out. Even Henderson, the six-foot-four-inch excommando, streetfighter, and hogpuncher, confesses that he has "never been at home in life", that all his "decay has taken place upon a child" (*HRK* 84). As children, as strangers to the world, Bellow's heroes can avoid choosing any fixed purpose in life. Like Joseph, they all long to give themselves away, to know their purpose, but at the same time they are afraid to commit themselves to any fixed state of being and drift into "endless becoming". To mature is to admit change and consequently to admit death. To "be" is to accept limits and consequently to admit death.

Behind the walls, Bellow's heroes boil over in an inner fury of self-revenge and self-justification. They retreat from external strife into internal strife which is staged as an enclosed drama. The life of the mind becomes a substitute for creative life. One part of the self replays its experience before another critical self that continually analyzes and evaluates the performance. Joseph is so lost in this internal drama of consciousness that he objectifies a part of himself into the "spirit of alternatives". Much of the same thing happens to Asa and Herzog. Asa replays his self-conflict with Allbee, his own double. Herzog spends his days writing letters to himself. Even Augie March is at last driven to a life of interior labour, "Hard, hard work . . . And none of this work is seen from the outside. It's internally done . . . All by yourself! Where is everybody? Inside your breast and skin, the entire cast" (*AM* 323). This internal work builds nothing, leads no-where. It is a treadmill of grievances as confining as the world it is meant to supplant.

But since perfect isolation is impossible this side of death, Bellow's heroes are periodically forced and attracted towards the society around them. Just as their interior lives become a kind of drama with the divided self as actor and audience, their public lives degenerate into theatre. Here again they are cast as actor and audience. The actor's main job is to put together a convincing dis-guise. This becomes a parody of their own desire to create an ideal self and of the heroic quest for self-perfection undertaken by the central characters in the fiction of the naturalists and realists. Over and over Bellow's heroes struggle to keep up appearances in order to hide what they consider their "real" but inferior selves: Tommy Wilhelm in his eighteen-dollar Jack Fagman shirt, Herzog in his macaroni sports ensemble, Sammler in his Kresge cap and seersucker suit, playing the war correspondent. Of course, the object is to play the fabricated self so well that it becomes genuine in the eyes of the world. But public life is a competition of actors, all trying to play their invented selves with more force than anyone else, and Bellow's heroes are not very successful in this free market of artificial souls. They live in continual fear that the rest of the cast is seeing through their disguise to the poor player beneath.

While all of Bellow's heroes make their reluctant appearances, the role they prefer is that of audience. They want to fix life within their vision, swallow up their environment in consciousness. Seeing is transformed into an alternative for living. Their compulsive visualizing is often close to being neurotic. Joseph and Asa spy on their neighbors. Herzog, like a peeping tom, peers through the bathroom window on his would-be victim, Gersbach. Even Sammler cannot resist the compulsion to "watch", as he returns to observe the black pickpocket enact his crimes. But what matters here is not so much the individual symptoms of Bellow's heroes as the social significance of these symptoms. Augie best understands and explains what this tyranny of watching and being watched means:

> When has so much damage been done by the gaze, and so much awful despotism belonged to the eyes? Why, Cain was cursed between them so he would never be unaware of his look in the view of other men. And police accompany accused and suspects to the can, and jailers see their convicts at will through bars and peepholes. Chiefs and tyrants of the public give no relief from self-consciousness. Vanity is the same thing in private, and in any kind of oppression you are a subject and can't forget yourself; you are seen, you have to be aware. In the most personal acts of your life you carry the presence and power of another; you extend his being into your thoughts, where he inhabits (AM 335).

Social life becomes a conspiracy of appearances. Each individual is reduced to a series of impressions that he makes upon an audience of jailers; he is never free of the necessity of making the strongest and best impression. At the same time each is a jailer, measuring and evaluating the impressions his neighbor gives out. And for all the observation little of any substance is really seen. No one, or almost no one, has the courage to live without disguise. In Bellow's streets even death is simply another show. Joseph tries to help a "fallen man" that he stumbles across in the Chicago winter, but as the police arrive he quickly becomes one of the crowd of "onlookers", reluctant to disengage themselves as the ambulance carries off the body. Much the same thing is reported in The Victim. Allbee tells of seeing a man pinned by a train to the subway walls. He screams for help as he slowly bleeds to death. The crowd sticks to the rules; it is an audience, and it watches him die. By the time we get to Mr. Sammler's Planet, we find that the impassivity of the crowd has changed to fascination, almost gratitude, as it watches crazy Eisen smash the thief with a sackful of bronze sculpture.

Because their external lives consist almost entirely of play-acting and passive observation, Bellow's heroes are filled with a sense of their own inconsequentiality. Their antidote is to seek out conflict. It works as a mental stimulant that for a moment relieves the interior suffering and produces an illusion of real existence. For example, Joseph continually seeks conflict in order to have consequences; "trouble like physical pain" makes him aware that he is really alive (*DM* 82). In one degree or another, all of Bellow's heroes use conflict in this same way. In *Mr. Sammler's Planet* it becomes one of the primary social forces. Almost every character in that novel is addicted to violent conflict, the square's LSD. Even gentle Sammler is hooked and compulsively moves toward danger because it momentarily ignites his consciousness. In fact Sammler has made the ultimate trip. Pushed almost to the point of death he recharged his own being by shooting a disarmed German soldier: "It was joy. . . . When he fired his gun, Sammler, himself nearly a corpse, burst into life" (*SP* 140). Everyone of Bellow's heroes would understand Sammler's joy, and his sudden burst of life. They are all passive; they are all filled with restraints and walled up love for their fellowman; at the same time they all have a hidden potential for extreme violence.

An important part of this climate of potential violence is an all-pervasive sense of betrayal. In their darkest moments Bellow's heroes are tempted to see society as a complicity of betrayal. Society brings people together for purposes of mutual exploitation. The blood guilt of mass murder hangs over it. The hero as an individual member of his society is an accomplice in this betrayal and at the same time a victim. For example, Asa Leventhal fears that the meaning behind social reality is betrayal, the blacklist and the crematorium. While he continually sees himself as a victim of betrayal, he just as surely sees himself as guilty of it. Treason becomes for Asa, just as for Joseph, "a medium, like air, like water" (*DM* 56). It determines his relationship with collective society and more importantly with those closest to him. Underlying all his relations with his wife, his family and his friends is fear and guilt. The rest of Bellow's heroes know this same fear and guilt. Over and over the love for father, brother, friend, wife is poisoned by the suspicion of mutual betrayal. Each of Bellow's heroes realizes that an obsession with betrayal is close to moral insanity. But this realization doesn't allow them to establish easy boundaries between the delusions of paranoia and reality.

Now if Bellow had stopped here, if he had allowed his heroes to die within the walls of their conflicts, his view of reality and of the individual's relationship to it would be very close to that of the naturalists and realists. But Bellow refuses to abandon his central characters to a futile and destructive quest for perfection or to an anonymous death within the ordinary self. Through his career he makes a desperate effort to push through this impasse, and in doing so he moves away from both the spirit and the law of the naturalist-realist tradition. The resolution that Bellow's heroes move towards springs from a triumph over the ego rather than the simple destruction of it. They go beyond their own striving for absolute perfection and in so doing experience the sense of a new reality. The external world comes to them not as a paradigm of death, but as a mystery. This mystery has little to do with hope or despair or with any intellectual formulation of these states. Bellow's heroes see that both pessimism and optimism are rackets, and their commitments, like Bellow's, are to something "far more rudimentary than any 'position' or intellectual attitude might imply".[7] What they arrive at is not an explanation but a sense of mystical atonement with life and reality which is independent of any final judgment of good or bad. In spite of all their resistances, Bellow's heroes discover moments of freedom when they escape from behind the walls and encounter reality. This freedom comes first in "isolate flecks", instants of intense perception which they do not really know what to do with. It grows to an experience of their relationship with all other men and to the beginnings of a morality centered in a sense of duty to other men. In Bellow's other work, it leads finally to a fleeting sense of identification with God. At this point it must be emphasized that none of this brings any final solution. For Bellow "final solutions" always mean somebody's death. The inner divisions of his heroes are never totally healed over. Their instincts for withdrawal and their fears of reality are never completely overcome. They never find any permanent point of contact with God or with the world of other men. At best they accept the mixed condition of their humanity and, as Henderson puts it, they pick up some gains along the way.

One of the recurrent moments of freedom that Bellow's heroes realize springs from a sudden emotional acceptance of the inherent limits of life. It begins with a surrender to the knowledge that there is no way of beating these limits, that striving against them is futile. For a moment the self emerges from the ego, with its demands of absolute freedom, and experiences reality. The two best examples of this process show up in *The Adventures of Augie March* and *Seize the Day*. Augie, the career auditor, makes a lengthy declaration to his friend Clem Tambow, which is probably the most important statement of his own beliefs that appears in the course of the novel:

> I have a feeling . . . about the axial lines of life, with respect to which you must be straight or else your existence is merely clownery, hiding tragedy. I must have had a feeling since I was kid about these axial lines which made me want to have my existence on them, and so I have said "no" like a stubborn fellow to all my persuaders, just on the obstinacy of my memory of these lines, never entirely clear. But lately I have felt these thrilling lines again. When striving stops, there they are as a gift. I was lying on the couch here before and they suddenly went quivering right straight through me. Truth, love, peace, bounty, usefulness, harmony. And all noises, and grates, distortion, chatter, distraction, effort, superfluity, passed off like something unreal (*AM* 454).

Augie goes on to explain that his "ambition of something special and outstanding", his struggles to know everything and to hold the world together by explanation carried him away from the axial lines of reality and into the walls of his own being. To return to these lines he has had to reject his own striving after self-perfection in order to be regenerated as "man himself, finite and taped as he is" (*AM* 455).

In the final scene of *Seize the Day*, Tommy Wilhelm has a similar experience, but it is presented in a far more dramatic way. With a lifetime of striving after "special distinction" behind him, Tommy ends up a bankrupt among the multitude. As he hurries along Broadway, he is swept up in "the inexhaustible current of millions of every race and kind" (*SD* 115). The crowd carries him into a "dark and cool" chapel where a funeral is taking place. He joins the line slowly moving towards the coffin and "the face of the dead". As he gazes down upon the corpse of a stranger, all of his resistances suddenly dissolve. He begins to cry and is soon carried "past words, past reason, coherence" to the "source of all tears". In the midst of this powerful emotional seizure, the chapel music, like the tide of death itself, floods through Tommy and he sinks "deeper than sorrow, through torn sobs and cries toward the consummation of his heart's ultimate need" (*SD* 118).

These two crucial experiences are of course similar in a number of ways. Both are essentially passive experiences. They are not achieved. They simply come as a gift, when the ego is beaten and striving is abated.[8] Both focus on an irrational, emotional acceptance of the limits inherent in human nature. Tommy and Augie have *known* all along about these limits, but momentarily, at least, they have stopped pounding their heads against them. Finally both of these experiences end in a mystical union with reality. Augie feels the force of "truth, love, peace, bounty, usefulness, harmony". Tommy encounters "the consummation of his heart's ultimate need". Paradoxically freedom comes with the acceptance of limits. For a moment both are at home in their own natures. Without the burden of infinite hopes or the obligation to perfect themselves they are free to know and feel their finite humanity. They are freed from endless becoming into being.

Scattered through Bellow's work are numerous moments of such transcendence: Joseph lying in bed and suddenly perceiving in the icicles and frost patterns on his window a "world without deformity or threat of damage" (*DM* 118–119); Asa Leventhal throwing open his window to catch a glimpse of "beautiful night" (*V* 66); Augie looking out upon the Ozarks with "original eyes" (*AM* 330); Henderson catching in the African dawn the "voice of objects and colors" (*HRK* 101) and the vision of a world alive. There is a recurrent pattern in each of these moments; they all come in passive instants when the brain surrenders its labour of ordering and interpreting. The conflict between the self and the world subsides. In a span of heightened perception, the imagination becomes one with the object world. As Herzog puts it, the individual is "easily contained by everything about him" (*H* 325). Reality is seen, not as a death trap, but as a living mystery, "some powerful magnificence not human, (*HRK* 101). In each case there is, as John Clayton points out, a momentary return to a state of innocence.[9] The hero looks out through the eyes of a child or an animal, freed from the "protective chitin of melancholy, and by-product of [the] laboring brain" (*H* 313).

Just as Bellow's heroes break through to moments of union with the world of objects, they have isolated visions of their union with the rest of mankind. Here they see their fellow men not as a multitude that bears them down but as brothers. This vision can only come when the hunt for "special distinction" and a "separate fate" subsides. For an instant the individual steps out of the lonely obsession with individual uniqueness and experiences the sense of a collective soul that contains all men. This vision recurrently comes to Bellow's heroes when they are most painfully aware of their own self-confinement and feel the walls of their own being crushing them. The first example in Bellow's work shows up in *Dangling Man* when Joseph records a strange dream that is set in a "low-pitched long room", a kind of "vault" (*DM* 120). He has come to reclaim the body of a victim of some massacre, and he walks among rows of baskets in which the corpses are lying. Suddenly he is filled with a guilty sense of his own complicity with victim and murderer alike. This is the first of a series of underground visions in Bellow's work which focus on the inescapable bond that links men. In *The Victim* it comes with more positive force. Asa emerges from a similar nightmare in which he is lost in a subway corridor. In a state of semi-consciousness he experiences a moment of "great lucidity", "a rare pure feeling of happiness" (*V* 169). He is convinced that he suddenly sees the truth in all its simplicity: "But it was supremely plain to him that everything, everything without exception, took place as within a single soul or person" (*V* 169). Tommy Wilhelm encounters much the same truth. As he thinks upon the Babel of individual wills that surrounds him in New York City, he realizes that "there is a larger body and from this you cannot be separated" (*SD* 84). He recalls that his first sense of this "larger body" came in the "underground corridor" beneath Times Square: "all of a sudden, unsought, a general love for all these imperfect and lurid-looking people, burst out in Wilhelm's breast. He loved them . . . they were his brothers and sisters. He was imperfect and disfigured himself, but what difference did it make if he was united with them by his blaze of love" (*SD* 84–85). Bellow returns to this idea of humanity as a "larger body" or "single soul" in *Herzog* and in *Mr. Sammler's Planet*. Herzog explains to his friend Lucas that "brotherhood is what makes a man human. . . . Man liveth not by Self alone but in his brother's face. . . . Each man shall behold the Eternal Father and love and joy abound" (*H* 272). While Sammler doubts that human brotherhood has much relevance in everyday action, he nonetheless has a deep sympathy for the "belief that there is the same truth in the heart of every human being, or a splash of God's own spirit" (*SP* 189).

The concept of humanity as a "larger body" or a "single soul" is central to the morality that is implicit in all of Bellow's novels. All of his heroes want to embody what in the simplest terms can be called "true nobility". The meaning of this quest is explored most fully in *Henderson the Rain King* and *Mr. Sammler's Planet*. Henderson's whole life moves towards the recognition that nobility is real. It is a part of the human mixture, a capacity within everyman for "high conduct". As Henderson puts it "the eternal is bonded onto us. It calls out for its share" (*HRK* 318). And Henderson knows, as do all of Bellow's heroes, "that there will never be anything but misery without high conduct" (*HRK* 264). The problem is that the eternal is by no means the only thing that is "bonded on to us". The ego carries us after power; it demands that we make ourselves interesting, original, unique, perfect. It makes the creation of the self a pursuit of madness. As Sammler puts it "human beings, when they have the room, when they have liberty and are supplied also with ideas, mythologize themselves. They legendize, they expand by imagination and try to rise above the limitations of the ordinary forms of common life" (*SP* 147). What is needed is the recognition that the self cannot be created out of nothing; it must be created in imitation of models.[10] If we are following the ego we choose debased models or debase the models we choose. If we are giving the eternal its share we choose proper models, "archetypes of goodness" (*SP* 136). What this good is, we know instinctively. It does not come as prize for a lifetime of philosophical inquiry; it is not something we dream out of the darkness in spite of ourselves. It is simply following our best instincts and "trying to live with a civil heart. With disinterested charity. With a sense of the mystic potency of humankind" (*SP* 136). One expresses a "civil heart" and "disinterested charity" by serving his fellow man and by having the courage to contain his own suffering. None of Bellow's heroes is satisfied that he has or can act out his own capacity for nobility. Given their mixed humanity certainly none of them could purely embody it. Elya Grunner probably comes closer than any of Bellow's central characters. In the concluding passage of *Mr. Sammler's Planet*, Sammler looks down upon the corpse of Elya, his friend and benefactor, and tries to sum up his life:

> At his best this man was much kinder than at my very best I have been or could ever be. He was aware that he must meet, and he did meet—through all the confusion and degraded clowning of this life through which we are speeding—he did meet the terms of his contract. The terms, which in his inmost heart, each man knows. As I know mine. As all know. For that is the truth of it—that we all know, God, that we know, that we know, we know, we know (*SP* 313).

That *Mr. Sammler's Planet* should end in prayer indicates the growing importance of the religious sense in Bellow's work. The heroes of his later novels all experience what Sammler calls "God Adumbrations" (*SP* 237). Since *Seize the Day*, the force and significance of these "adumbrations" have increased with each subsequent novel. None of Bellow's heroes arrives at any intellectual belief in God. It would even be inaccurate to say that any of them achieves or has faith. God is not a conclusion. He has nothing to do with proofs or convictions. Bellow's most recent heroes simply experience *in isolated moments of illumination* a sense of God's presence. In fact this mystical sense of God's presence frees them from the necessity of proofs, explanations, intellectual constructions and from the mental burden of holding the world together. As Herzog puts it "Synthesize or perish! Is that the new law? But when you see what strange notions, hallucinations, projections, issue from the human mind you begin to believe in Providence again" (*H* 322). As Herzog ceases to strive to order reality, he discovers that he doesn't have to: "God ties all kinds of loose ends together. Who knows why" (*H* 305). God is also seen as the deliverance from the imprisoned self caught in the snares of the ego and the will. Tommy

Wilhelm, Henderson, Herzog and Sammler all pray to be released from their own wills into the will of God. The clearest sense of this prayer being answered is seen in *Herzog*. In his final pilgrimage to Ludeyville he feels himself within the "hollowness of God", momentarily content with his life, "satisfied to be, to be just as it is willed" (*H* 325, 340).

No one who has read Bellow with care will make the mistake of believing that his central characters achieve any state of final beatitude. Even within "the hollowness of God", Herzog knows that "the bitter cup [will] come round again, by and by" (*H* 326). The ego cannot stand much of reality, of humanity, of God. For Bellow's heroes the moment of mystical union can never become a place of permanent residence. It is at best a corrective to the pure states of ego-mania and despair and to the illusion that these states correspond to reality, a reminder that the true country lies beyond the American Eden and also beyond the American Wasteland. In refusing his claim to these mystical estates, Bellow, inevitably, has been accused of selling his heritage.

Through the late sixties and early seventies, Bellow's reputation began to slide among the young and among some of the older critics who praised his first work. The most hostile bluntly accused him of selling out to the middle-class. He had betrayed the tradition kept alive by the naturalists and realists, the tradition of shouting "No, in thunder" as the phrase now has it. But no one need worry about Bellow's integrity. He has not slept with the "fat Gods". In fact he offers the most sustained and most penetrating criticism of contemporary American life of any novelist of his generation. Bellow's sin is that he has refused to be a prophet. But who can really blame him for this in a country where prophecy appears to be the one resource that is infinitely renewable. It is difficult to "speak in thunder" without announcing either the New Jerusalem or the "abomination of desolation". But as Bellow has remarked, "Prophecy is nice work if you get it".[11]

Notes

1. Saul Bellow, "The Writer as Moralist," *Atlantic Monthly*, 211 (March, 1963), 59.

2. Bellow, "Writer as Moralist," 59.

3. Bellow, "Writer as Moralist," 59.

4. This article was written before the publication of *Humboldt's Gift*.

5. Saul Bellow, *Dangling Man* (New York: Vanguard Press, 1944), p. 88. Subsequent references to Bellow's novels will be cited in the text to the following editions: *The Victim* (New York: Vanguard Press, 1947); *The Adventures of Augie March* (New York: Viking Press, 1953); *Seize the Day* (New York: Viking Press, 1956); *Henderson the Rain King* (New York: Viking Press, 1959); *Herzog* (New York: Viking Press, 1964); *Mr. Sammler's Planet* (New York: Viking Press, 1970).

6. A number of critics have discussed this pattern of alienation and flight from death in Bellow's heroes. For example see Keith Opdahl, *The Novels of Saul Bellow* (University Park: Penn State University Press, 1967), pp. 2 ff., 34–35. John Clayton, *Saul Bellow: In Defense of Man* (Bloomington: Indiana University Press, 1968), 49ff., 97ff.

7. Bellow, "Writer as Moralist," 62.

8. Several critics discuss this surrender of the ego in Bellow's heroes. For example, see Opdahl, pp. 5–6, 14, and Clayton, pp. 115 ff., 135–136.

9. Clayton, pp. 180 ff.

10. Bellow explicitly subscribes to the idea that "all things that come to much" are suggested by earlier models in "Distractions of the Fiction Writer" in *The Living Novel: A Symposium*, ed. Granville Hicks (New York: Macmillan, 1957), p. 17.

11. Bellow, "Writer as Moralist," 61.

INDEX

"Address by Gooley MacDowell to the Hasbeens Club of Chicago," 74

Adventures of Augie March, The, xxiii n.30, 33, 34, 52, 189; alienation in, 38; atmosphere of, 14; Bellow on creation of, 20; and Brueghel's *The Misanthrope,* 83–88; characterization in, 13; and *Dangling Man,* 14; eagle episode in, 9–10; faults of, 13, 15, 16, 33, 34; and *Henderson,* 20, 52; language in, 15, 33; love in, 16, 28; new fictional style of, 33, 38, 52; as parable of American optimism, 17–18; point of view in, 9; reviews of, 8–10, 11–13, 14–18; structure of, 38; typifies revisionist liberalism, 37; verbalism in, 34; and *The Victim,* 13, 14; winner of National Book Award (1954), 27; women in, 13, 16, 28

Africa, in *Henderson,* 19–20, 24

Aldridge, John W., xv, 51–56

Alienation: and the artist, xxi; in *Augie March,* 38; Bellow and, xiii, xv, 35–36, 38, 53; in *Dangling Man,* 38; in *Herzog,* 35–36, 53; of modernists, ix, 35

American: artist in, 164–65, 166; in *Augie March,* 8–9, 10, 17–18; Bellow's, 165–66. *See also* American dream; American experience

American dream: Augie March as symbol of, 17; Bellow on, 18

American experience, ix, 181

American literature: Bellow on, xiii, 181, 183

Anthroposophy, xix, 55, 173 n.19. *See also* Steiner, Rudolf

Anti-Semitism: in *The Victim,* 5–6

Art, 44; Bellow on, xi, xii, xviii, 165

Artist: and alienation, xxi; in America, 164–65, 166; Bellow on role of, xii, xiii, 160

Baker, Robert, 26–29

Bellow, Saul, 181–94; career of, 30, 33, 37–38, 41, 51, 188; as caricaturist, 16, 31, 40; as creator of character, 13, 16; education of, 58; in fifties, x, xi, 38; in

forties, 37; influences on, 52, 58; interview with, 57–72; Jewish heritage of, 41, 47–48, 158; as novelist of ideas, 47–48, 51, 58; optimism of, 54, 55; philosophy of, xiv, 54, 56, 59; protagonists, (*see* Protagonists); on psychiatry, 95; on psychology, xvii, 33–34, 58–59, 94; quoted, ix, xi, xvi, xvii, xix, 101, 131, 166; readers of, xi, 22, 62–64, 129; in sixties, xvii, 42, 43. *See also* Bellow, Saul, writings of

Bellow, Saul, writings of: compared, 38, 41, 53; concept of humanity in, 191–92; early, xviii, 11–12, 42; endings of, 28–29, 34, 54, 127–28, 171; later, xviii, 31; rhetorical technique, xvi, 73–82; short fiction, xvi, 73–82; style, xi, 13, 33–34, 147; technique, 32–33, 51–52, 75; themes, xi–xii, xvi, 34, 54 159–60; use of language, 15, 25, 27–28, 33, 47, 74, 79. *See also* Bellow, Saul; titles of individual works

Berryman, John, 65, 68–69

Bildungsroman: Augie March as, 27

Black humor, xx, 51, 56, 159, 163

Blacks: in *Mr. Sammler's Planet,* 44–45, 123–25

Boyers, Robert, 122–40

Bradbury, Malcolm, 158–59

Brans, Jo, xx, 57–72

Brueghel, Pieter, 15, 83–84, 86; *The Misanthrope* and Augie March, xvi, 83–88; *Netherlandish Proverbs,* 86

Chicago, xxii n.10, 60, 69, 74, 75, 81, 159, 163, 184

Citrine, Charlie *(Humboldt's Gift),* xix, 55–56, 70; as Bellow, 66; Bellow on, 66, 67, 70–71; character of, 159, 160–64, 166–68, 170; as Jew, 168; and Rudolf Steiner, 167, 169; significance of name, 164, 173 n.11; as "undergrouud man," 170; urban background of, x; as victim, 55

City: in Bellow's work, x–xi, xxii n.10; as symbol, xxi n.8; as symbol of death, x, xxii n.8, 184. *See also* Environment, urban

195